Manuel Neri

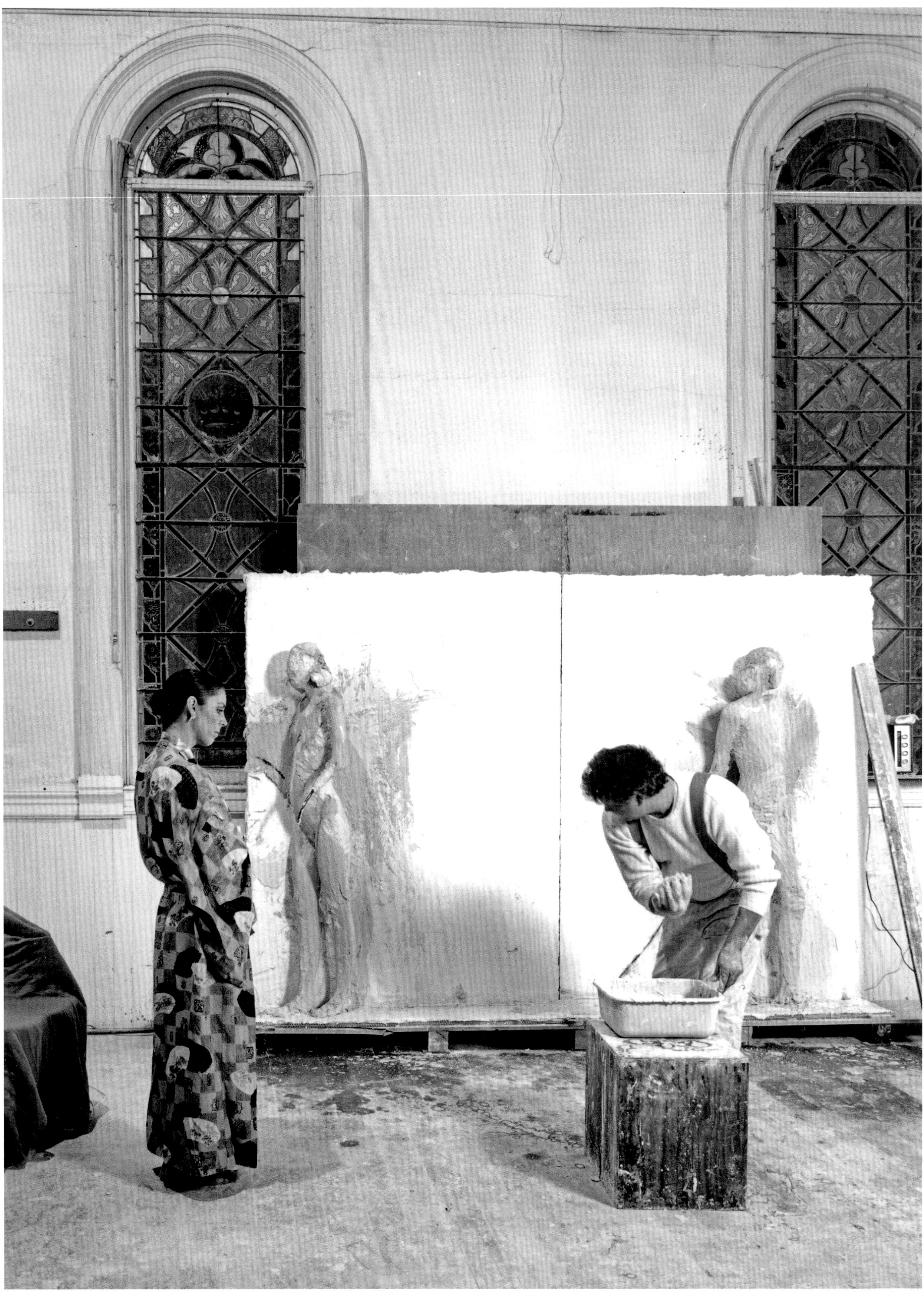

Manuel Neri

The Human Figure in Plaster and on Paper

Jock Reynolds

Yale University Art Gallery
New Haven

Distributed by Yale University Press
New Haven and London

Publication made possible by the Joann and
Gifford Phillips, Class of 1942, Fund; the Raymond
and Helen Runnells DuBois Publication Fund;
the Rosalee and David McCullough Family Fund;
the Stephen S. Lash Fund; and the Wolfe Family
Exhibition and Publication Fund.

First published in 2018 by the
Yale University Art Gallery
1111 Chapel Street
P.O. Box 208271
New Haven, CT 06520-8271
artgallery.yale.edu/publications

Distributed by
Yale University Press
302 Temple Street
P.O. Box 209040
New Haven, CT 06520-9040
yalebooks.com/art

Published in conjunction with the exhibition
*Manuel Neri: The Human Figure in Plaster and on
Paper*, organized by the Yale University Art Gallery.

Yale University Art Gallery
March 2–July 8, 2018

Tiffany Sprague,
Director of Publications and Editorial Services

Christopher Sleboda,
Director of Graphic Design

Project editor: Madeline Kloss Johnson
Proofreader: Stacey A. Wujcik

Set in Minotaur
Printed at GHP, West Haven, Conn.

ISBN 978-0-300-23302-5
Library of Congress Control Number: 2018935051

10 9 8 7 6 5 4 3 2 1

Cover illustration: Manuel Neri at his studio,
Benicia, California, 1982
Frontispiece: Mary Julia Raahauge and Manuel Neri
in the artist's studio, Benicia, California, 1985
Essay frontispiece: Manuel Neri in his studio,
Benicia, California, 1995

Contents

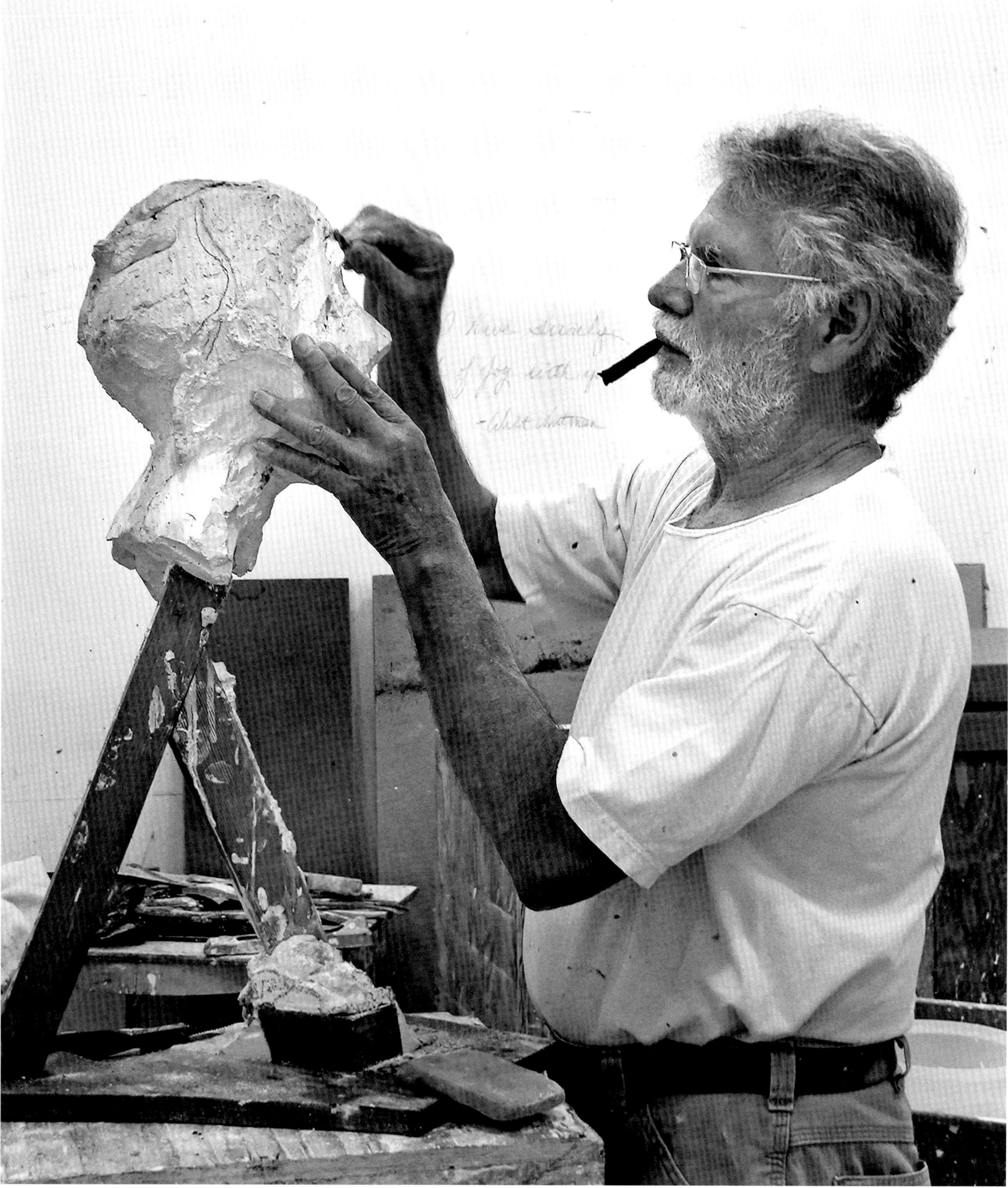

Manuel Neri:
A Tribute

Manuel Neri was born in 1930 in the small town of Sanger, near Fresno, in California's Central Valley.[1] His parents, who had emigrated from Mexico to escape the political chaos still resonating from the Mexican Revolution, were primarily employed as farm workers.[2] Neri became the male head of the household at a young age—his elder brother died from pneumonia in 1943 and his father from tuberculosis in 1944—and he dropped out of high school to help support his mother and two sisters. Following World War II, Neri's mother moved the family to Oakland, California, and secured a new job working in an electronics factory. Neri also gained employment installing equipment for the Western Union Company, but he yearned to resume his high-school education. After taking summer courses, he eventually graduated from high school in 1950, at the age of twenty. He immediately enrolled in San Francisco City College (SFCC), determined to earn enough pre-program credits to gain admission to the University of California, Berkeley, as an engineering major.[3]

That same year, Neri took a ceramics course from Roy Walker at SFCC. Walker encouraged him to audit courses at the California School of Fine Arts, which was soon to be renamed the San Francisco Art Institute (SFAI). These courses gave Neri a swift and formidable introduction to the world of art, as he learned from Clyfford Still, Mark Rothko, and other notable artists then teaching at the school. A year later, in 1951, while still taking some pre-engineering courses at SFCC, Neri also audited a ceramics course at the Oakland campus of the California College of Arts and Crafts (CCAC). There he met Nathan Oliveira and Peter Voulkos—both of whom would become lifelong friends and go on to become prominent figures in Bay Area artistic circles—and fully committed himself to life as a professional artist.[4] His artistic training was briefly interrupted when he was drafted into service in the Korean War, but immediately upon returning home in 1955, he returned to CCAC, this time as a full-time art student.[5] Two years later, in 1957, he transferred to SFAI.

It was at this juncture in Neri's life that he met Gurdon Woods, a sculptor who in 1955 had been hired to direct SFAI as its president. Woods quickly came to admire and encourage Neri as a student and thereafter as a young artist. A little more than a decade later, Woods went on to do the same for me—I became one of his first students at the University of California, Santa Cruz (UCSC), after he founded the school's art department in 1966. I took his first studio course in sculpture as a sophomore in 1967, and it was through Woods that my connection to and knowledge of Neri developed.

Woods had a classical method of teaching, in which he urged my fellow students and me to engage our eyes, minds, and hands while working with plaster and clay to fashion the human figure from the live models he brought in to pose for us in his studio classroom. Once he sensed our eagerness to learn more about sculpture, he then

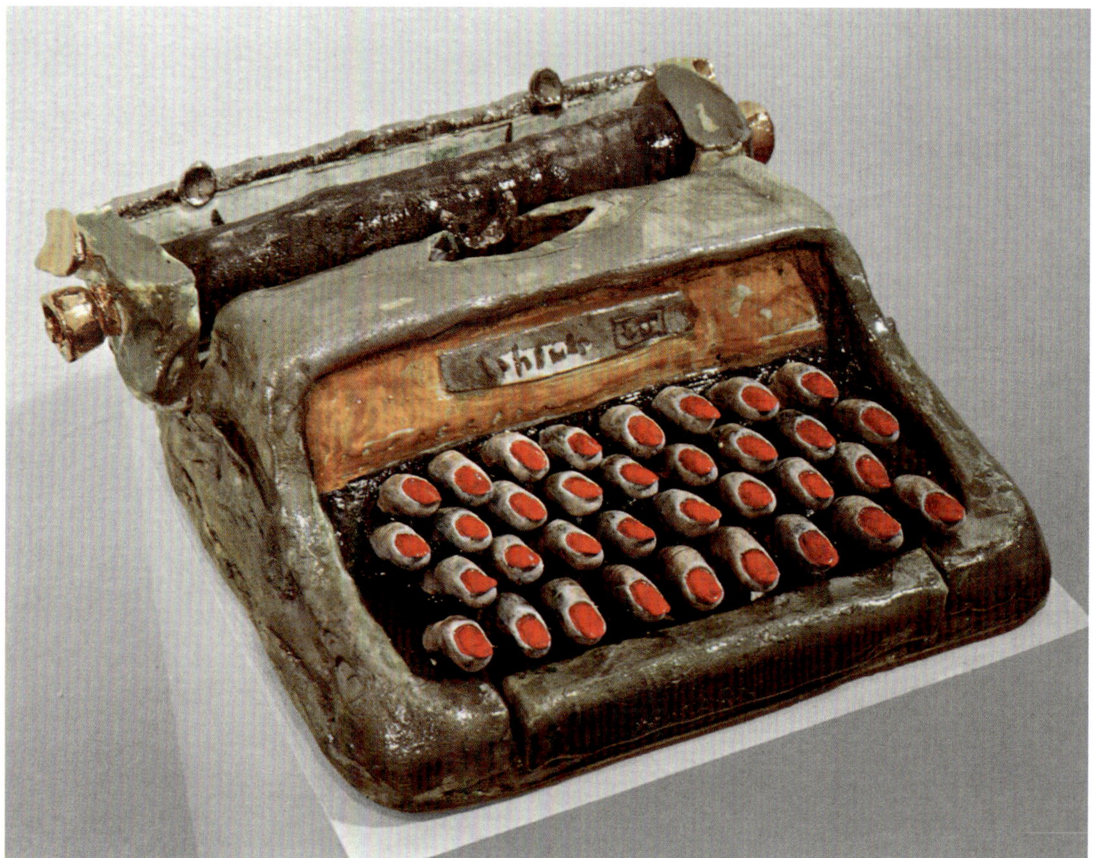

Fig. 1. Robert Arneson, *Typewriter*, 1965. Ceramic, H. 10 × W. 12 in. (25.4 × 30.5 cm). Private collection. From: Peter Selz, *Funk*, exh. cat. (Berkeley: University of California, Berkeley, 1967), 14

taught us how to create artworks with wax, make molds of them in plaster, and eventually cast them in bronze, which we did together in a small bronze foundry that Woods established in an abandoned blacksmith shop long extant on the campus's expansive ranch land.

Woods soon invited me to assist him in his own off-campus studio on weekends, and he continued to mentor me in courses and on trips we began taking together to museums, galleries, and artists' studios in San Francisco and Berkeley. It was on one such early trip, in the spring of 1967, that I had the formative experience of first viewing artworks created by Neri—as well as by many other artists based in the Bay Area, such as Robert Arneson, Joan Brown, Bruce Conner, Robert Hudson, William T. Wiley, and Voulkos. They were on view in the now legendary *Funk* exhibition, curated by Peter Selz at the Berkeley Art Museum (fig. 1).[6] Selz had founded the museum just two years prior, after leaving his position as a curator of paintings and sculpture at the Museum of Modern Art, New York. He was a dynamic force and, upon arriving in Berkeley, he immediately understood the creative pulse of the Bay Area artists' community and supported it strongly. When the *Funk* exhibition opened, it caused a sensation. The works were humorous, freewheeling, and irreverent, reflecting the Beat sensibility that inspired and permeated the culture of the Bay Area. The two works by Neri that I saw in the exhibition were from his *Ceramic Loop* series, part of a brief foray into abstraction in clay that Voulkos had inspired (figs. 2-3).[7] A year later, in 1968, Woods took me

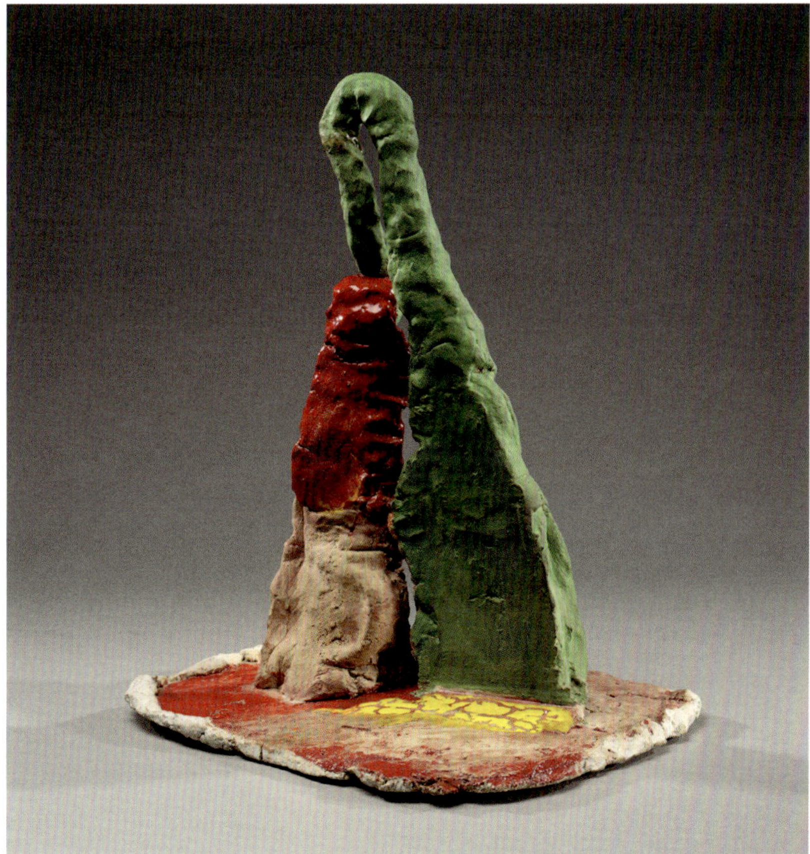

Fig. 2. Manuel Neri, *Ceramic Loop IV*, ca. 1956-61. Glazed ceramic with epoxy, 24 × 20 ½ × 19 ¾ in. (61 × 52.1 × 50.1 cm). Yale University Art Gallery, Janet and Simeon Braguin Fund, 2018.4.2

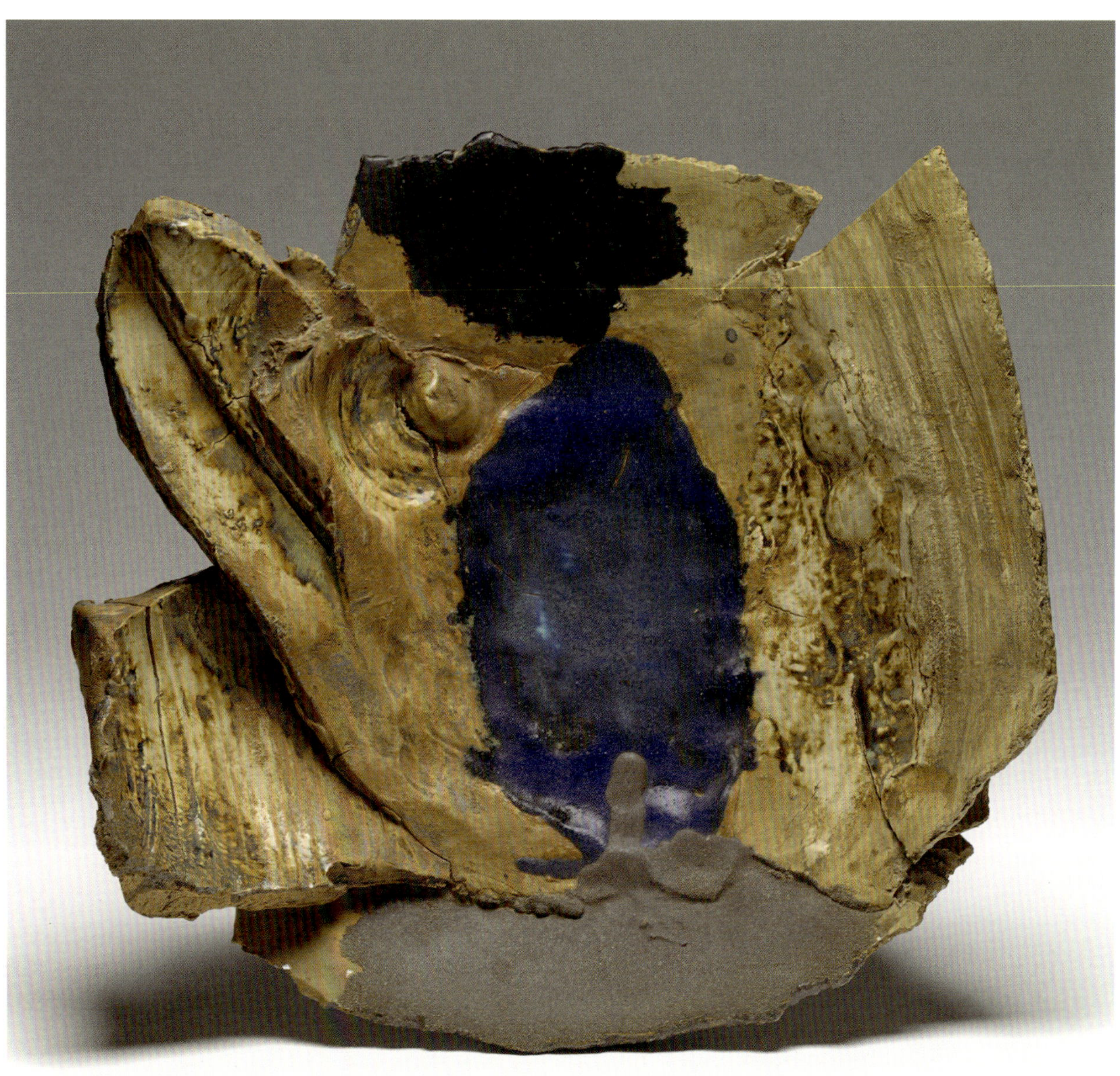

back to Berkeley for a studio visit with Voulkos, who was then a young faculty member in the art department at the University of California, Berkeley. Voulkos could not have been kinder to me, and I admired his astounding work ethic, creative production in multiple media, and devotion to working closely with students via hands-on demonstration.

From Woods, I also learned more about Joan Brown, another young artist he had first encouraged as a student. She had met Neri in 1957 while enrolled at SFAI, and the pair instantly began to work, travel, and show together (fig. 4); they also married and had a son, Noel.[8] Neri and Brown were profoundly inspired by—and subsequently became essential members of—what came to be known as the Bay Area Figurative School, which was already flourishing under artists such as Elmer Bischoff, Richard Diebenkorn, and David Park (figs. 5-6).[9] The artists of this slightly older generation were also devoted teachers, and they soon befriended Brown and Neri and respected them as peers. Even

10

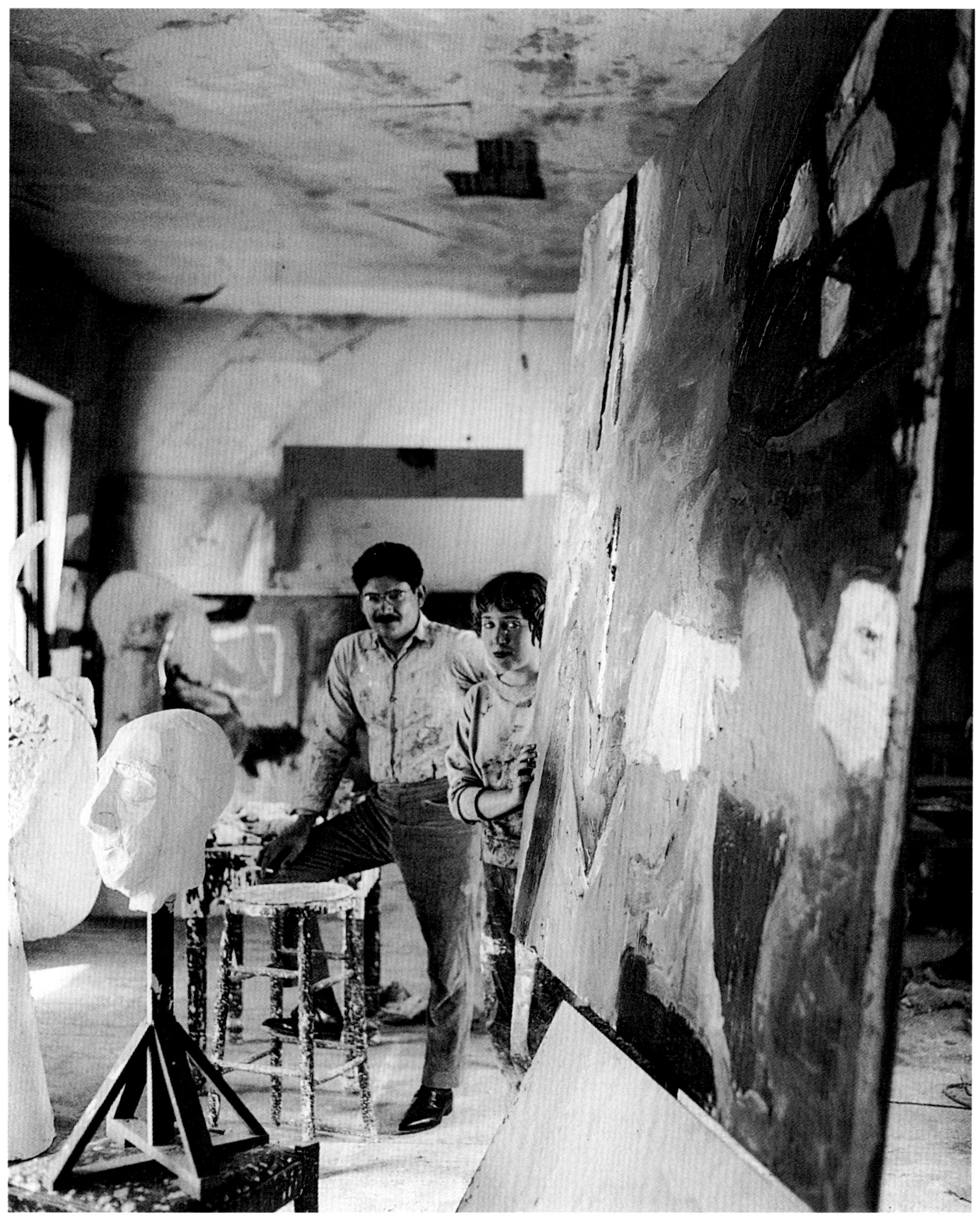

Fig. 4. Manuel Neri and Joan Brown in their studio on
Mission Street, San Francisco, 1959

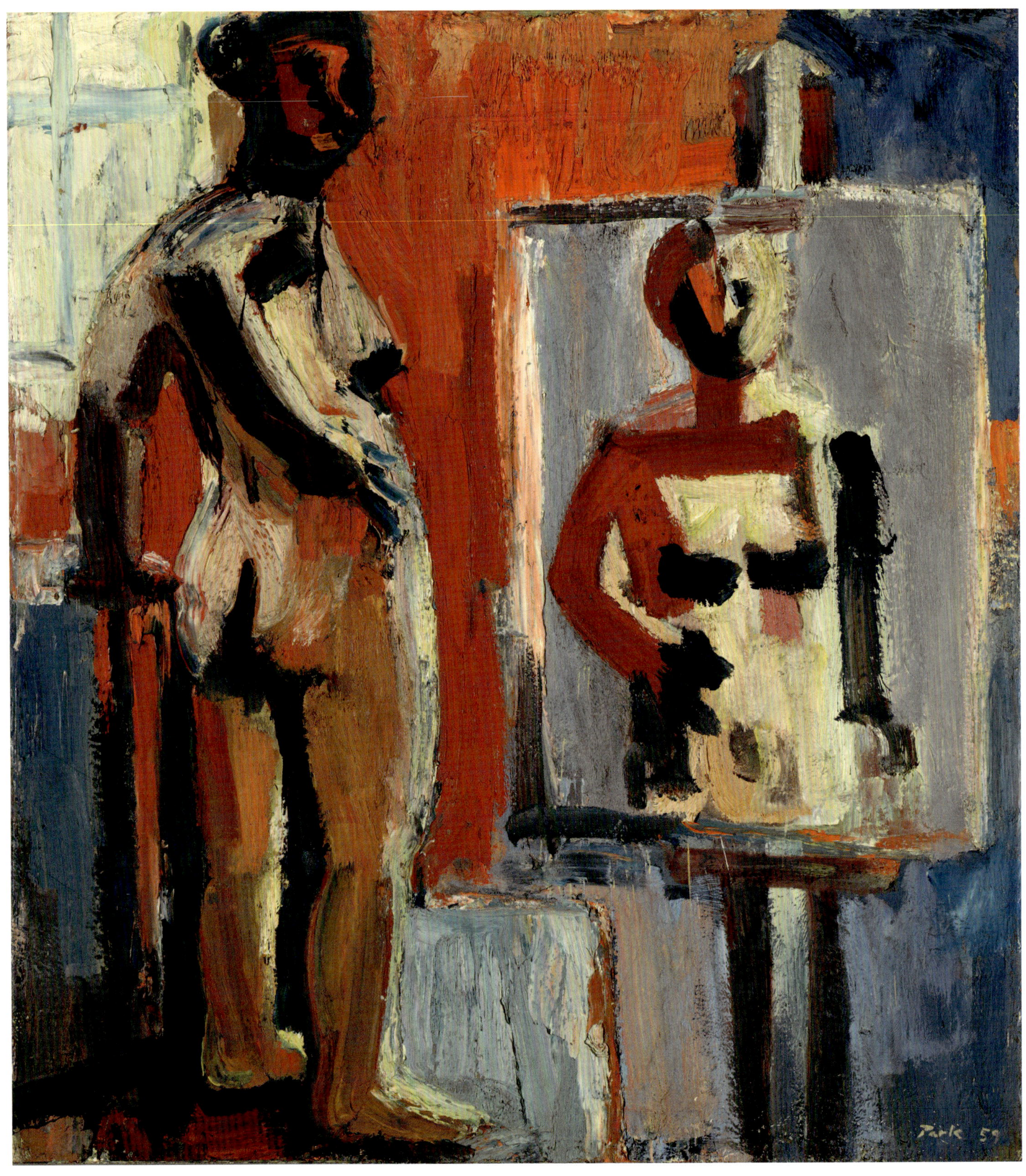

Fig. 5. David Park, *The Model*, 1959. Oil on canvas, 66 ½ × 59 in. (168.9 × 149.9 cm).
Yale University Art Gallery, Gift of Karen, Lawrence, and Ellen Eisner, in memory
of their mother, Anita Brand Eisner; gift of Laila Twigg-Smith, by exchange; and
purchased with Charles B. Benenson, B.A. 1933, Fund; Walter H. and Margaret
Dwyer Clemens, B.A. 1951, Fund; Director's Discretionary Fund for the Yale
University Art Gallery; Leonard C. Hanna, Jr., Class of 1913, Fund; The Iola S.
Haverstick Fund for American Art; The Heinz Family Fund; Katharine Ordway
Fund; Joann and Gifford Phillips, Class of 1942, Fund; and George A., Class of 1954,
and Nancy P. Shutt Acquisition Fund, 2014.71.1

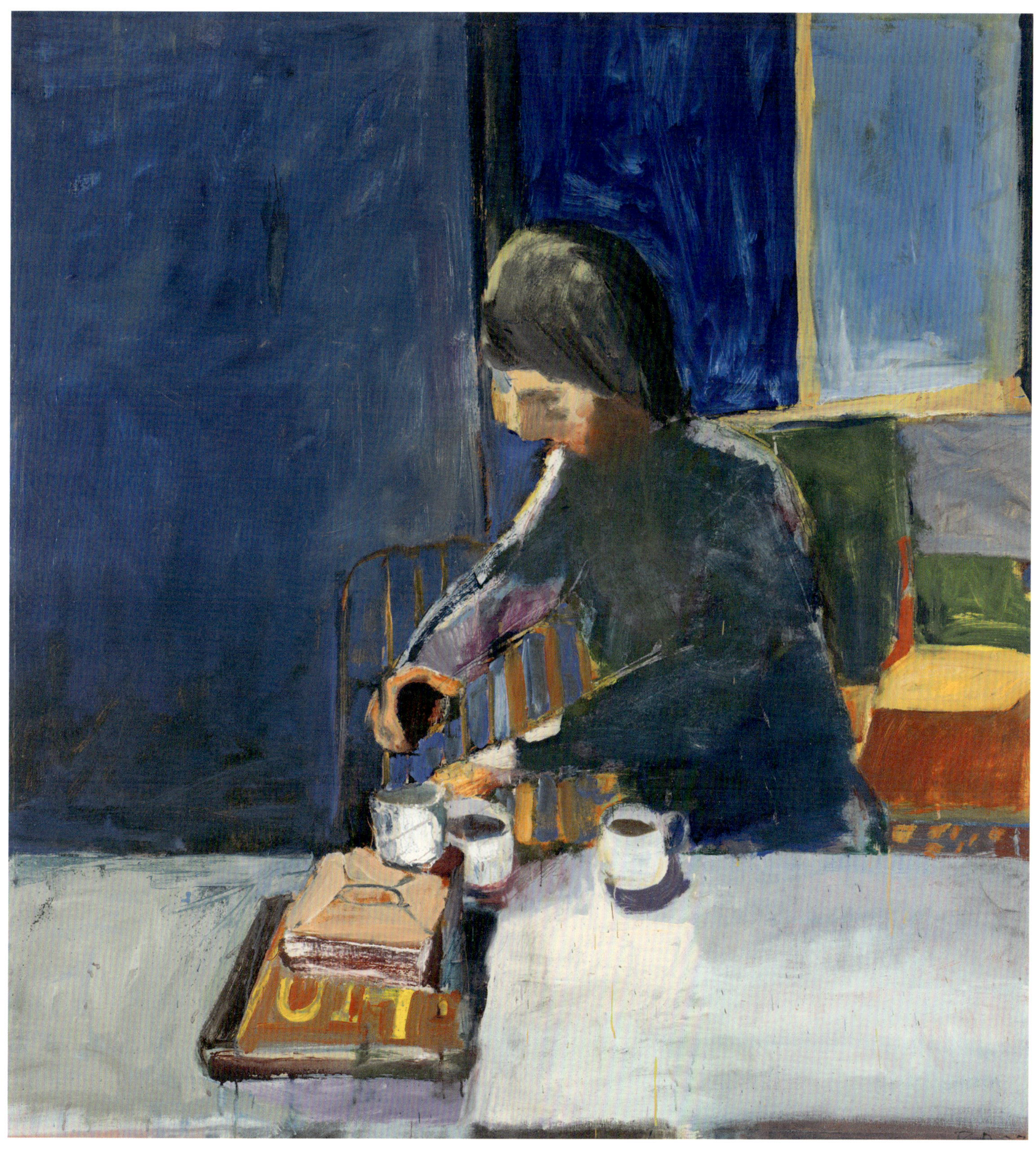

Fig. 6. Richard Diebenkorn, *Girl with Cups*, 1957. Oil on canvas, 59 × 54 in. (149.9 × 137.2 cm). Yale University Art Gallery, Gift of Richard Brown Baker, B.A. 1935, 1975.110.1

after divorcing in 1966, Neri and Brown remained good friends and admirers of each other's work, and Brown's bold, improvisational handling of paint and use of a full range of color in her figurative work quickly established her as a major artist (fig. 7). Her work had a great impact on Neri that never diminished. She was clearly his first muse and was portrayed in a number of Neri's most important early sculptural heads and full figures realized in plaster (fig. 8). Neri also integrated some aspects of Brown's technique—including her heavy impasto, vibrant colors, and dashing paint strokes—into his own sculptural creations, and never ceased doing so.

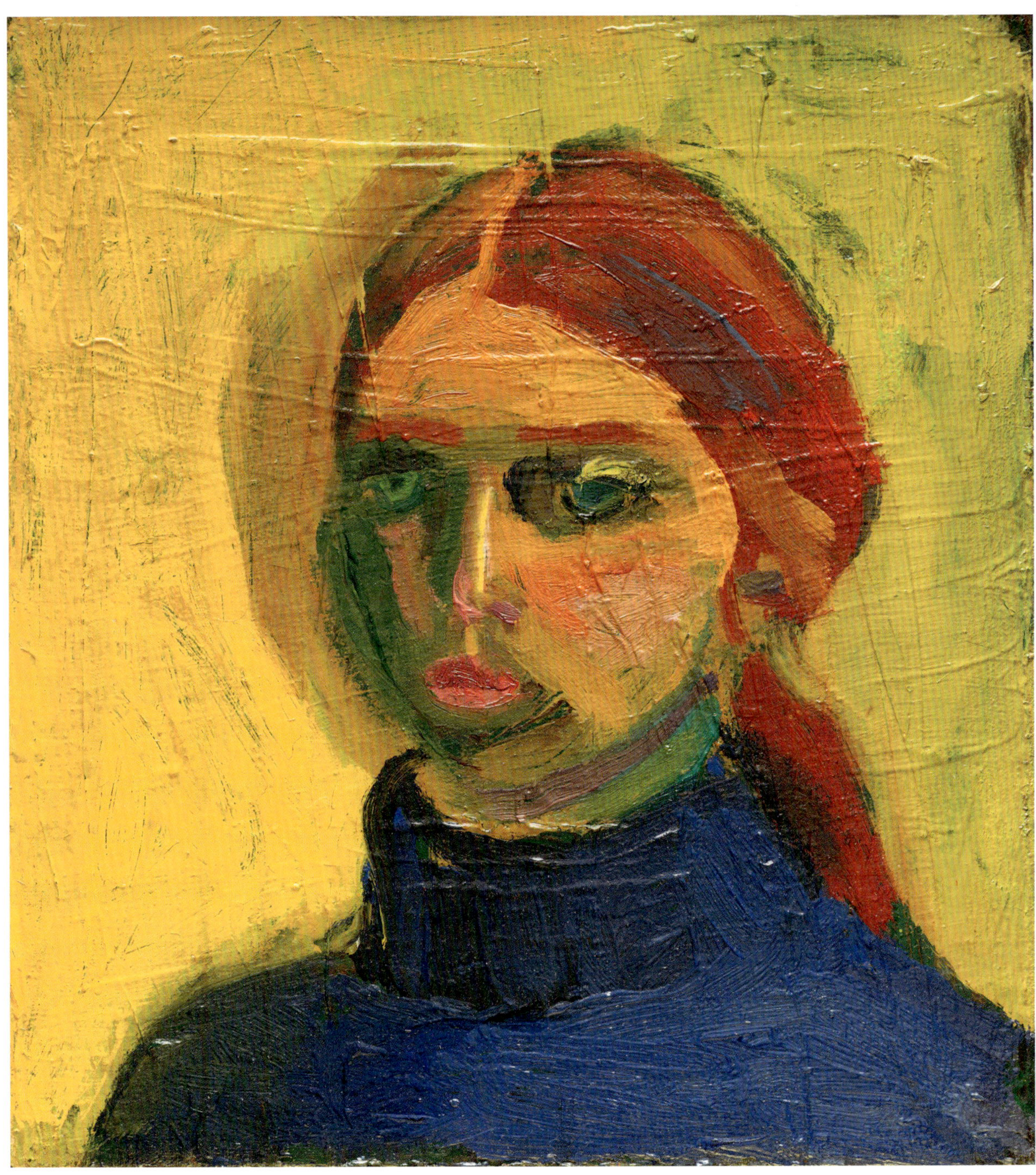

Fig. 7. Joan Brown, *Self-Portrait*, ca. 1959. Oil on canvas, 15 × 13 in. (38.1 × 33 cm). Yale University Art Gallery, Promised gift of The Manuel Neri Trust

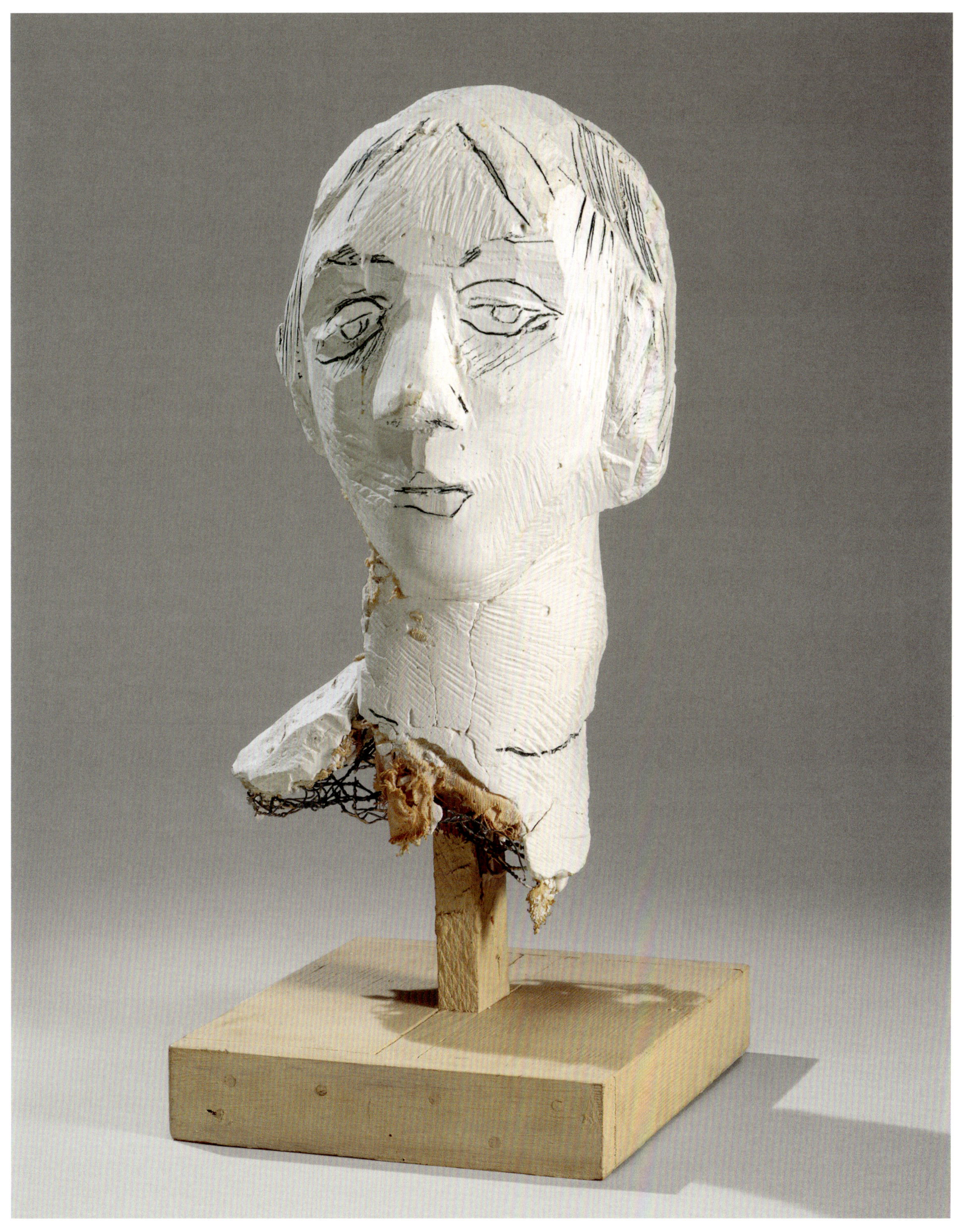

Fig. 8. Manuel Neri, *Head of Joan Brown*, ca. 1959. Plaster with graphite, 16 × 7 × 8 in. (40.6 × 17.8 × 20.3 cm). Yale University Art Gallery, Janet and Simeon Braguin Fund, 2018.4.1

Back at UCSC in 1968-69, I continued to spend many weekends working as an assistant to Woods in his studio, learning a great deal about the materials and tools that he employed to fashion his artwork. Woods also owned an extensive personal library of art books and catalogues, and it became a regular practice for us to discuss some of them together during lunch breaks. I can't remember the specific little catalogue containing a discussion of Neri's early plaster figures that came up one Saturday, but I still vividly recall Woods telling me how he had first met Neri, shortly after Neri had transferred to SFAI in 1957. One day the technician in charge of overseeing SFAI's sculpture classrooms had burst into Woods's office in a very agitated state, repeatedly and insistently exclaiming, "You have to come with me and stop him!" Urged to follow the technician to the sculpture studios, Woods soon beheld a large array of full-scale figurative works that Neri had created in a single week—a whirlwind of sculpting that had exhausted the entire inventory of plaster meant to last for the remainder of the semester. Woods calmed his colleague down and simply told him to immediately buy more plaster, as much as Neri and the other students might need for the rest of the semester. Amazed by Neri's remarkable creative productivity, Woods closely followed his artistic development thereafter and, as he described to me during another of our lunchtime discussions, later made visits to Neri's studio on Connecticut Street, in San Francisco's Potrero Hill neighborhood. There he observed how Neri's plaster figures and plaster heads continued to be produced in great abundance, and, once they filled up his work space, many of them would be broken apart and shoveled off his loading dock to make room for more new work to come to life (figs. 9-11).

By the time I graduated from UCSC in 1969, fully intent on pursuing a life in the arts, Woods had urged me to spend a year assembling a strong portfolio of work and then apply to the M.F.A. program at my hometown university, the University of California, Davis. He recommended that, if accepted, I return to Davis to study with Neri, Robert Arneson, Wayne Thiebaud, William T. Wiley, and the other talented young artists who had recently been hired by Richard Nelson, the chairman of UC Davis's newly founded art department whom Woods held in high esteem.

At this point—still the early years of Neri's creative development—the artist was embarking on an important body of work dealing with an entirely different subject that came to interest him: ancient Mayan and Incan architecture and temples. In the summer of 1969, he took a trip to Central and South America to explore his family's Mexican heritage and to visit the ancient ruins in Tula

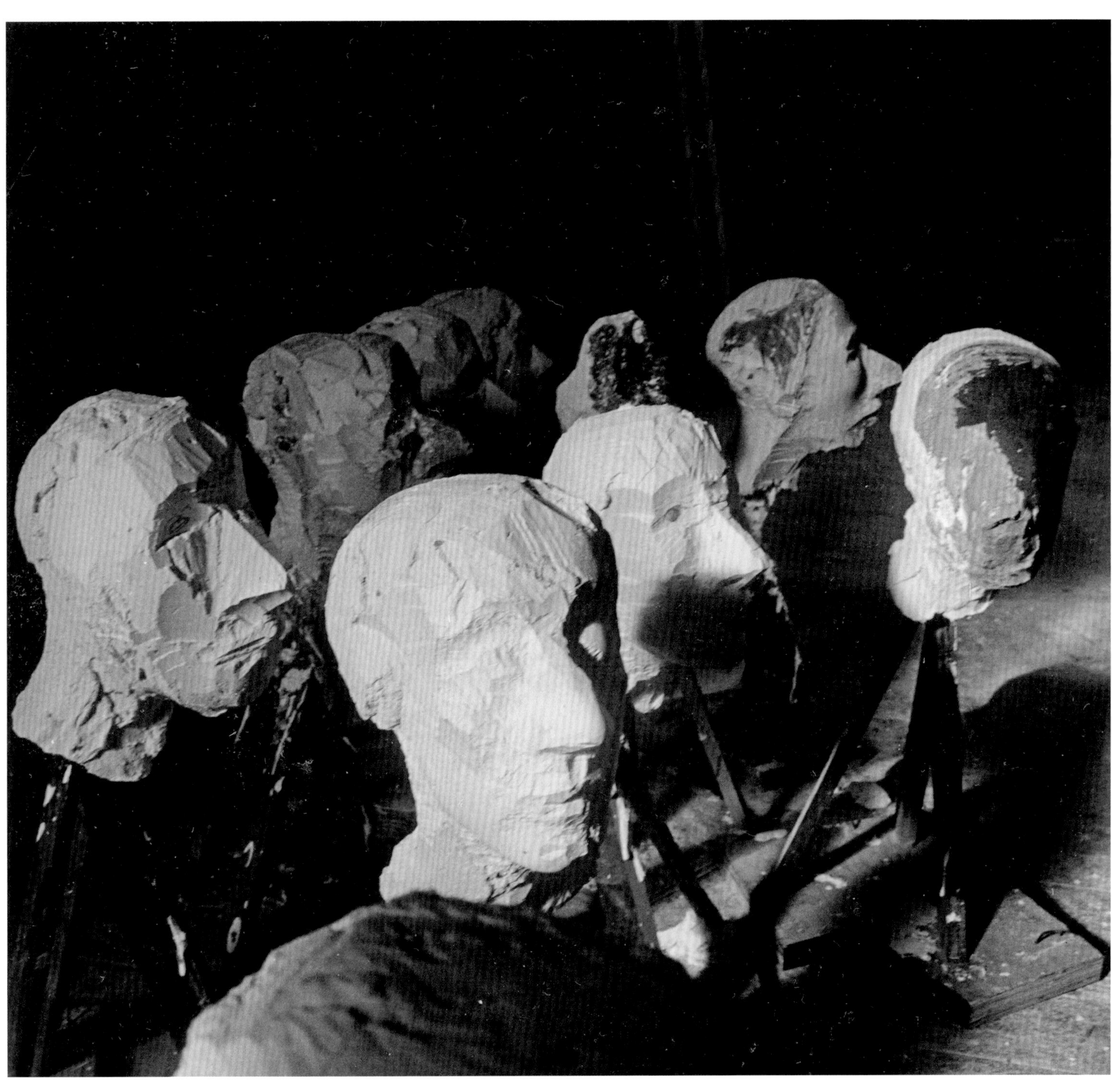

Fig. 9. Plaster heads in Manuel Neri's studio, Benicia,
California, 1972

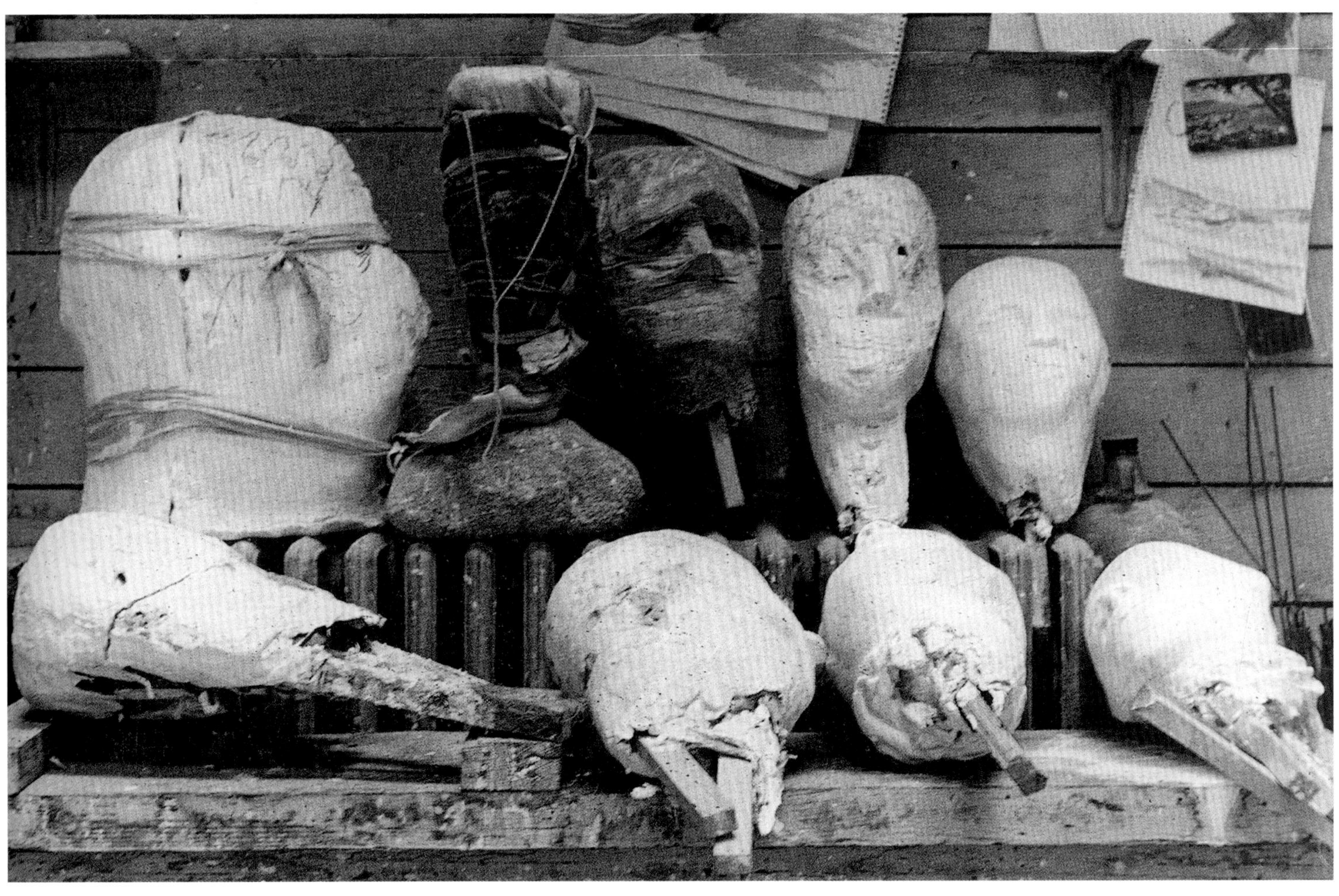

Fig. 10. Plaster heads in Manuel Neri's studio,
San Francisco, ca. 1957

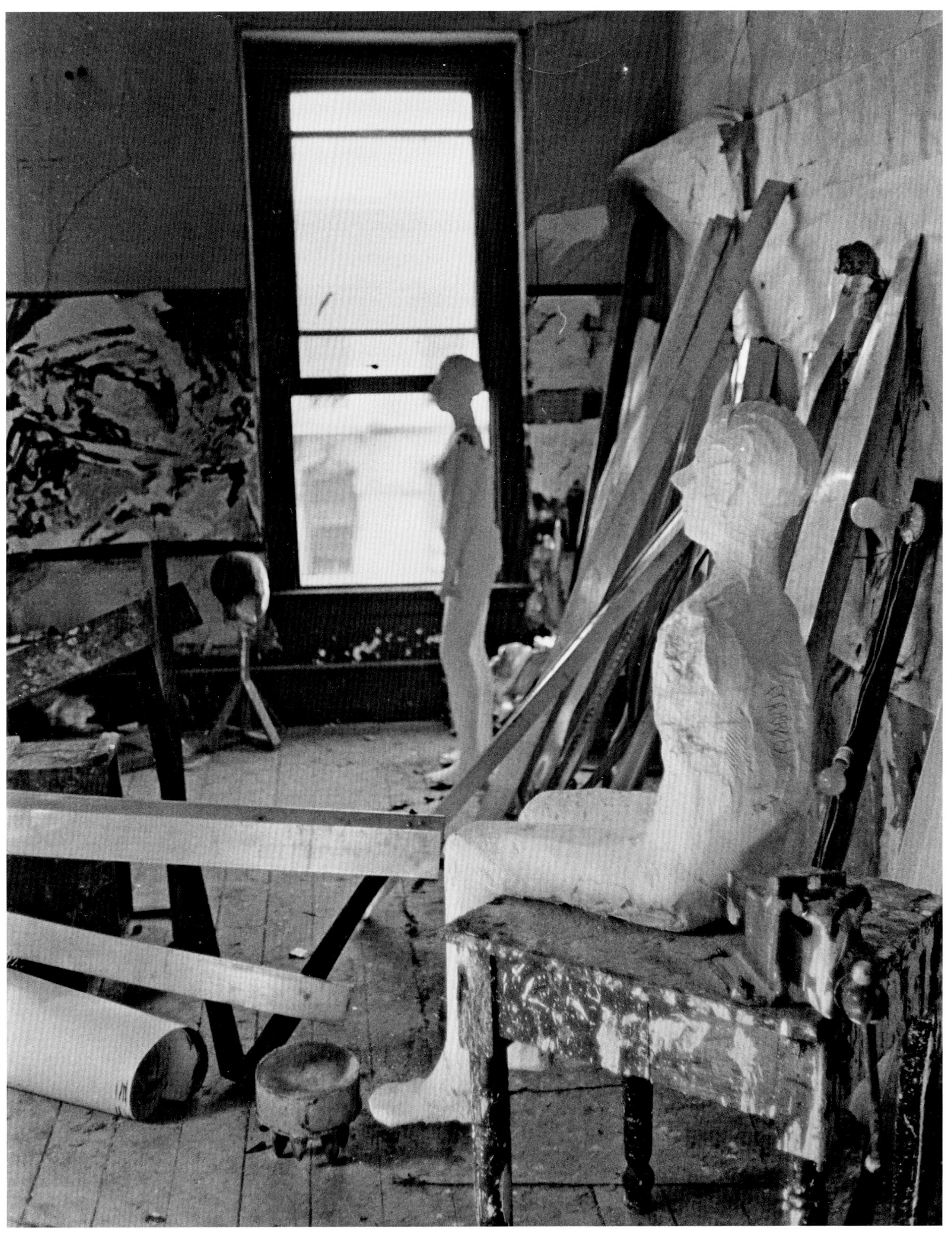

Fig. 11. Manuel Neri's Connecticut Street studio,
San Francisco, 1959

and Tikal. Upon returning to UC Davis that fall, Neri began generating a beautiful group of works on paper and later on some very handsome geometric sculptural forms made from wood, wire screen, and cast magnesite, which he named for the architectural forms and ruins that had captured his attention in Tula.[10] Some of these serial and quite minimalist artworks were titled *Repair of the Great Steps of Tula*, insinuating his belief that a ruin could indeed come to life again via the imagination of an artist (fig. 12).[11] Neri also worked with the human figure all the while, continuing to craft, carve, and paint singular heads or full figures, some standing, others seated, and still others crouching (figs. 13–15).

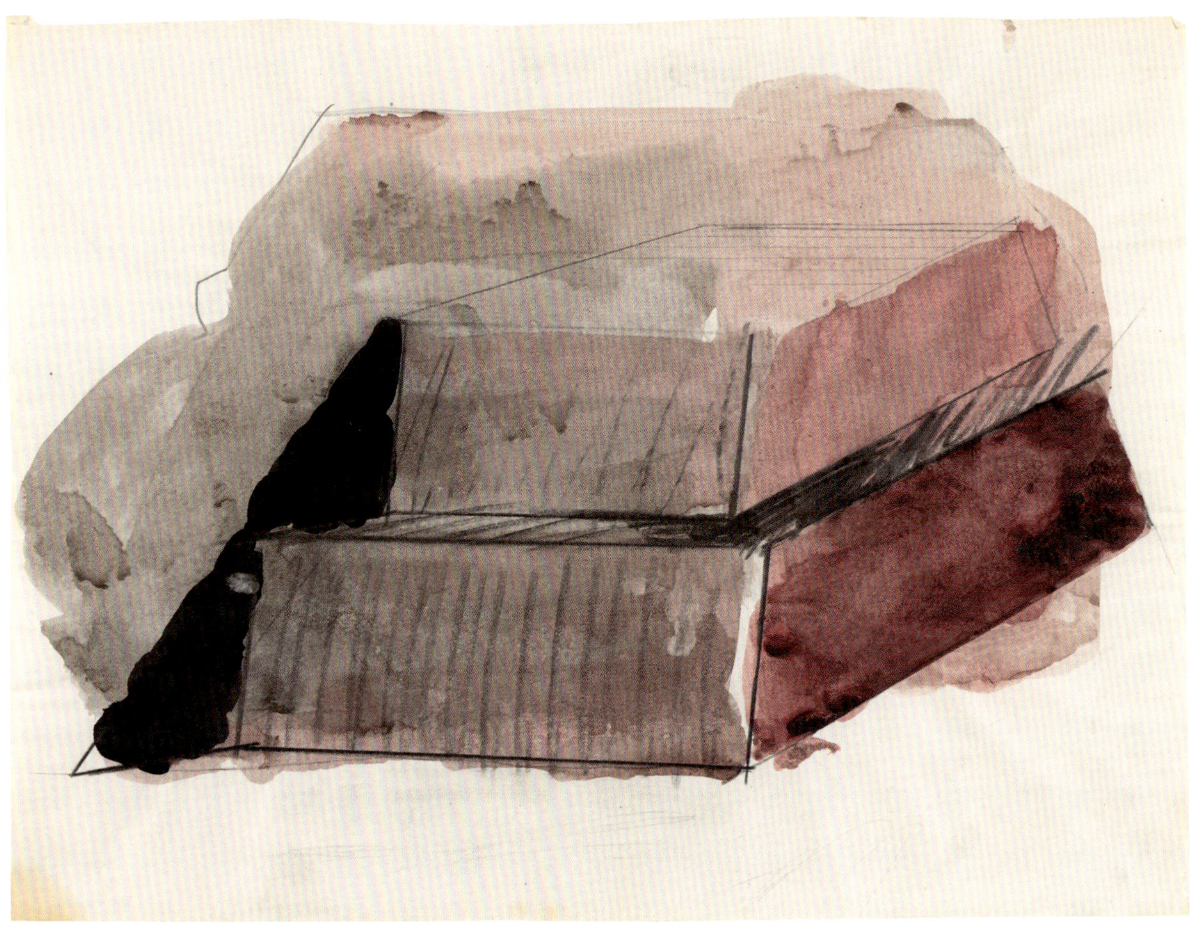

Fig. 12. Manuel Neri, *Architectural Forms-Repair of the Great Steps of Tula No. 1*, 1969. Watercolor, ink, and graphite on paper, 10 13/16 × 13 15/16 in. (27.5 × 35.4 cm). Yale University Art Gallery, Gift of The Manuel Neri Trust, 2017.88.101

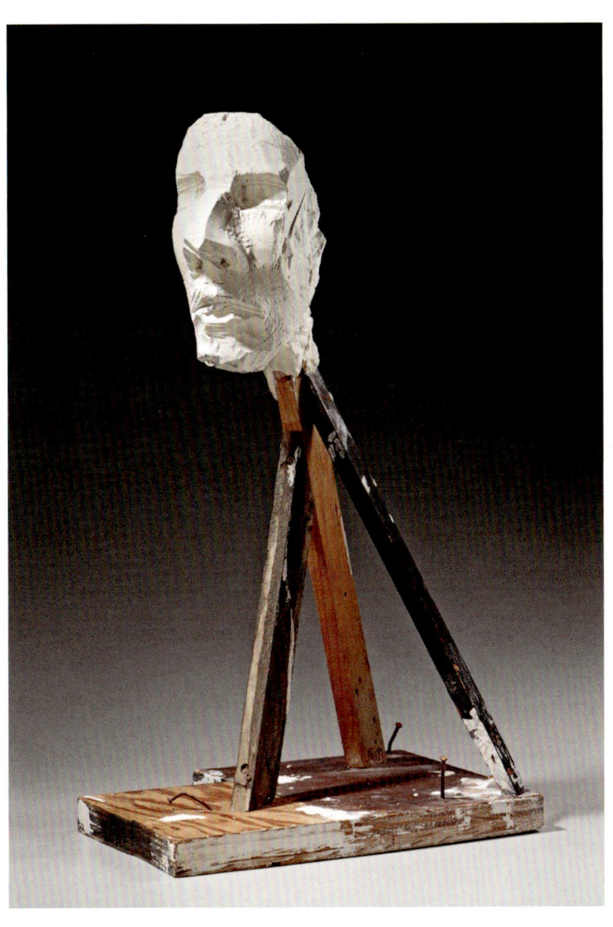
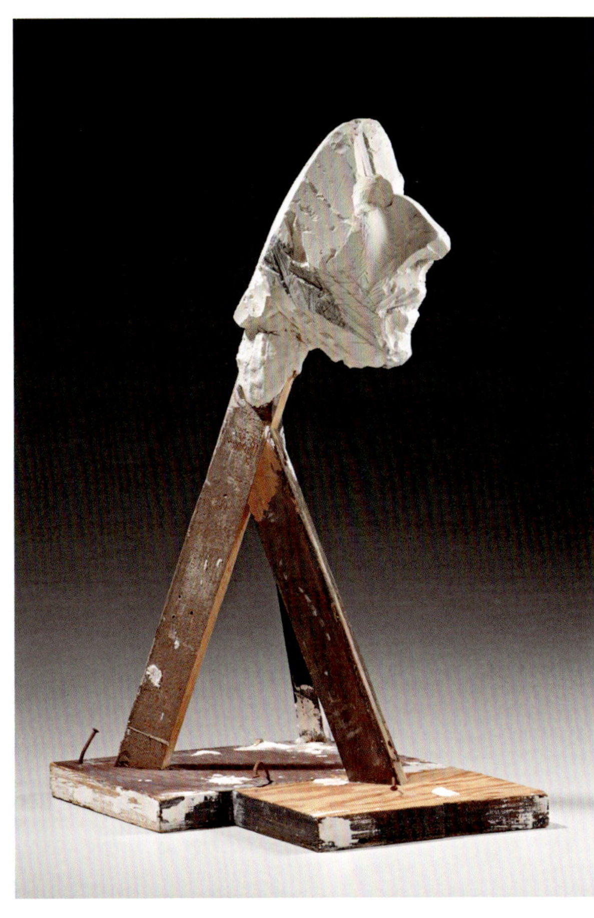

Fig. 13. Manuel Neri, *Male Head No. 1*, 1969. Plaster with graphite, 27 ¼ × 12 ¼ × 16 in. (69.2 × 31.1 × 40.6 cm). Yale University Art Gallery, Gift of The Manuel Neri Trust, 2017.88.4

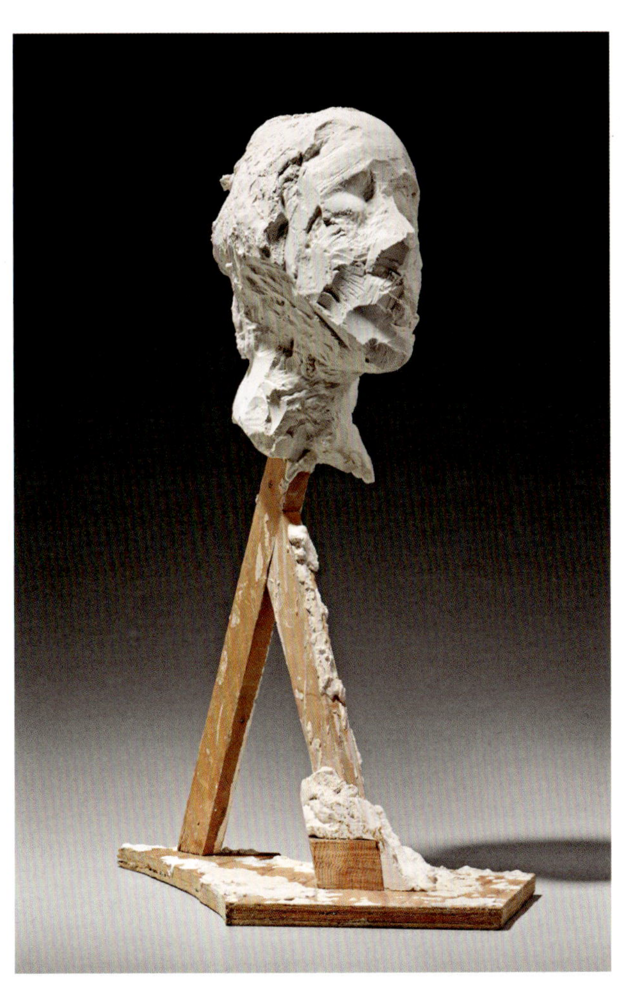
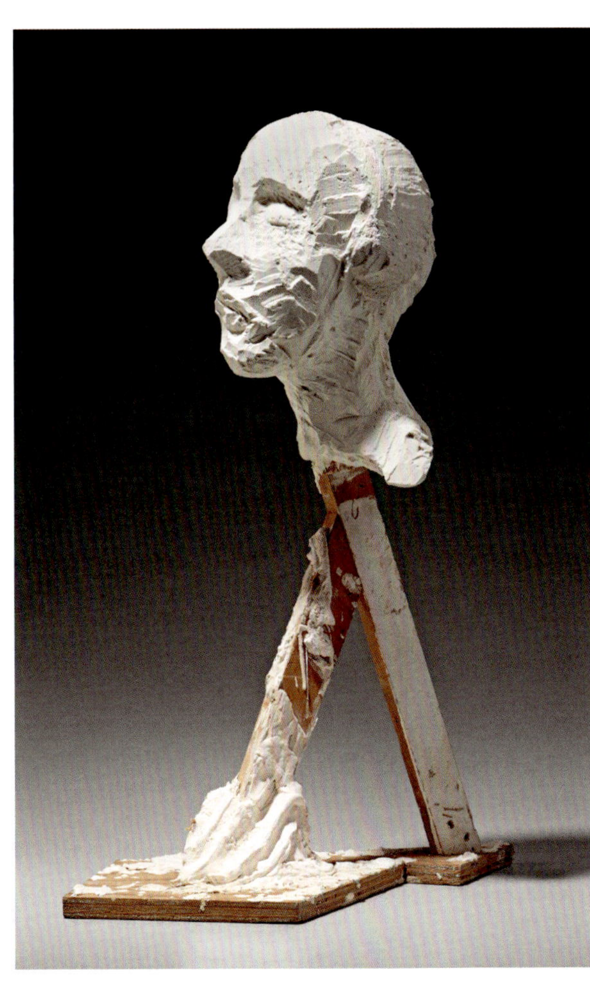

Fig. 14. Manuel Neri, *Female Head No. 1*, ca. 1969, reworked 1972–74. Plaster, water-based pigment, and graphite, 28 × 13 × 17 in. (71.1 × 33 × 43.2 cm). Yale University Art Gallery, Gift of The Manuel Neri Trust, 2017.88.2

Fig. 15. Manuel Neri, *Bull Jumper III*, 1989. Plaster with water-based pigment, 30¼ × 21½ × 42 in. (76.8 × 54.6 × 106.7 cm). Yale University Art Gallery, Gift of The Manuel Neri Trust, 2017.88.32

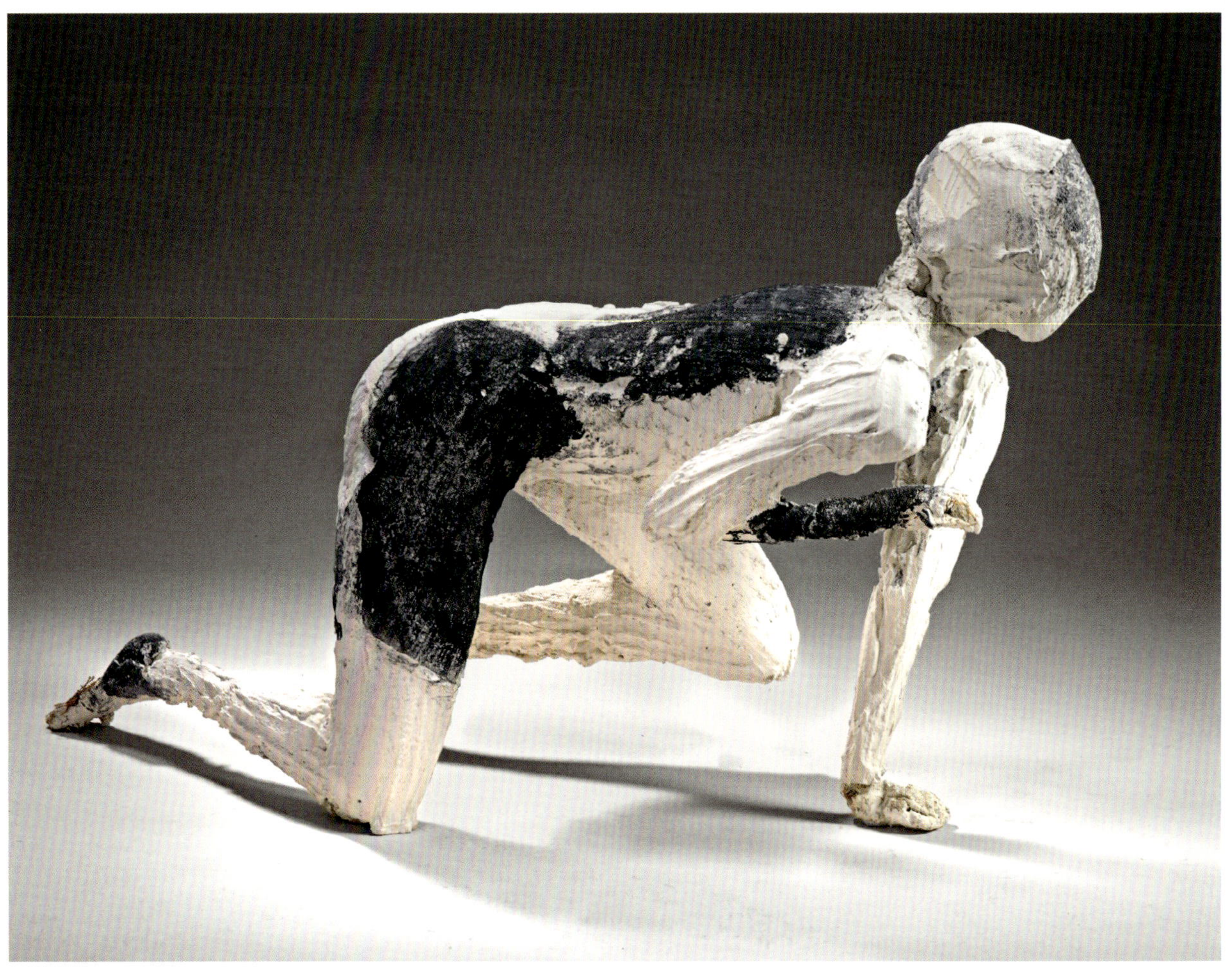

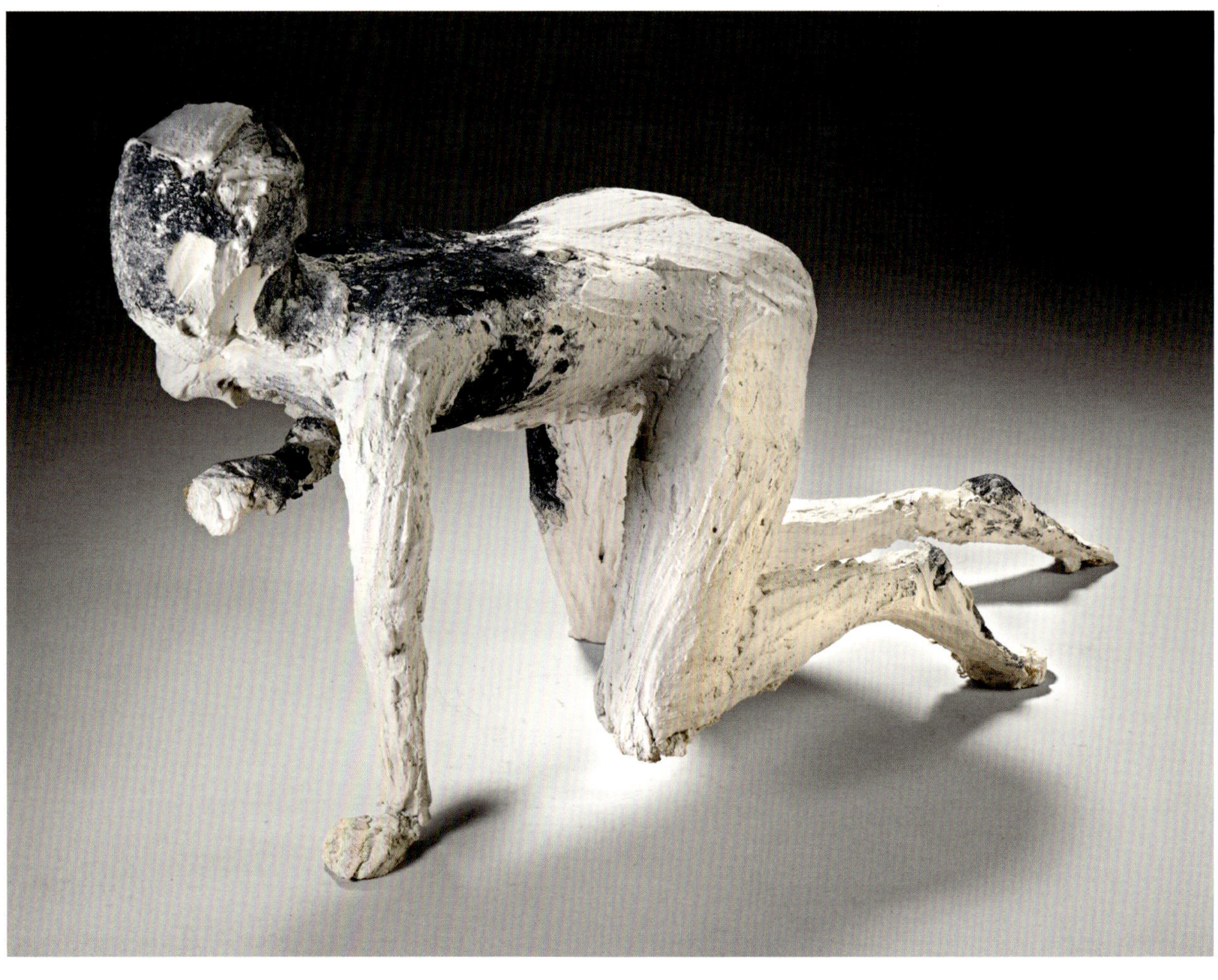

I was fortunate to gain admission to the UC Davis M.F.A. program in 1970, and that year I was able for the first time to view an array of Neri's sketchbooks, gouaches, and drawings in his studio, which are still not widely known to many admirers of his sculpture (figs. 16–18). I was also surprised during that year that the next example of Neri's art that I encountered was very different from anything of his I had seen before. Neri had recently moved into a new studio, a vacant wooden church he had purchased in the town of Benicia, just north of San Francisco, and it turned out that a colony of wild honeybees had established itself and grown a large hive within the walls of the church. In time, the hive became such a nuisance that Neri had the building fumigated, which caused a flurry of bees to desperately pour out of his studio walls and die in great numbers on the floor. I knew nothing of this incident until later that year, when a number of us graduate students and faculty members were invited to create a group exhibition together in the public gallery in the UC Davis student union.[12] For his contribution to the show, Neri scattered hundreds of what he titled *Dead Bees* over the large, unoccupied central area of the gallery floor. He had fashioned the deceased foragers' heads and bodies from crumpled paper, attached scissor-cut cardboard wings to them with string, and finally splashed their enlarged corpses with a lightly tinted coating of either varnish or

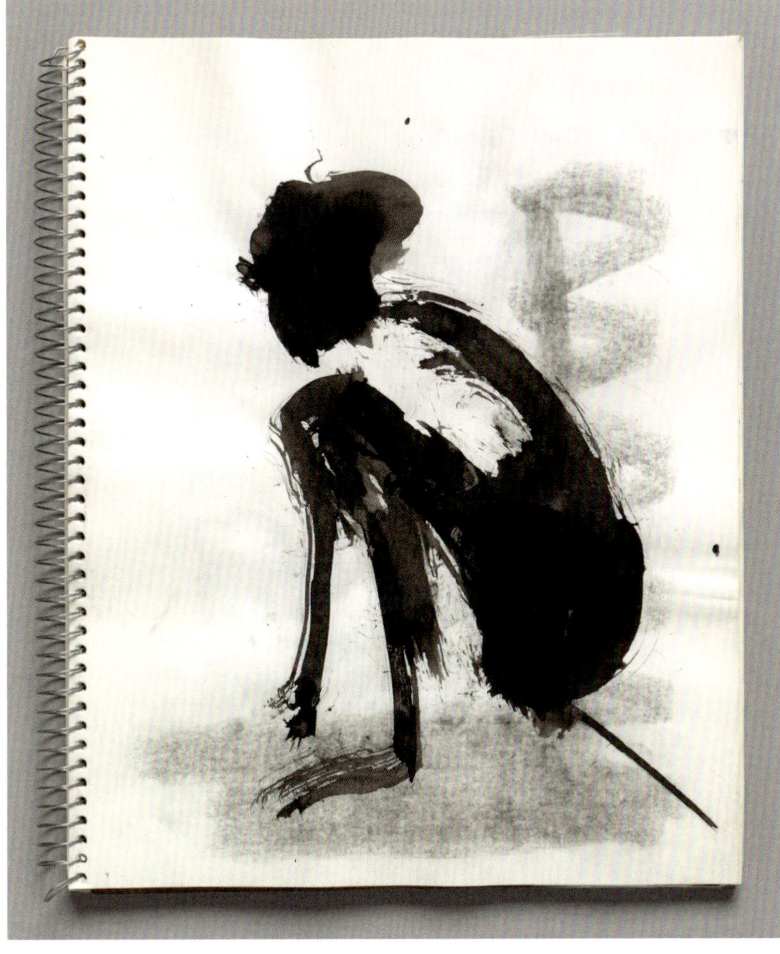

Fig. 16. Manuel Neri, page from *Strathmore Sketchbook*, ca. 1987. Sketchbook with ink, oil stick, graphite, and charcoal, 14 × 11 in. (35.6 × 28 cm). Yale University Art Gallery, Gift of The Manuel Neri Trust, 2017.88.137

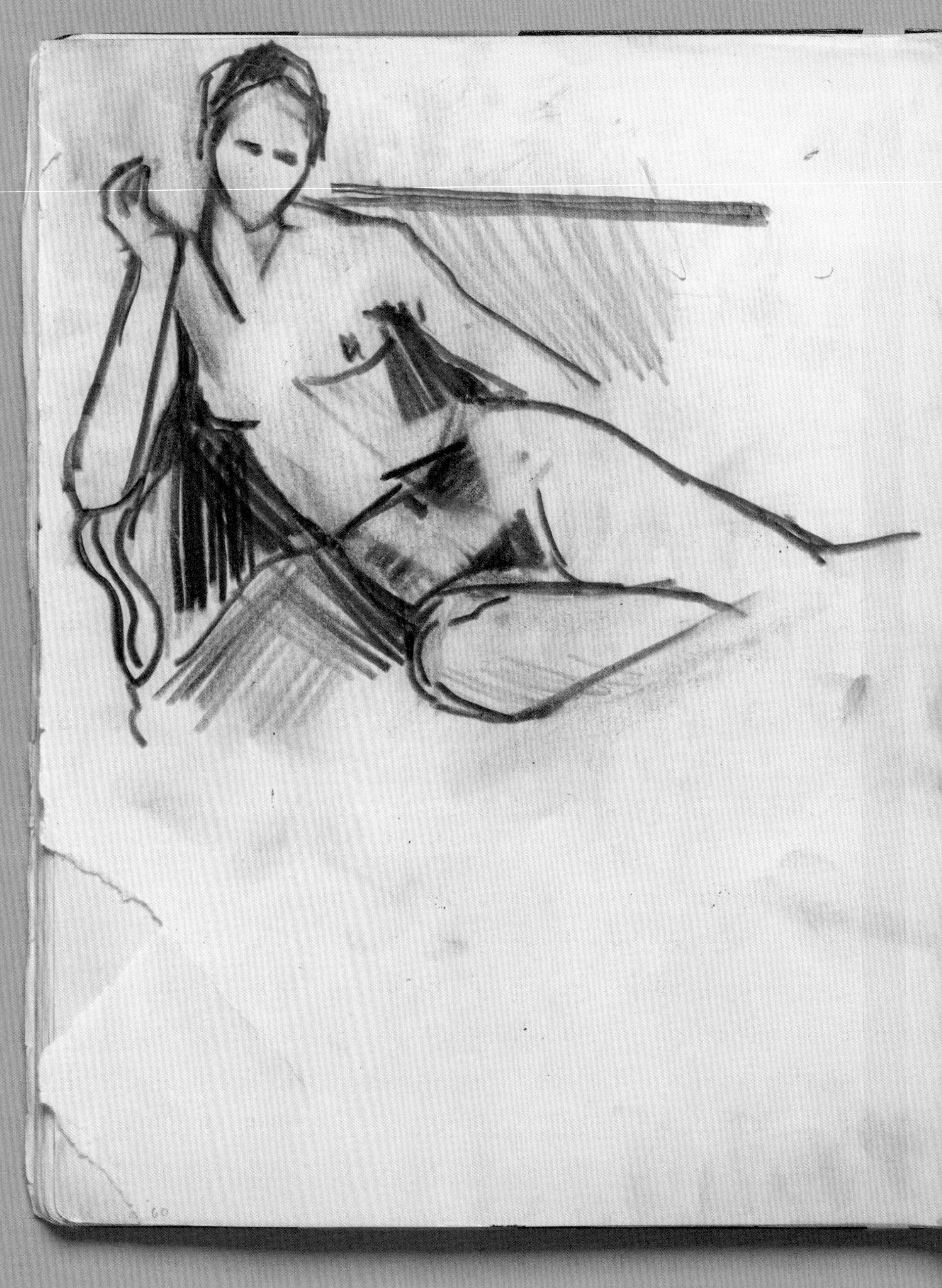

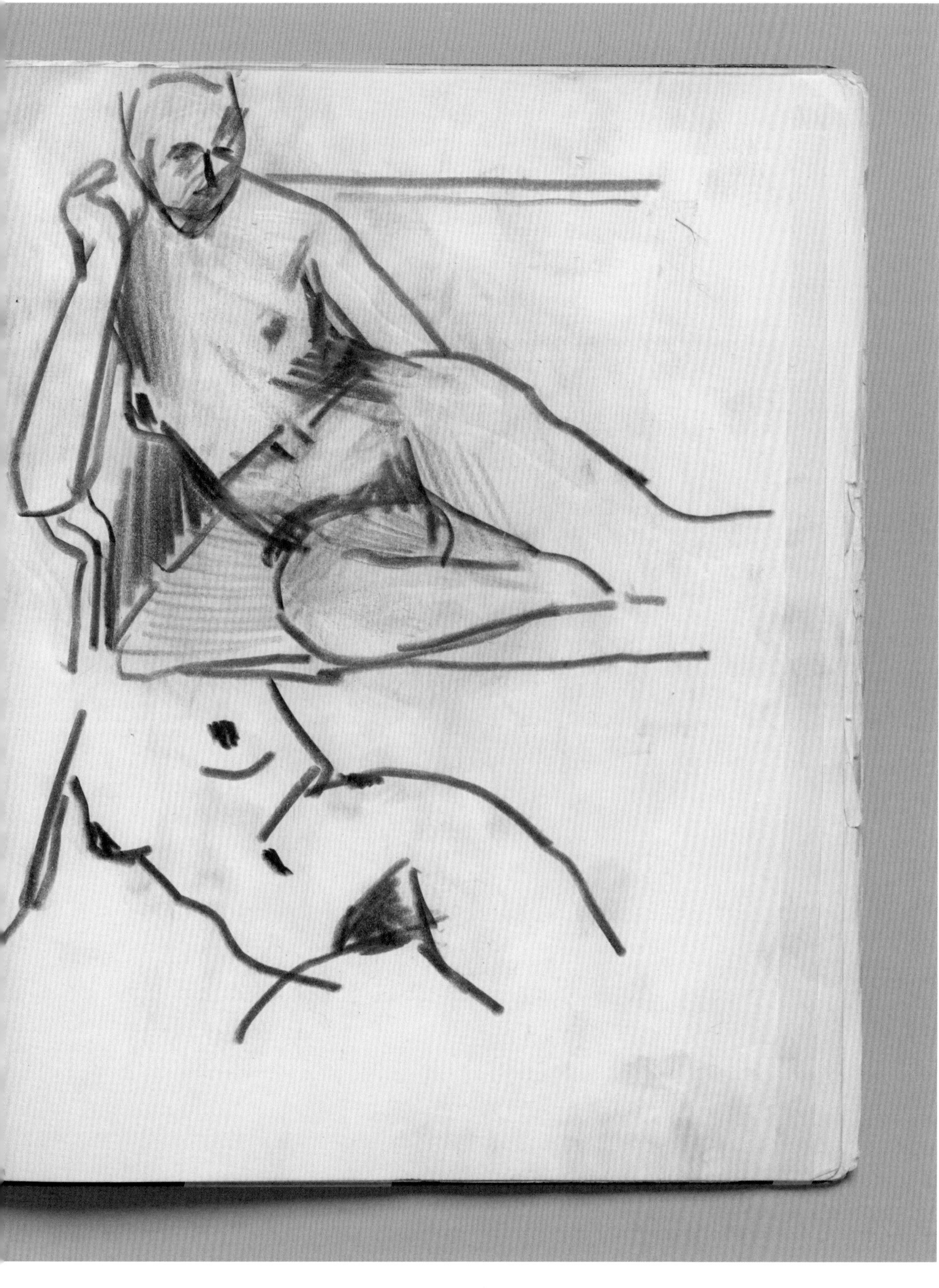

Fig. 17. Manuel Neri, spread from *Casting Sketchbook*, ca. 1959. Sketchbook with graphite, ballpoint pen, oil pastel, and ink, 10⅞ × 8½ in. (27.6 × 21.6 cm). Yale University Art Gallery, Gift of The Manuel Neri Trust, 2017.88.131

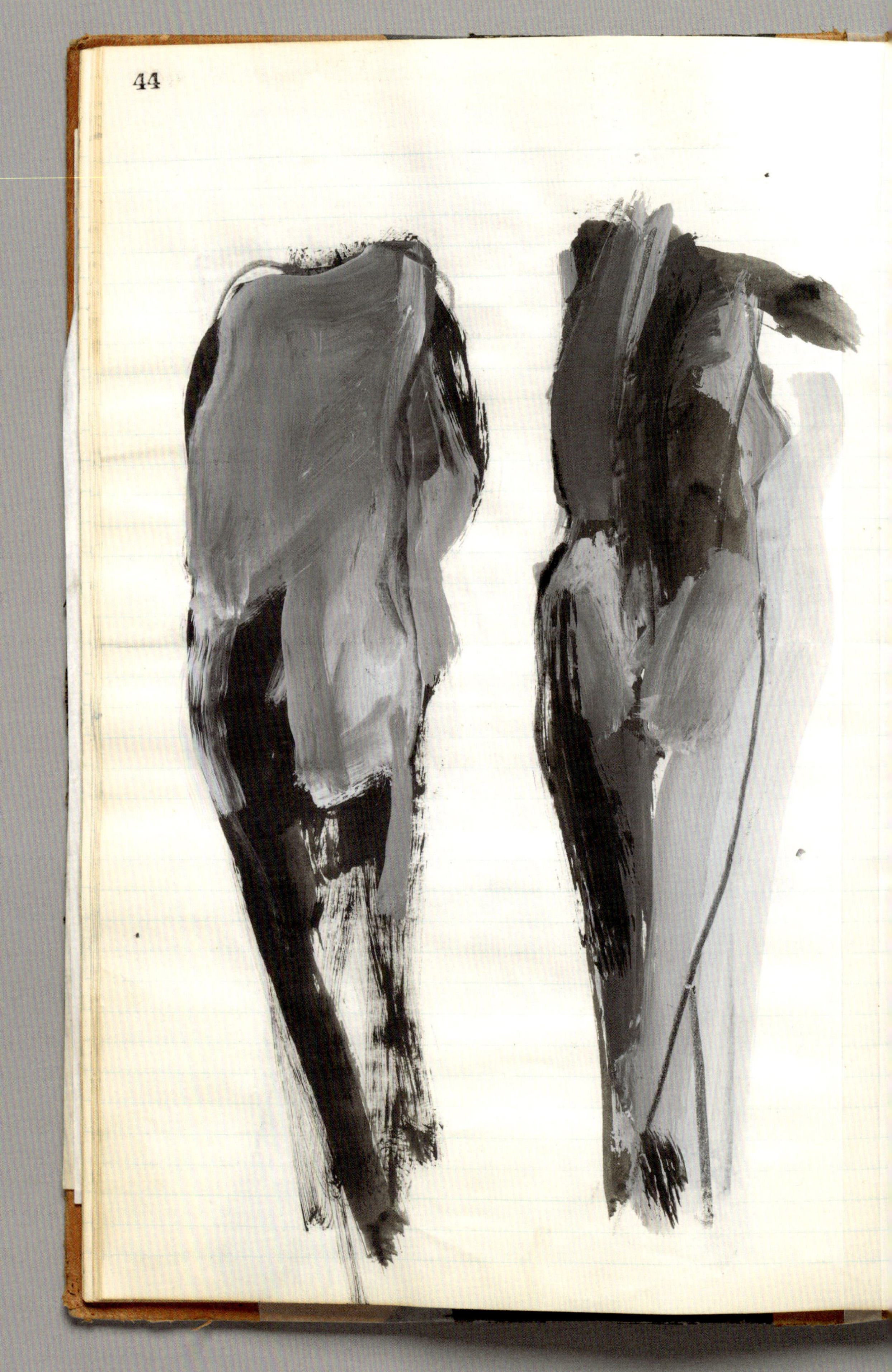

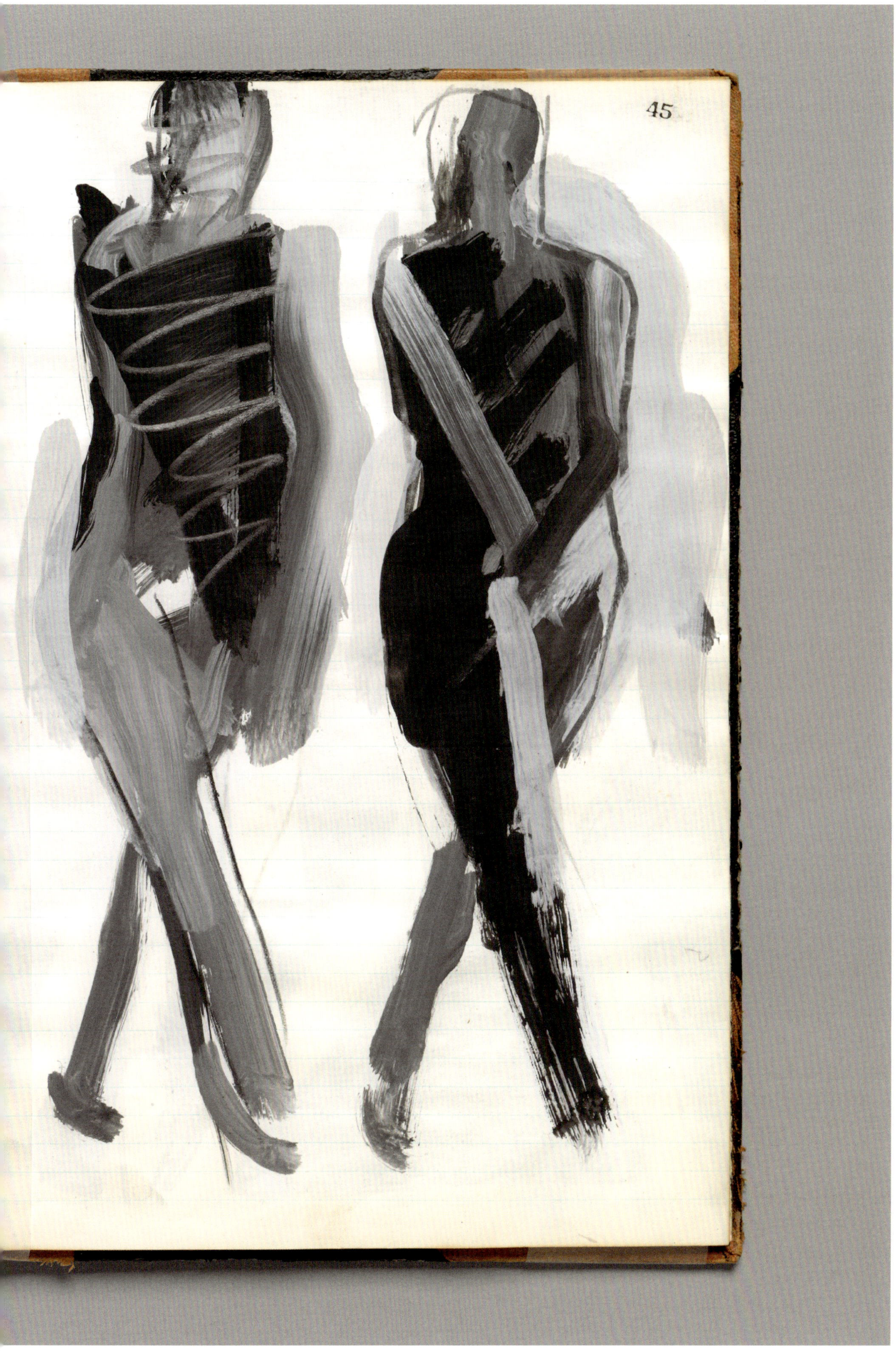

Fig. 18. Manuel Neri, spread from *Unos Actos de Fe Sketchbook*, ca. 1974–76. Sketchbook with graphite, water-based pigment, ink, cut and pasted paper, and red pencil, 13 × 8 ½ in. (33 × 21.6 cm). Yale University Art Gallery, Gift of The Manuel Neri Trust, 2017.88.136

paint thinner. The display of hundreds of Neri's *Dead Bees* was in many respects the first example of installation art I had encountered but yet had no name for. That this artwork was sourced from one of Neri's real-life experiences truly intrigued me, as did his statement that a formal exhibition space could be occupied by sculptural objects that needed no plinths or pedestals, and could instead lay still, scattered on the floor much as Neri's real bees had come to rest after meeting their death in his studio. Interestingly, Neri later mailed many of us students and friends small cardboard boxes that were rubber-stamped with the words "DEAD BEE" (fig. 19). Within each box was one of the bees Neri had taken back to his studio and then chosen to present yet again in a different manner, as individual works of art.[13]

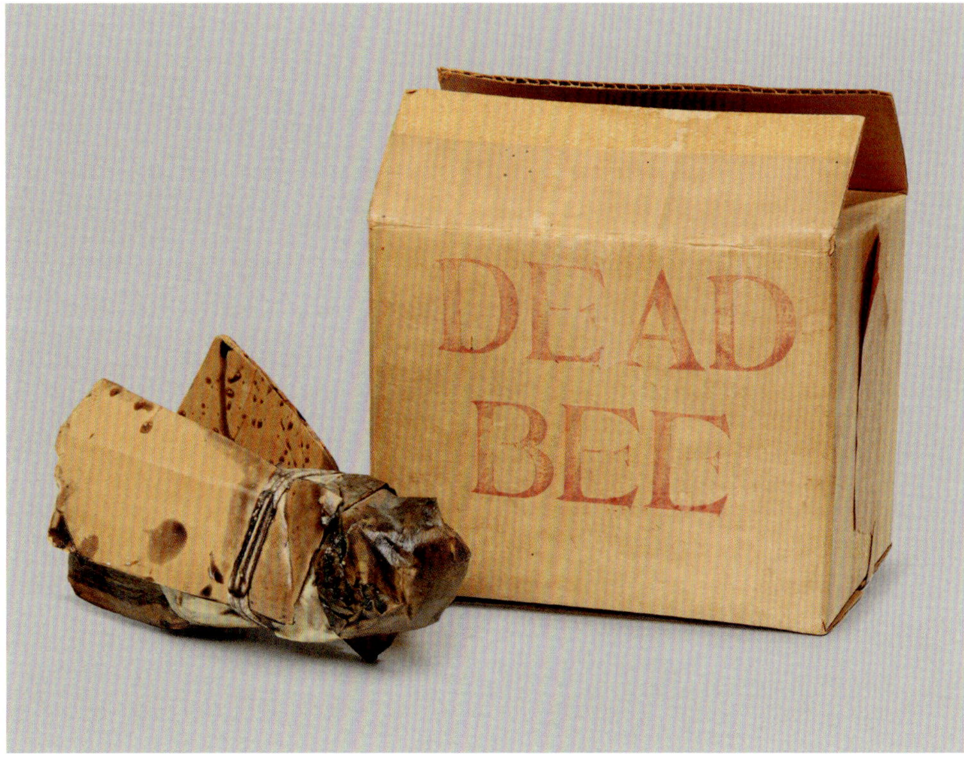

Fig. 19. Manuel Neri, *Dead Bee*, ca. 1970. Mixed media on paper and cardboard, 6 × 3 × 3 in. (15.2 × 7.5 × 7.5 cm). Fine Arts Collection, Jan Shrem and Maria Manetti Shrem Museum of Art, University of California, Davis, Gift of Jock Reynolds, 2007.004.208

The great blessing of studying at UC Davis during its art department's early years was that our teachers, all young artists themselves, were also very busily finding their way. We students were continuously able to observe how our mentors developed the subject matter for their creative endeavors, which more often than not were—like Neri's *Dead Bees*—directly inspired by experiences drawn from their daily lives. They encouraged us to do the same and essentially treated us as peers. They often worked either alongside some of us or, at times, directly with us, and they were always willing to have us observe any of their classes and, in numerous instances, become their teaching assistants when they had the need for such help. Becoming a teaching assistant for Neri was something I yearned for and achieved in my second year of graduate study.

That year, I taught an undergraduate studio course alongside
Neri—which met once a week for three hours—in which we challenged
our students to represent the human figure in plaster from a live model
(fig. 20). First the model held a series of different poses, and the students
drew each one swiftly; then the model held a long pose, and the students
were asked to render a figure in three dimensions using plaster as their

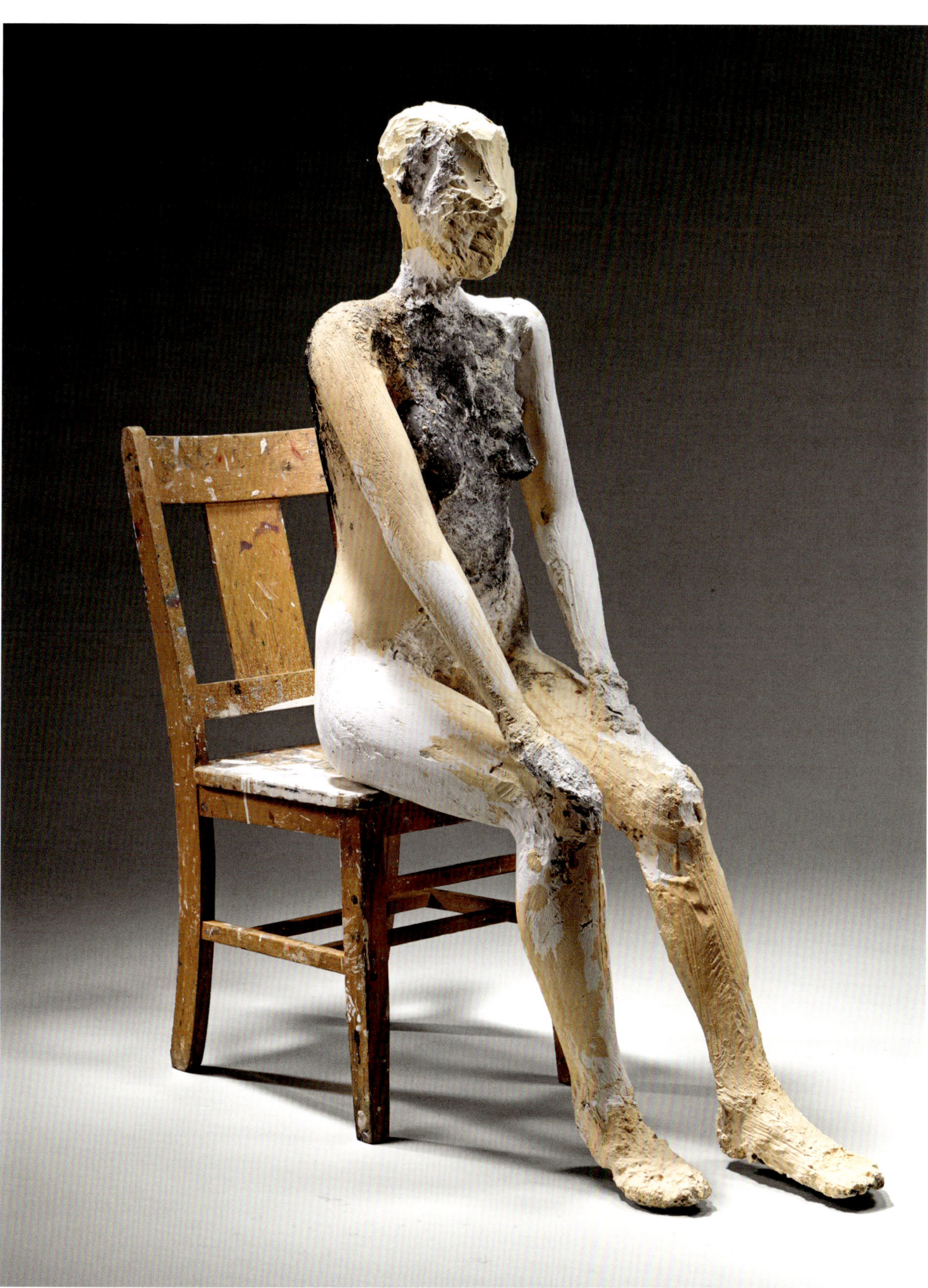

Fig. 20. Manuel
Neri, *Re-making
of Mary Julia
No. 6*, 1976. Plaster
with pigment, 52 ×
17 × 38 in. (132.1 ×
43.2 × 96.5 cm).
Yale University
Art Gallery, Gift of
The Manuel Neri
Trust, 2017.88.35

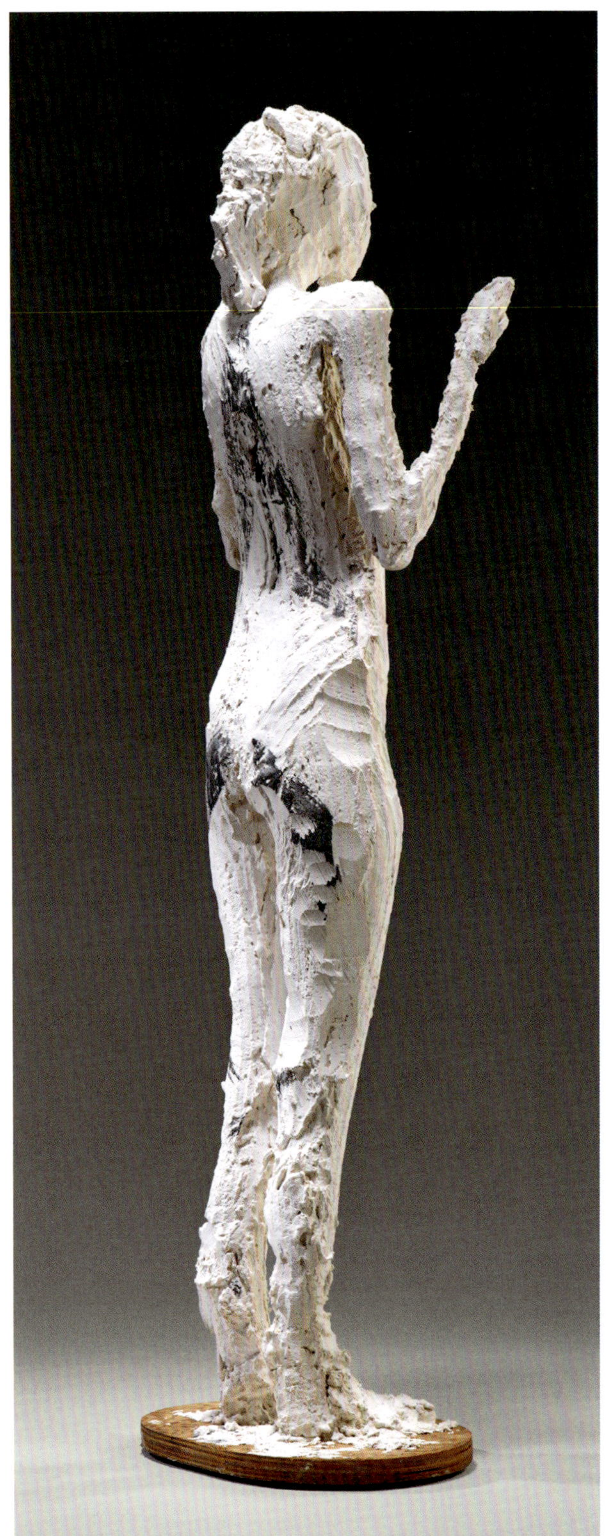
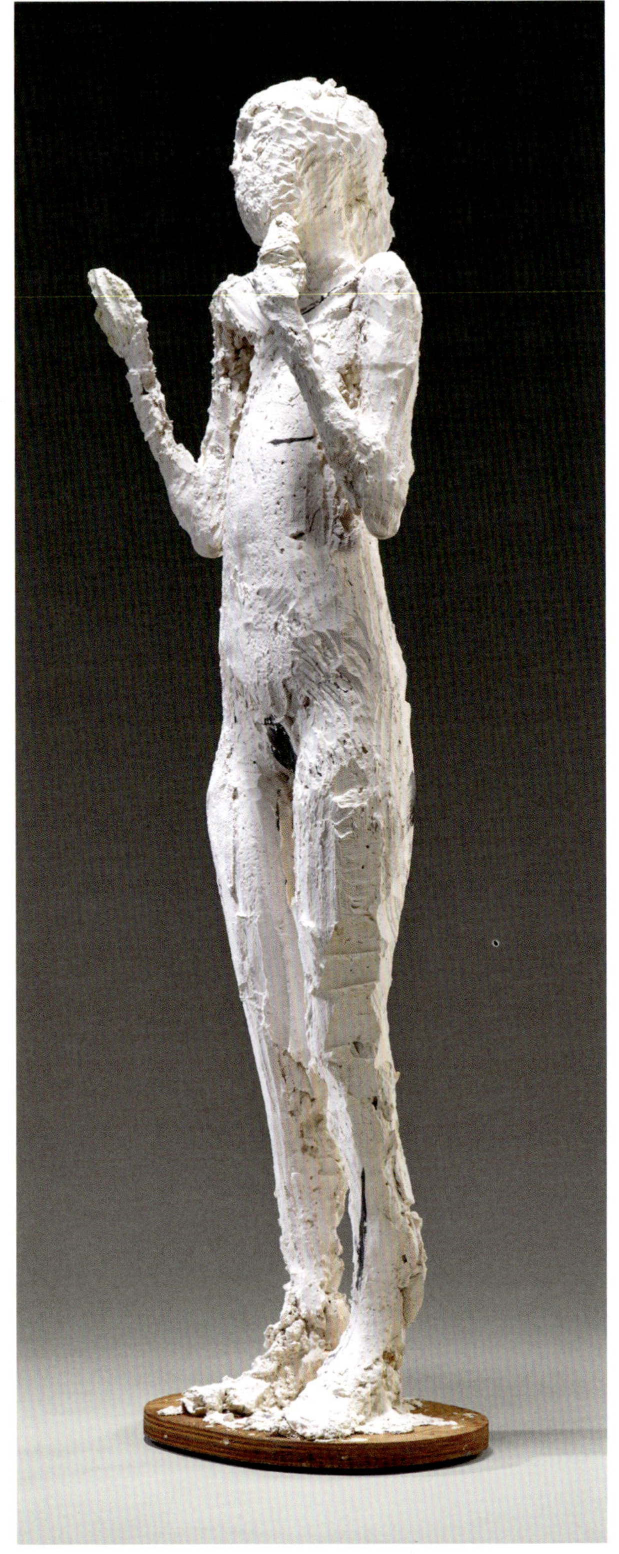

medium (plaster being one of the most versatile materials sculptors
have used throughout the history of art). Neri was himself a master of
such work. During our semester spent teaching together he also invited
me to visit his studio in Benicia, where I readily observed how his own
creative work with a model was conducted. It happened to be that my
studio visit coincided with the moment when Mary Julia Raahauge had
become Neri's second great muse (Joan Brown being his first) and thereafter virtually the only—and very passionate—subject of much of his
full-scale figurative work (figs. 21-22).[14]

30

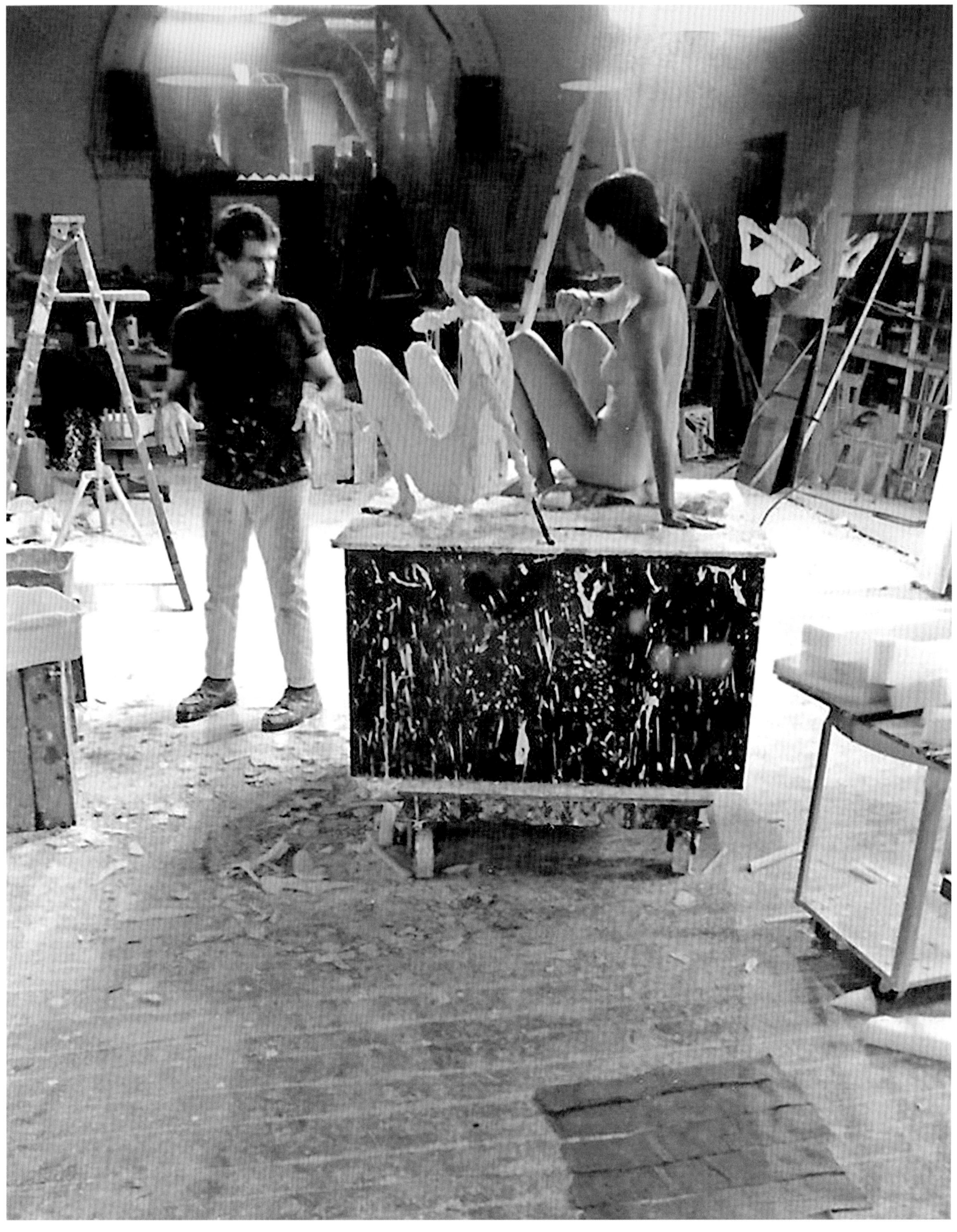

Fig. 22. Mary Julia Raahauge posing for Manuel Neri in his
studio, Benicia, California, 1979

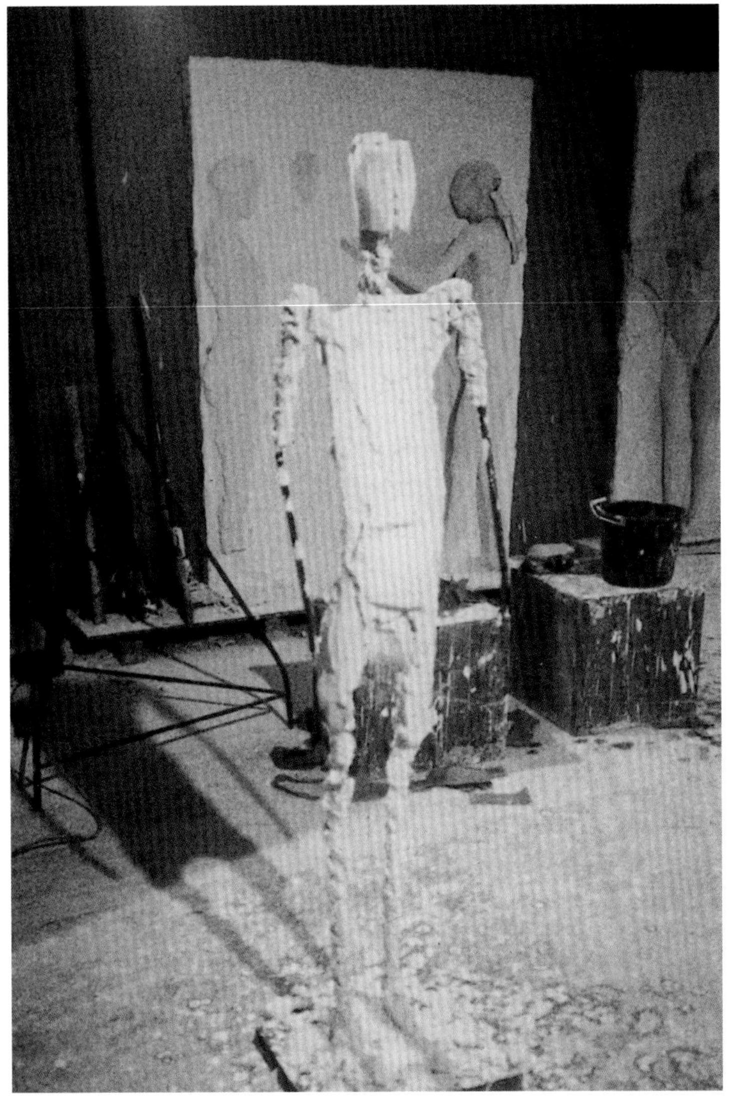 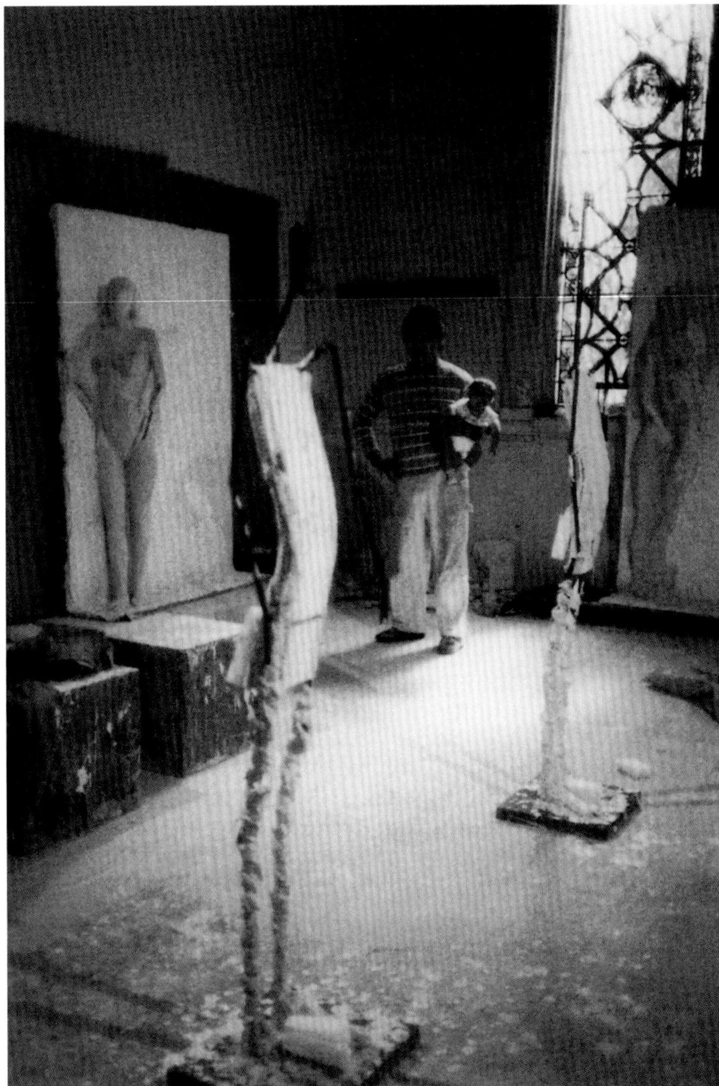

Fig. 23. Plaster sculpture in progress in Manuel Neri's studio, showing the steel armature, Benicia, California, 1985

Fig. 24. Manuel Neri with plaster sculptures in progress in his studio, Benicia, California, 1985

When embarking on a new body of work, Neri would usually begin with a series of what he calls "starts"—drawings of his model in different poses, executed in rapid succession. Then, he would go back and rework the starts—frequently five or six at a time—to add color and emphasize the line of the pose or gesture. For sculptures, Neri would decide on a pose with the model, then draw it or sometimes just begin constructing a basic figurative armature from wire, wood, steel, cardboard, and burlap (figs. 23-24). Then, working quickly with wet plaster, Neri would apply the material with his bare hands to build up his model's pose and form over the entire armature (fig. 25), at times either mixing multiple batches of plaster to finish an individual work in such a manner or letting the plaster figure harden to the point where it could be easily shaped, carved, or otherwise finished with a variety of hand tools: rasps, chisels, hammers, hatchets,

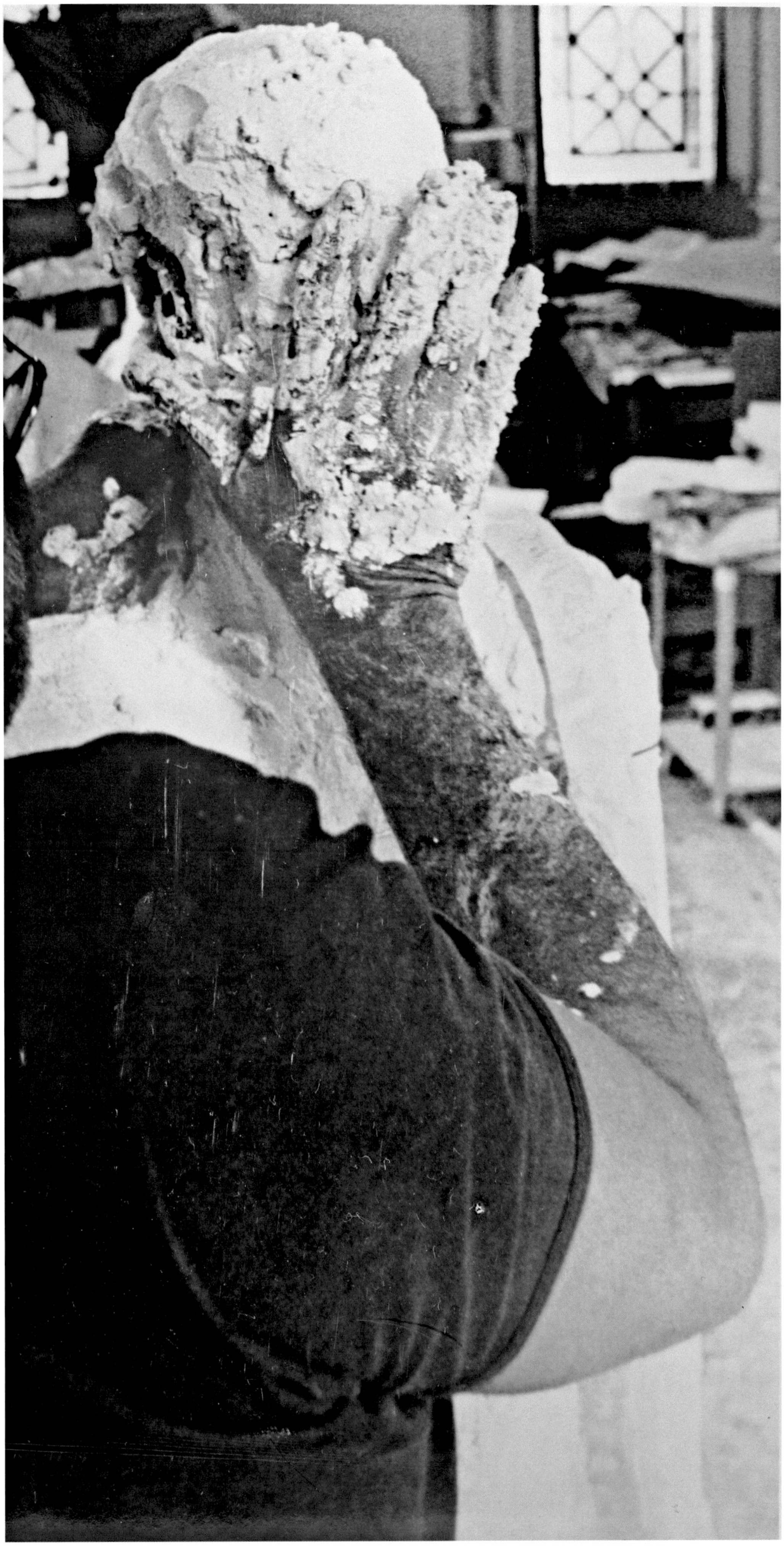

Fig. 25. Manuel Neri working in his studio, Benicia, California, 1980

adzes, brushes, spatulas, sandpaper, and more (fig. 26). Additional layers of plaster, as well as powdered pigments and paint, were also applied to a good number of Neri's figures and heads (fig. 27). As with his drawings, Neri would often work on several pieces simultaneously. His creative process when working with plaster was especially intense and even physically exhausting due to the very nature of the material—it could be worked with easily and decisively when wet and soft, but often required much more aggressive handling when it hardened. Sometimes Neri would snap a dry arm off a sculpture, if its first gesture no longer seemed right to his eye, and then quickly build up a new one. At other times he might simply wire a bun of plaster hair onto one of the heads of his figures, to bring it to a point of visually satisfying completion. An active sense of improvisation was always present whenever I observed Neri working directly in plaster, something that truly fascinated me.

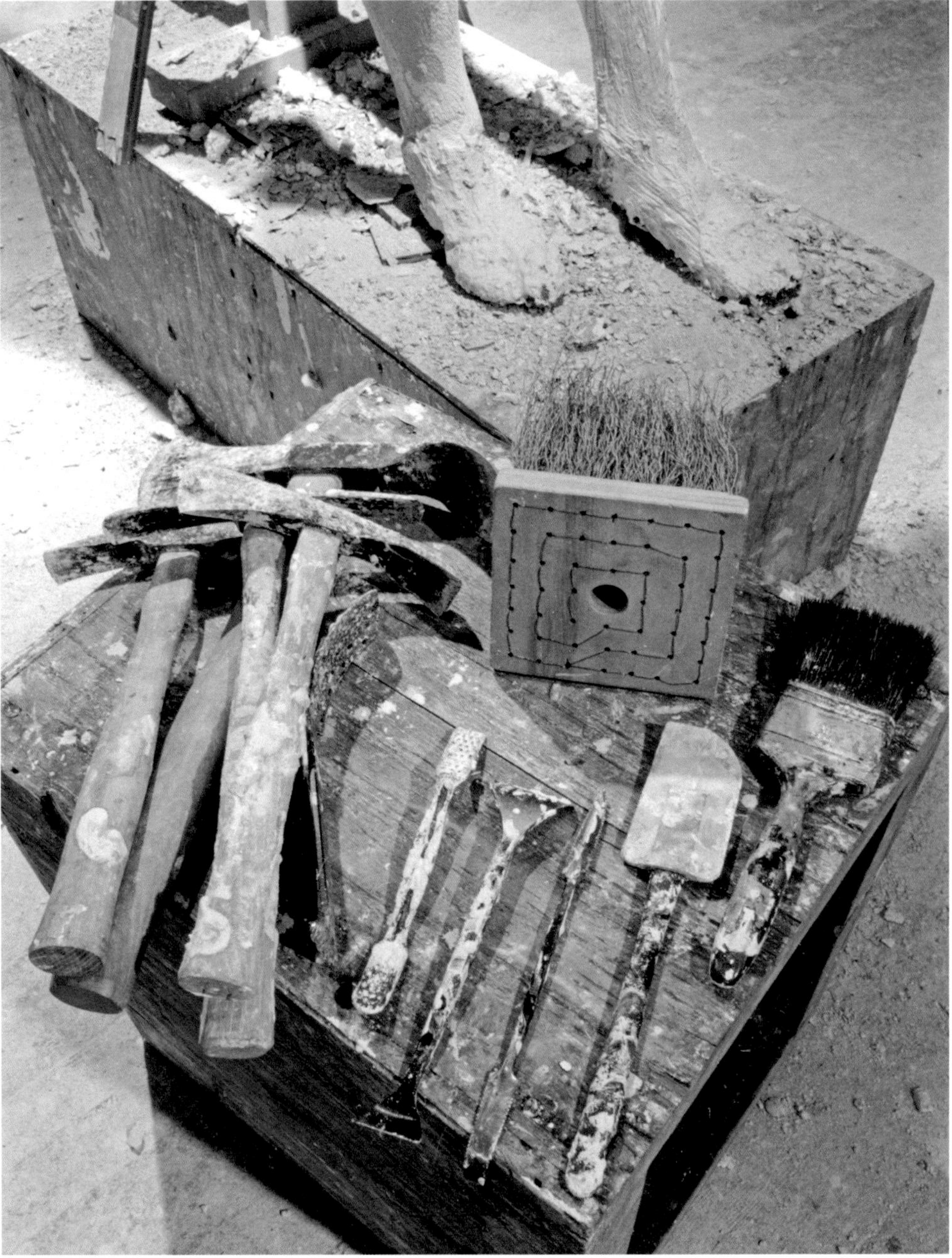

Fig. 26. Tools in Manuel Neri's studio, Benicia, California, 1987

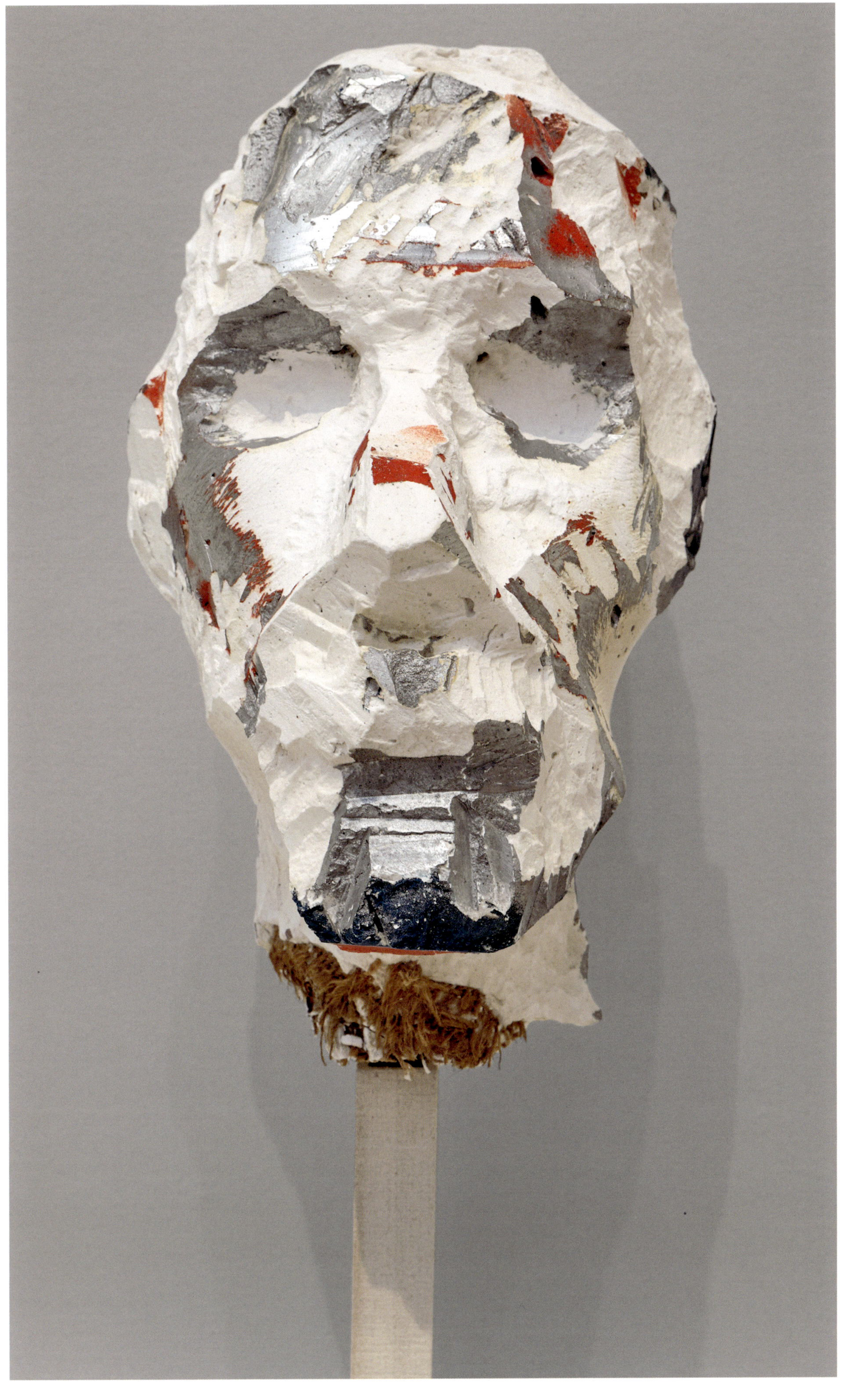

Fig. 27. Manuel Neri, *Head of Markos*, 1963. Plaster with metallic paint and oil-based enamel, 25 × 7 × 8¼ in. (63.5 × 17.8 × 21 cm). Yale University Art Gallery, Gift of The Manuel Neri Trust, 2017.88.3

I also watched Neri keep his eyes and hands active in another way, by both teaching and working at the same time. In the studio course we taught together, he would often sit toward the back of our classroom, observing and commenting to his students who were working on their figures, while simultaneously dipping a watercolor brush into a cup of strong black coffee with which he would quickly sketch the class model dozens of times on a pad of cheap paper. These images would float down to the floor one after another. I regularly swept up dozens of Neri's visual exercises and would then dispose of them—for he had no intention of keeping any of them—along with ample amounts of plaster debris that had accumulated by the time one of our class sessions ended. Neri simply wanted and needed to be creative whenever possible. He thus consistently demonstrated a remarkable work ethic to his students, and his studio in Benicia always abounded with drawings large and small, watercolors, and collages that were tacked to the walls (figs. 28-31).

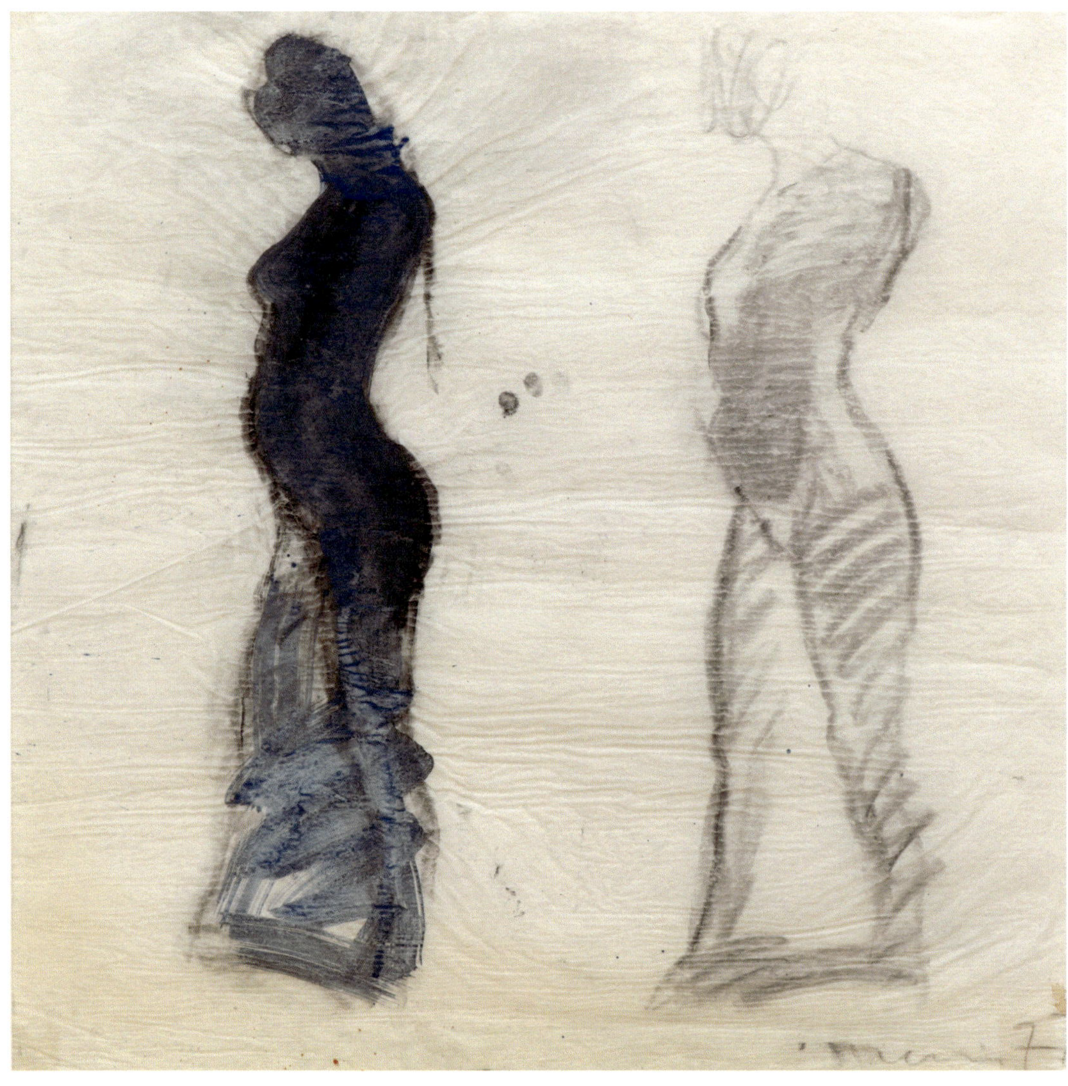

Fig. 28. Manuel Neri, *Twins: Double Figure Study*, 1977. Charcoal and watercolor on paper, 35³⁄₁₆ × 35¹⁄₂ in. (89.3 × 90.2 cm). Yale University Art Gallery, Gift of The Manuel Neri Trust, 2017.88.56

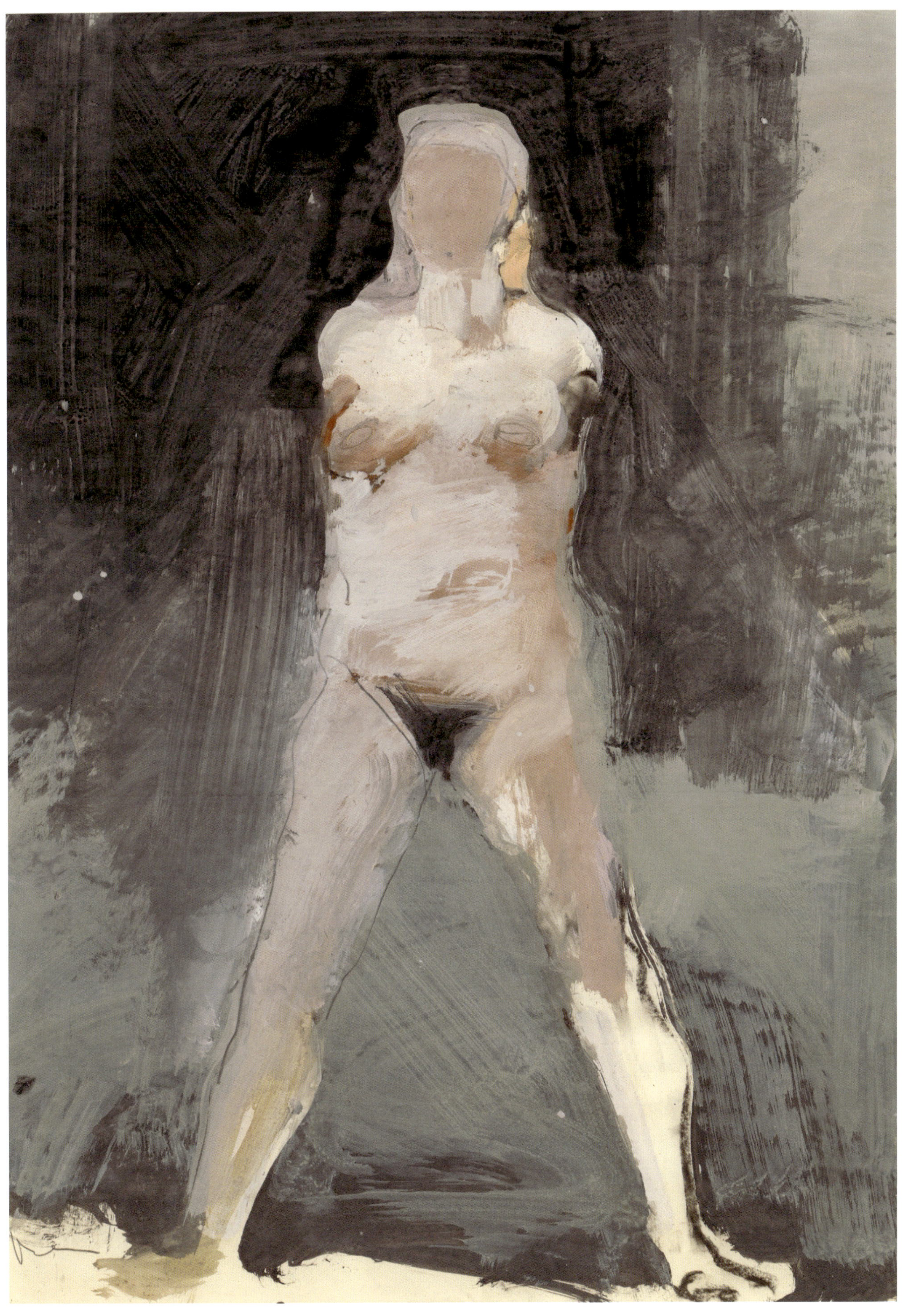

Fig. 29. Manuel Neri, *Mary Julia's Passion*, 1973. Watercolor, charcoal, graphite, and ink on paper, 41¾ × 30¼ in. (106 × 76.9 cm). Yale University Art Gallery, Gift of The Manuel Neri Trust, 2017.88.55

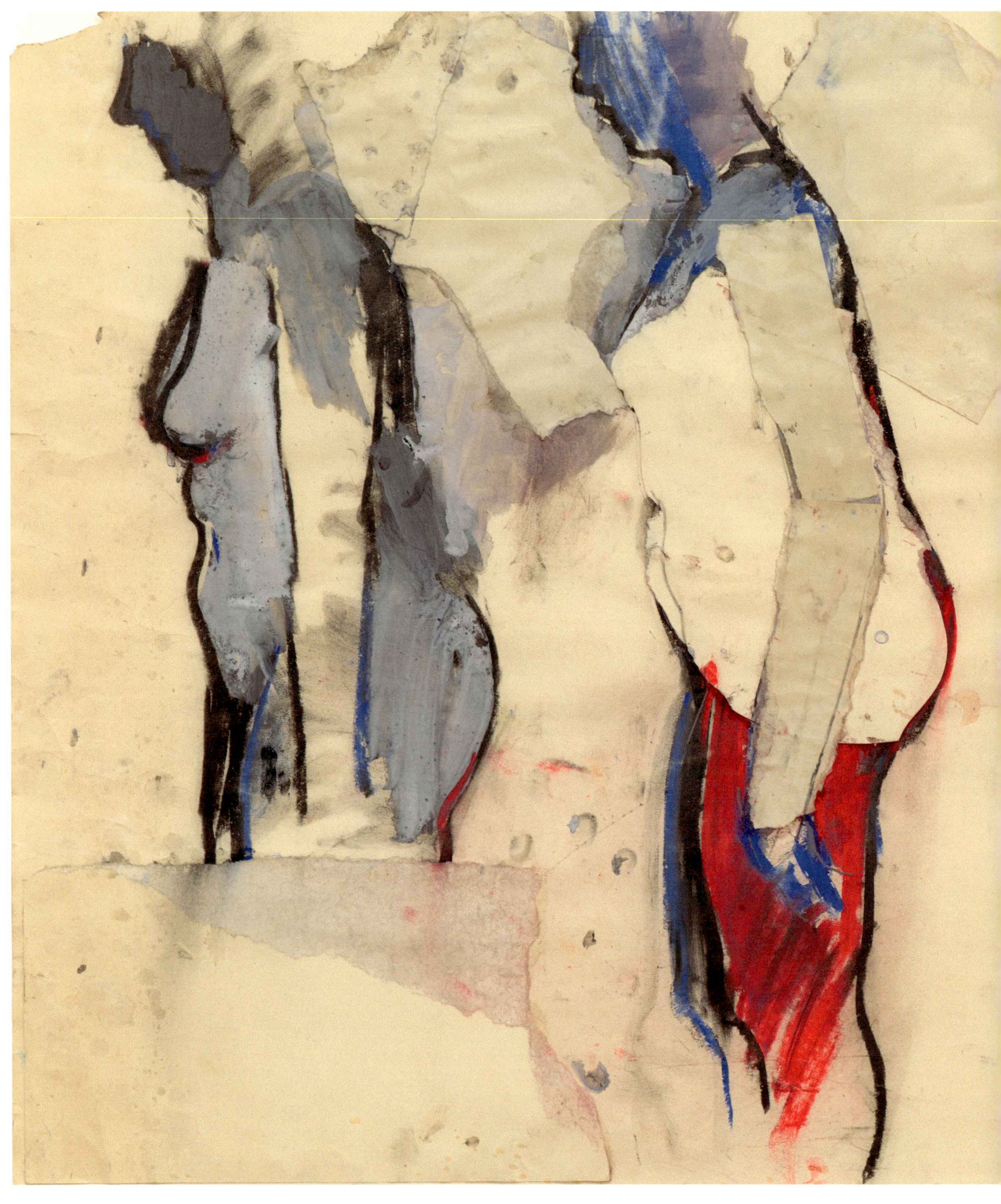

Fig. 30. Manuel Neri, *Torso Studies*, 1963. Mixed media with collage,
26 1/16 × 40 in. (66.2 × 101.7 cm). Yale University Art Gallery, Promised gift
of The Manuel Neri Trust

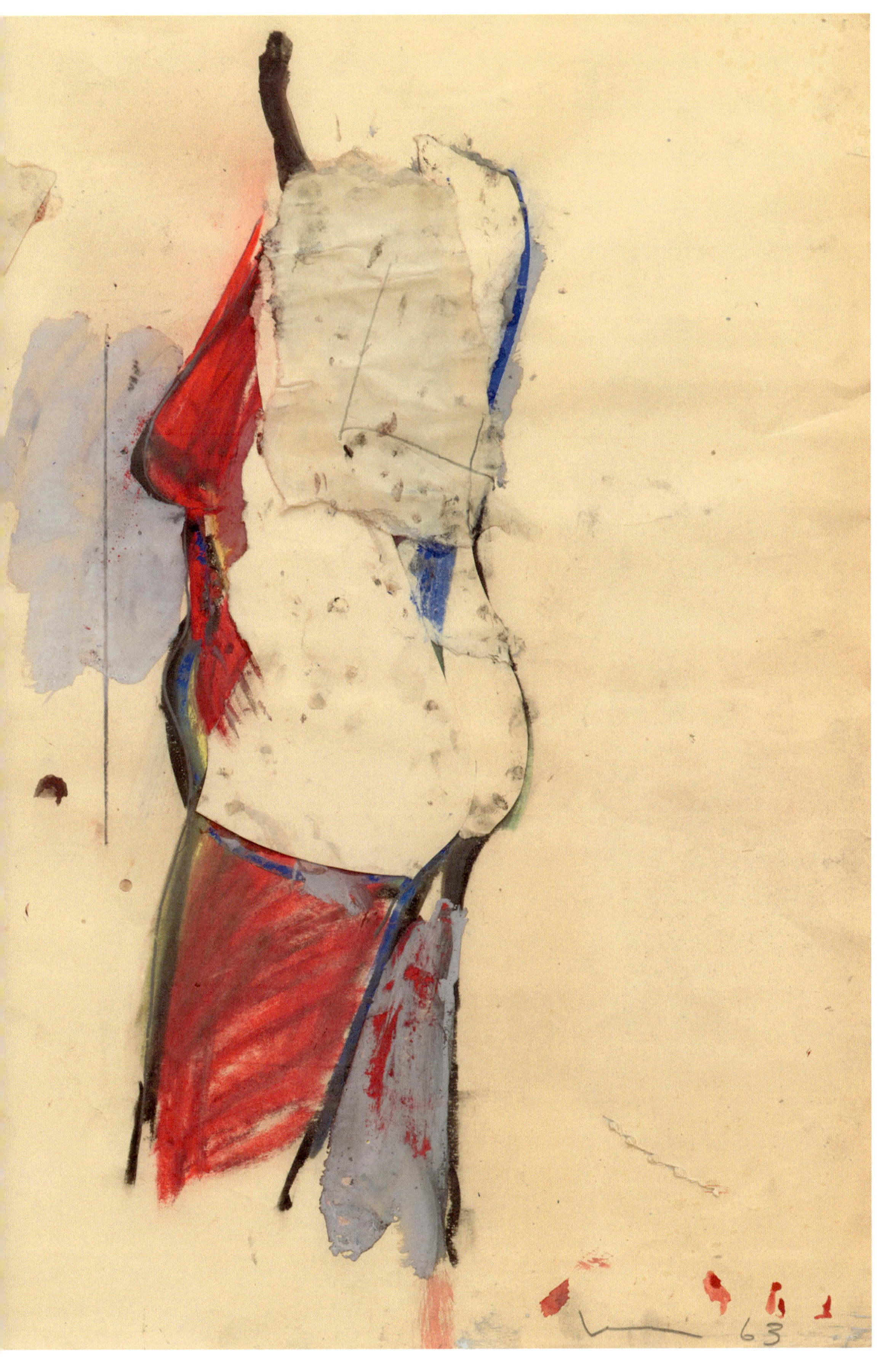

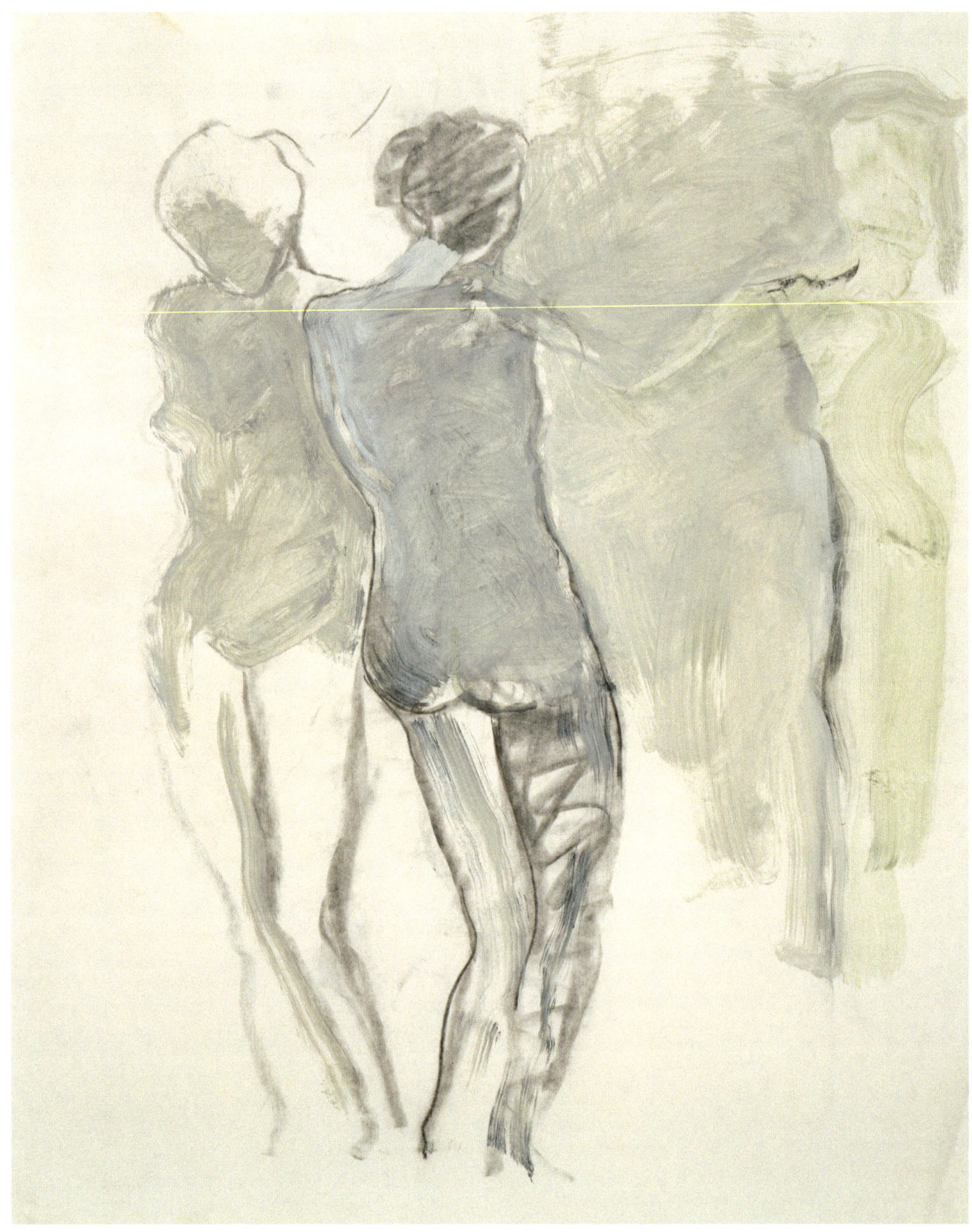

Also in 1972, Neri staged an installation at UC Davis—part of another faculty and student art exhibition—that displayed his creative process to the public and was closely tied to his teaching methods. In the central area of the art department's exhibition space, later named the Richard L. Nelson Gallery in 1976, Neri laid down and conjoined four full sheets of plywood and painted them to create a stage of sorts, upon which he fashioned a pair of full-length plaster figures. As part of the piece, Neri came to the gallery to work: every three days he altered the sculptures, and other times he merely sat on public view in a wooden chair, contemplating his figures and thinking about what he might wish to do to them next (figs. 32-34). It was soon apparent to me, and surely to others of Neri's students, that sitting quietly and considering what to do next was also a serious aspect of creative work, something we perhaps needed to pay more attention to in our own practices. Over the span of Neri's continued work on the figures, shards of plaster fragments accumulated in the space. Tools were also left here and

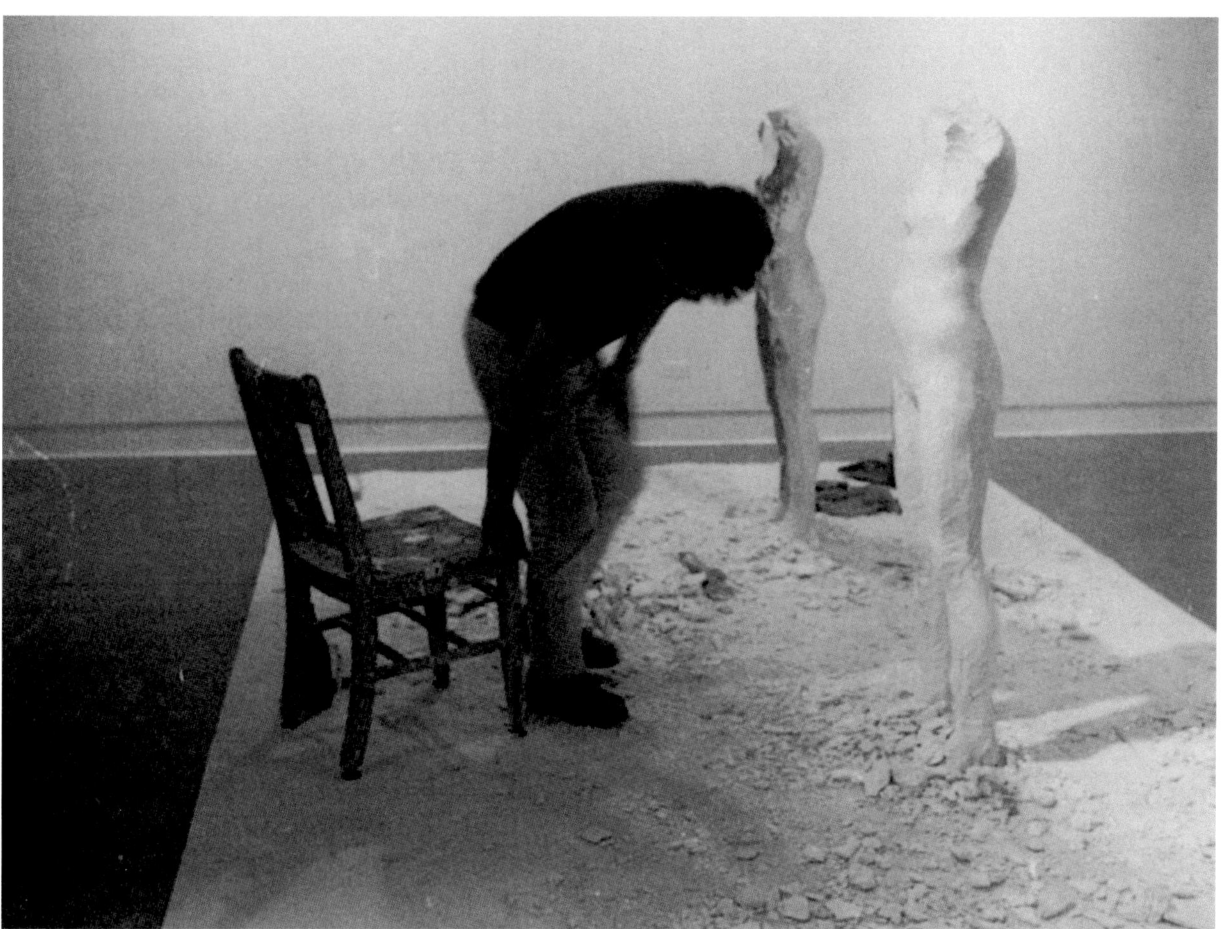

Fig. 32. Manuel
Neri's installation
at the University
of California,
Davis, 1972

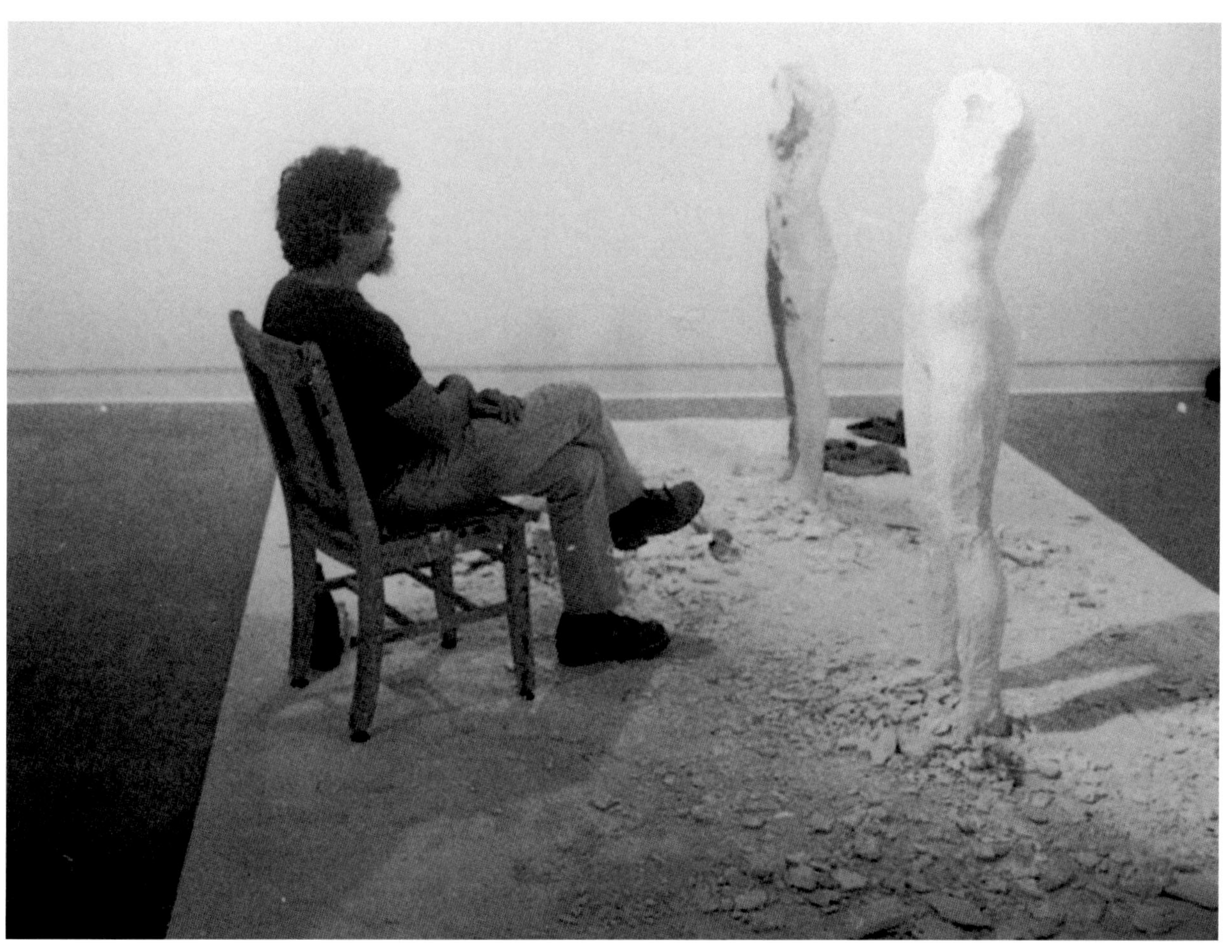

Fig. 33. Manuel
Neri's installation
at the University
of California,
Davis, 1972

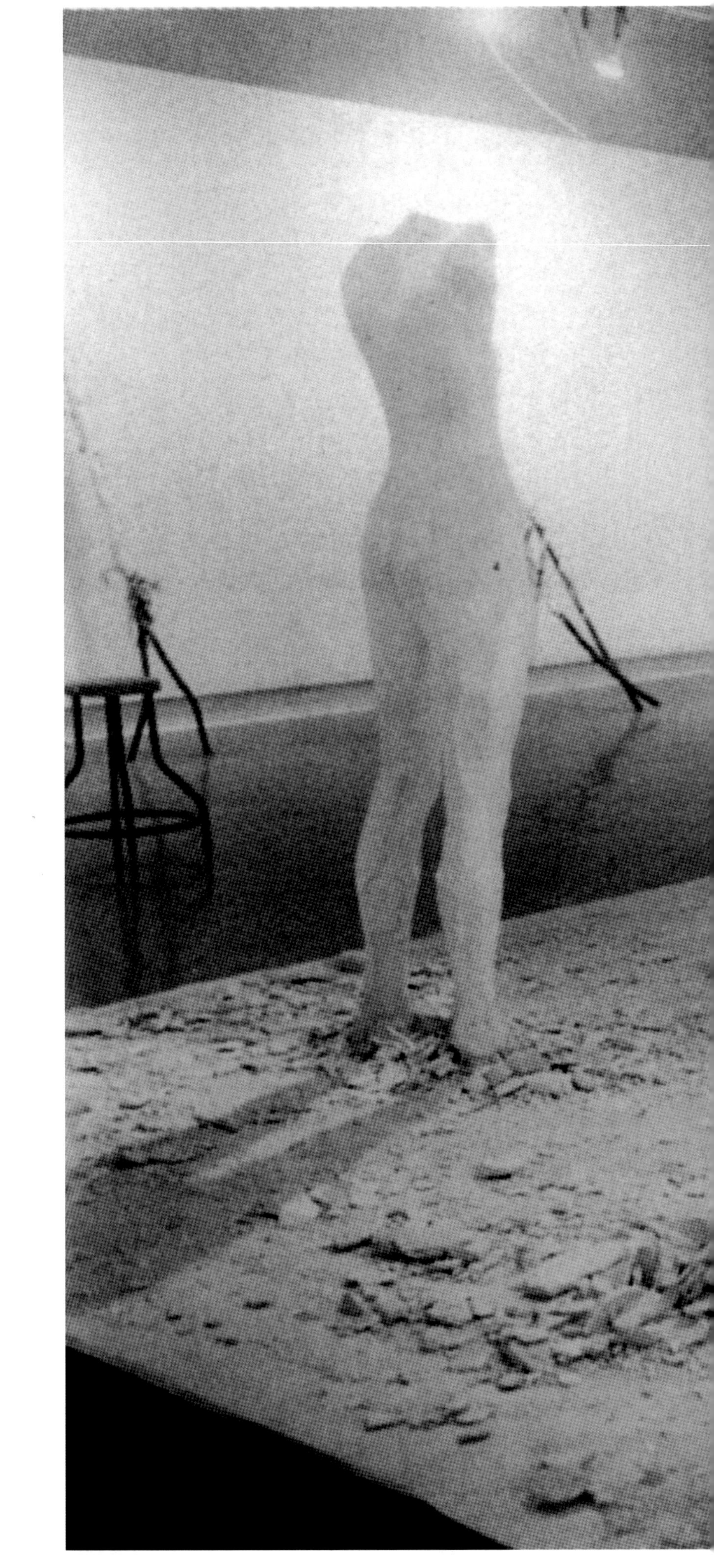

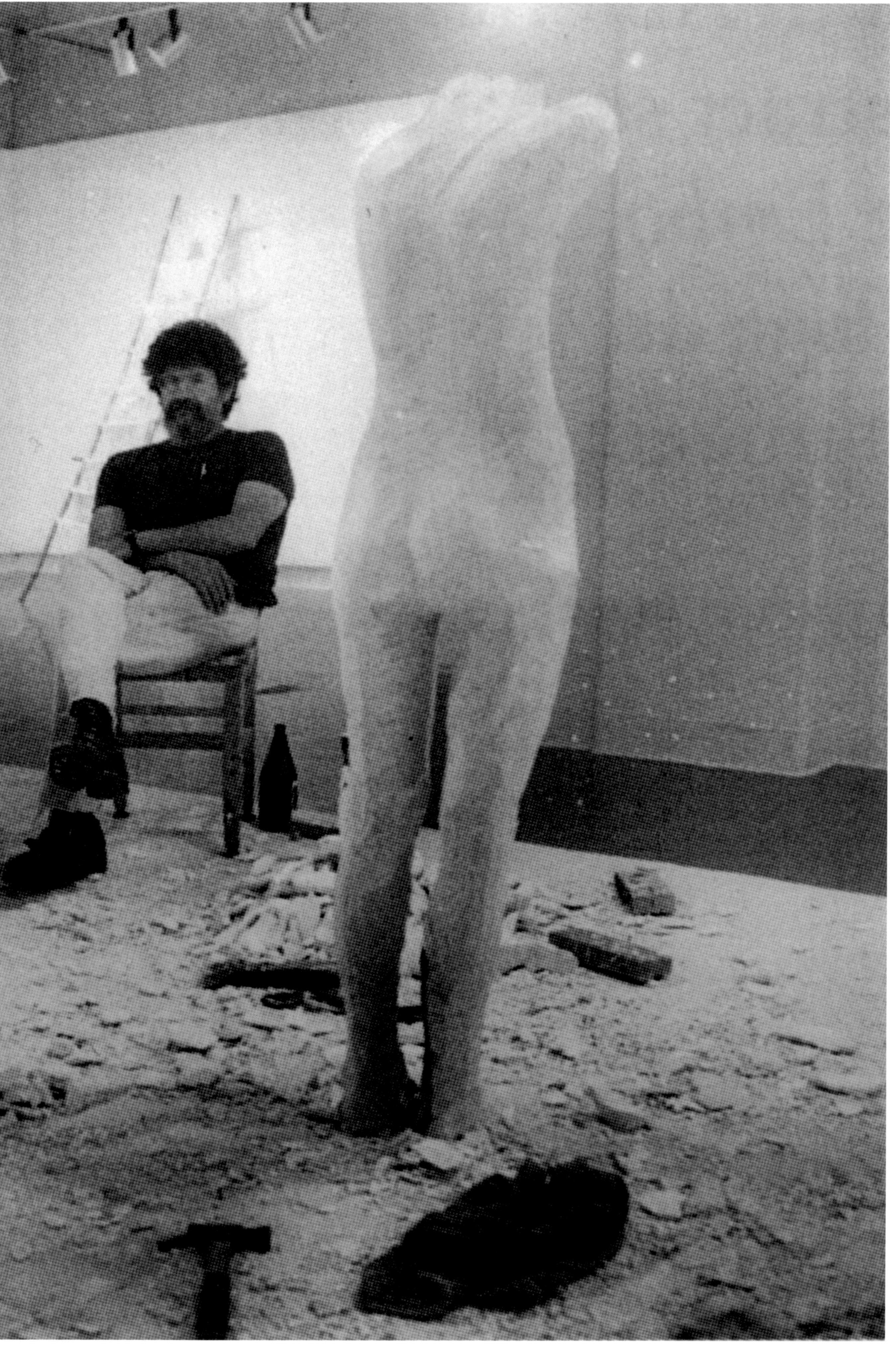

Fig. 34. Manuel
Neri's installation
at the University
of California,
Davis, 1972

there as Neri worked on the sculptures and then paused for further reflection. At other times Neri's chair was left vacant, but it still lent the sense of the artist's presence as the third figure in this formative installation.

One doesn't often gain such proximity to the creative process of a great artist and teacher, and hence I never forgot Neri once I left Davis in 1973 to begin my career as an artist and assistant professor at San Francisco State University. After living and working a while within a new artists' community, in 1975 I helped cofound 80 Langton Street, one of a number of so-called alternative artists' spaces then being established in San Francisco to help support living artists working across multiple disciplines. When, a year later, it became my turn to organize an exhibition there, I decided to invite Neri to create a full-scale sculptural figure in plaster every day for a little more than a week, resulting in an installation of eight figures surrounded—as in the demonstration to his students in the gallery at UC Davis—by all of the plaster shards and tools that accompanied their making (figs. 35-37). I knew that Neri would ask Mary Julia to serve as the live model for this endeavor, and I wanted my peers to see what a remarkable body of

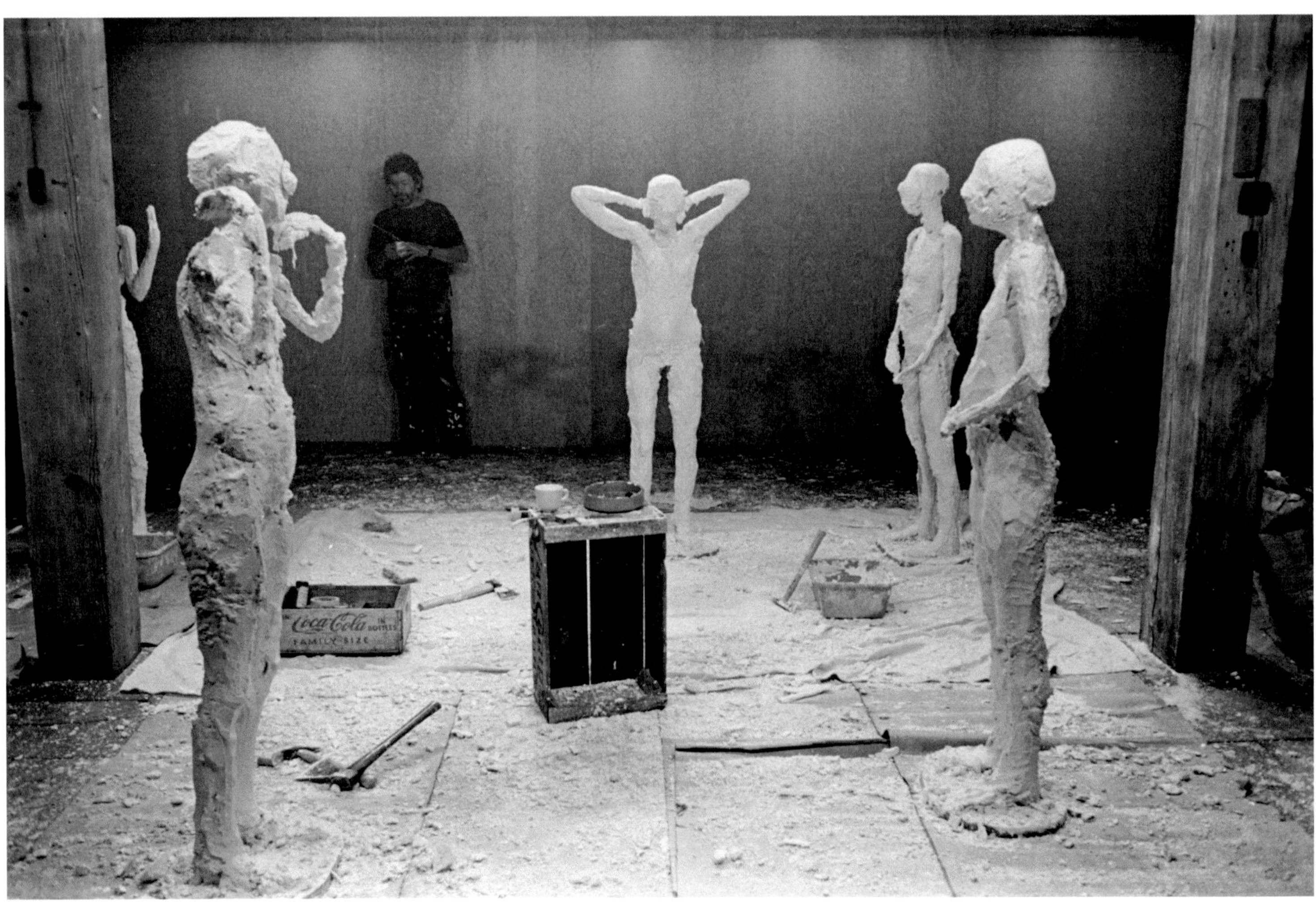

Fig. 35. View of *The Remaking of Mary Julia: Sculpture in Process* at 80 Langton Street, San Francisco, 1976

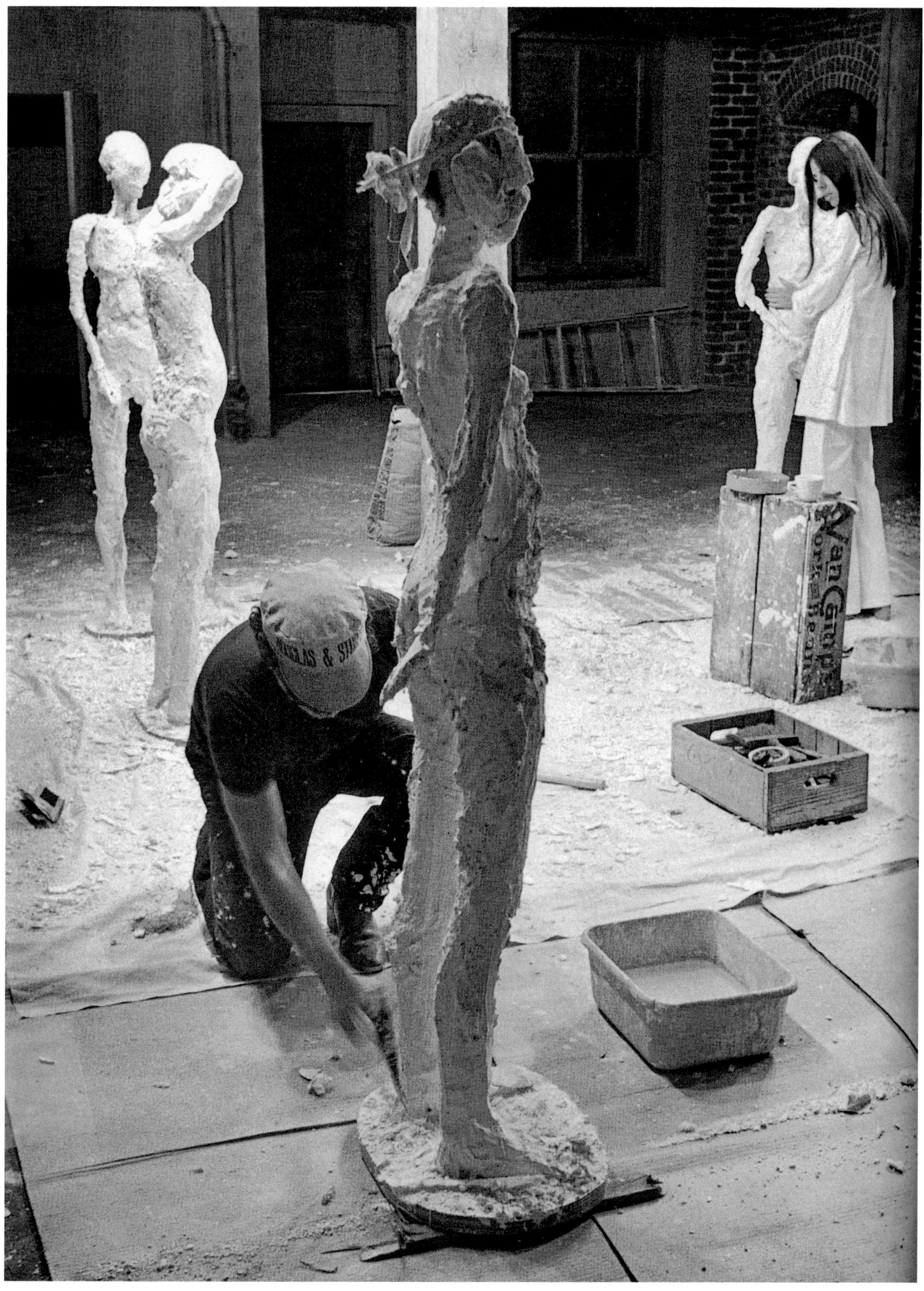

Fig. 36. Manuel Neri and Mary Julia Raahauge in *The Remaking of Mary Julia: Sculpture in Process* at 80 Langton Street, San Francisco, 1976

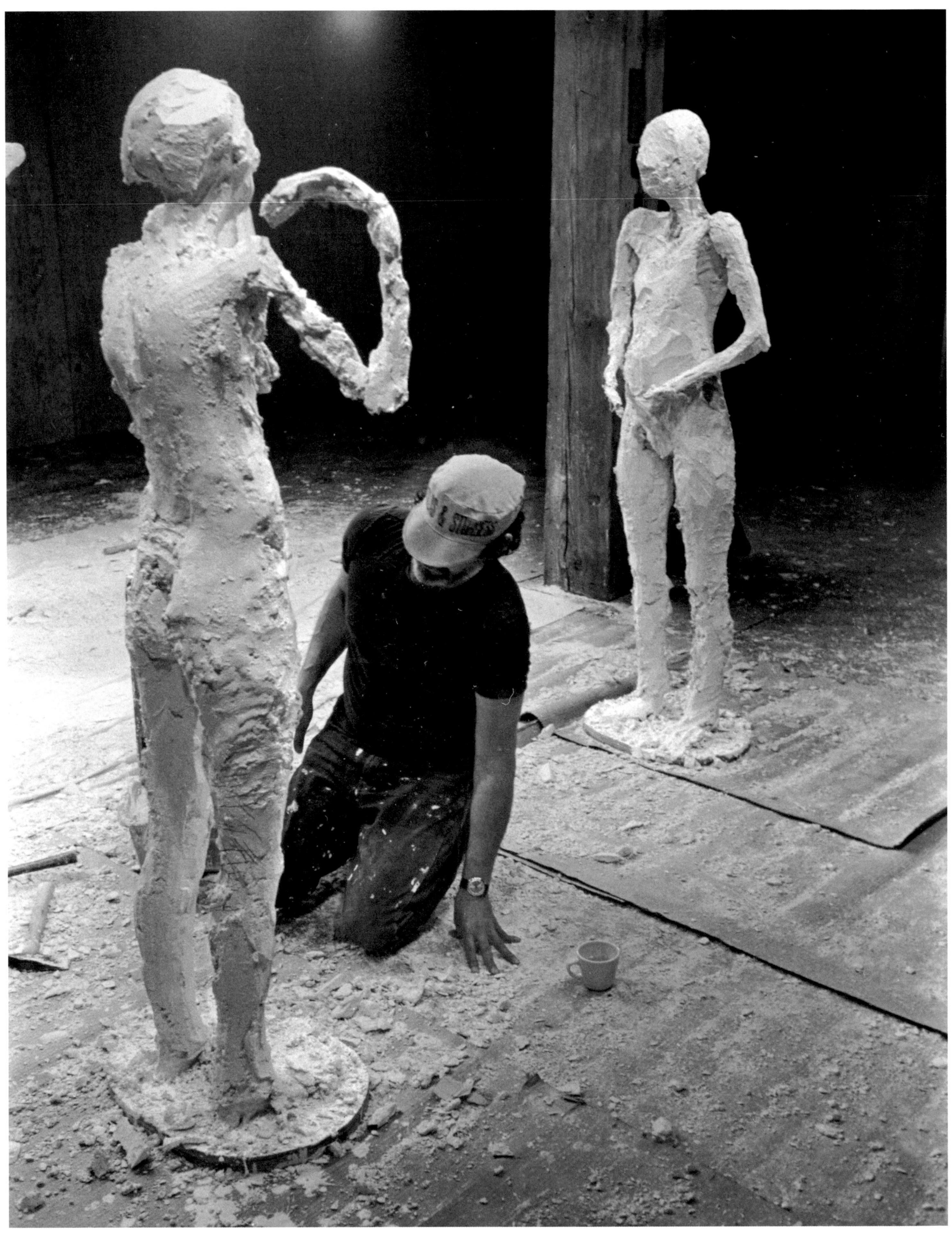

Fig. 37. Manuel Neri in *The Remaking of Mary Julia: Sculpture in Process* at 80 Langton Street, San Francisco, 1976

work my mentor and his great muse would produce within such a short burst of time. Neri and Mary Julia did exactly what I expected of them, brilliantly so. The exhibition was titled *The Remaking of Mary Julia: Sculpture in Process.*[15]

In the years that followed, including after I became director of the Yale University Art Gallery, I continued to stay in touch with Neri and track the development of his career, mounting exhibitions that included his work, such as *Five West Coast Artists: Bischoff, Diebenkorn, Neri, Park, and Thiebaud* and *The Ceramic Presence in Modern Art: Selections from the Linda Leonard Schlenger Collection and the Yale University Art Gallery.*[16] Nearly five decades after our first interaction, in 2017, Neri—along with Anne Kohs, who stewards The Manuel Neri Trust—astounded me by very generously gifting a large trove of his artworks to the Gallery. With this gift, the museum now holds more than 150 works by Neri, spanning ceramics, drawings, paintings, prints, sculptures, sketchbooks, and watercolors. When I traveled to California to select the specific sculptures and works on paper by Neri that I wished to add to the Gallery's collection, I made a decision to concentrate my selections on the figurative works that Neri realized in plaster and on paper. This choice reflects my conviction that it has been via his lifelong and fiercely direct engagement with these very common, inexpensive, and ultimately fragile materials that Neri's art has most often reached its highest aesthetic peaks, more elevated to my eyes than many of the very masterful and beautiful figurative works he either cast in bronze in the United States and Mexico or carved in Carrara marble in Italy from the mid-1970s onward. I know I am not alone in this judgment, for many of the artists who know Neri and his work most intimately agree with this assertion. We fully understand why most galleries and collectors generally shy away from works made of plaster, thinking them to be too easily broken and hard to keep clean, and sometimes assuming they are mere studies or primary works meant to be destroyed after being cast. Neri's figurative plaster sculptures also benefit greatly from being carefully examined in person; this allows the viewer to better understand their material presence and emotional power, for photographic reproductions of his sculptures in plaster and bronze can easily confuse one's eyes. There is much to be gained from taking a long and close look at all of the works included in this publication and the exhibition it accompanies. Doing so will yield a satisfying understanding of how fully these objects embody Neri's longtime passion for and creative engagement with the human figure.

1. For selected reading on Neri's life and art, see: Thomas Albright, *Manuel Neri*, exh. cat. (San Francisco: John Berggruen Gallery; Santa Monica, Calif.: James Corcoran Gallery; New York: Charles Cowles Gallery, 1988); Henry Geldzahler, *Manuel Neri: Sculpture, Painted and Unpainted*, exh. cat. (Bridgehampton, N.Y.: Dia Center for the Arts, 1993); Price Amerson et al., *Manuel Neri: Early Work, 1953–1978*, exh. cat. (Washington, D.C.: Corcoran Gallery of Art, 1996); Jack Cowart, *Manuel Neri: Paintings and Painted Papers*, exh. cat. (Washington, D.C.: Corcoran Gallery of Art, 2001); Bruce Nixon, *Manuel Neri: The Figure in Relief*, exh. cat. (Hamilton, N.J.: Grounds for Sculpture, 2006); Renny Pritikin, Jock Reynolds, and Simon Sadler, *You See: The Early Years of the UC Davis Studio Art Faculty*, exh. cat. (Davis: Richard L. Nelson Gallery, University of California, Davis, 2007); Bruce Nixon, *Manuel Neri: Matters of Form and Construction*, exh. cat. (Ames: Iowa State University Museums, 2017); Riva Yares, *Manuel Neri: Singularity of Form and Surface* (New York: Yares Art, 2017); and Bruce Nixon, *Manuel Neri and the Assertion of Modern Figurative Sculpture*, exh. cat. (Redwood City, Calif.: Anderson Collection and Stanford University Press, 2018).

2. The Neri family benefited from the ensuing Bracero Program, which was developed during the World War II years to bring a large contingent of Mexican guest workers to labor in California's fields. The *braceros* (manual laborers) helped harvest crops while many residents were serving as soldiers or working in factories to manufacture military equipment and munitions. After the war ended in 1945, many Mexican workers remained in California and were encouraged to become U.S. citizens by the ranchers and farmers who had employed them and admired their strong work ethic.

3. For the biographical details in this and subsequent paragraphs, see Amerson et al., *Manuel Neri: Early Work, 1953–1978*, in particular the section "Life of the Artist: An Illustrated Chronology," 299–395.

4. Neri and Voulkos spent the summer of 1952 in Helena, Montana, where they helped found the Archie Bray Foundation for the Ceramic Arts, a ceramics program for young artists interested in working with clay. Ibid., 305.

5. Neri's engineering talent and further training in the United States Army Signal Corps landed him a position as a communications specialist in Incheon, South Korea, where he was stationed until being honorably discharged in 1955. At this time, Neri was married to Marilyn "Miem" Hampson, a fellow art student at CCAC. They had a son, Raoul, who was born while Neri was overseas. Neri and Hampson separated in 1956, a number of months after their second child, Laticia, was born. Ibid., 305–7, 311.

6. Selz launched the Berkeley Art Museum with a major gift of funds and paintings from the artist Hans Hofmann, who had taught at the university decades earlier. The *Funk* exhibition was on view April 18–May 29, 1967, and was accompanied by a catalogue: Peter Selz, *Funk*, exh. cat. (Berkeley: University of California, Berkeley, 1967). "Notes on Funk," Selz's short essay for the catalogue, included quotes and statements contributed by a number of the artists in the exhibition. It also underscored the interconnection between the visual art, music, and poetry of the Bay Area.

7. *Ceramic Loop I* and *Ceramic Loop II* were loaned to the *Funk* exhibition from Voulkos's personal collection, and *Ceramic Loop I* was illustrated in the catalogue; Selz, *Funk*, 37.

8. Noel, who is also an artist, was born in 1962. Neri and Brown separated in 1965, just before Neri was first hired as a lecturer at the University of California, Davis. Neri went on to marry twice more and have four more children.

9.	The Bay Area Figurative artists ceased working in the Abstract Expressionist style, which dominated American art in the 1950s and 1960s, and instead returned to figuration. For more information, see Thomas Albright, *Art in the San Francisco Bay Area, 1945–1980: An Illustrated History* (Berkeley: University of California Press, 1985).

10.	Thanks to the generosity of The Manuel Neri Trust, a number of Neri's Tula and Tikal works now reside at the Gallery; see inv. nos. 2017.88.29–.30, .41–.42, .73–.75, .101–.129, and .142–.153.

11.	I was fortunate to have also encountered these early works by Neri while I was studying at UC Davis, and I remain amazed that they still have not received the full attention they deserve. They relate thematically to another great trove of artworks at the Gallery, created by the modern artists Anni and Josef Albers in response to their many outings to Central and South America and their particular fascination with the ancient ruins of the Zapotec culture that are still very visible in Oaxaca, Mexico. This body of work by the Alberses was addressed in a recent Gallery exhibition and publication; see Jennifer Reynolds-Kaye, *Small-Great Objects: Anni and Josef Albers in the Americas*, exh. cat. (New Haven, Conn.: Yale University Art Gallery, 2017). It remains for one of the Gallery's curators or curatorial fellows to engage these other seminal works by Neri in the future, and to perhaps display them alongside works created by the Alberses and some of the terrific Prehispanic objects—great in both quantity and quality—in the museum's collection of ancient art.

12.	Titled *Garden Show*, the exhibition was on view at the Memorial Union Gallery at UC Davis in January 1970.

13.	My *Dead Bee* is also illustrated in Pritikin, Reynolds, and Sadler, *You See*, 71. The *You See* catalogue contains a short essay I wrote, titled "Memory Lame," as a tribute to Neri and other faculty artists at UC Davis who had mentored me well; see ibid., 17–22.

14.	Neri met Mary Julia Raahauge in Benicia, where she was working as a hostess at a family restaurant. He asked her if she would be interested in posing for him. She was reluctant at first, but after talking to friends who knew him and finding out he was really an artist, she agreed. I thank Anne Kohs for this information.

15.	The exhibition was on view May 4–15, 1976.

16.	The Gallery's exhibitions *Five West Coast Artists: Bischoff, Diebenkorn, Neri, Park, and Thiebaud* and *The Ceramic Presence in Modern Art: Selections from the Linda Leonard Schlenger Collection and the Yale University Art Gallery* were on view March 28–July 13, 2014, and September 4, 2015–January 3, 2016, respectively.

Exhibition Highlights

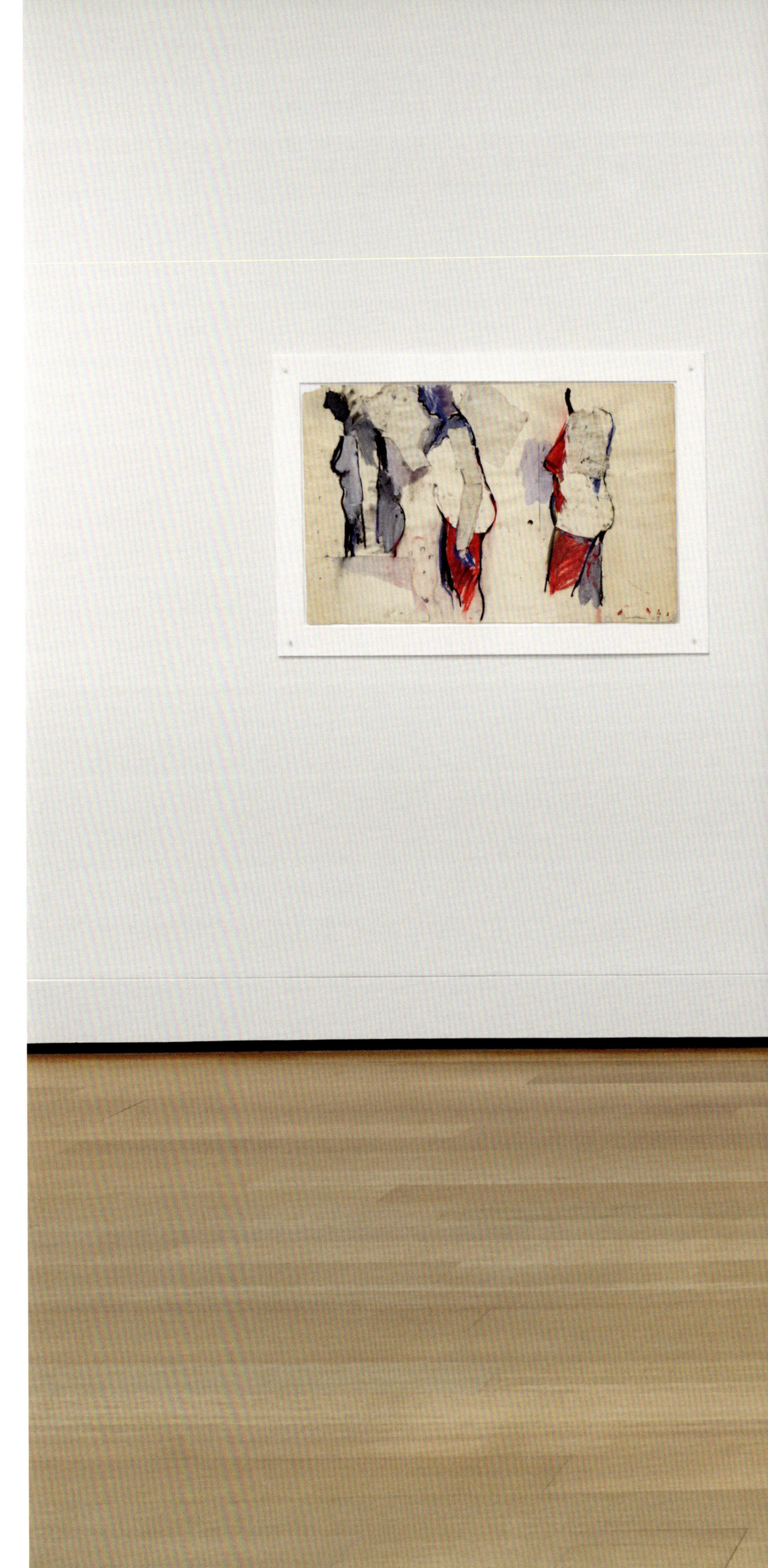

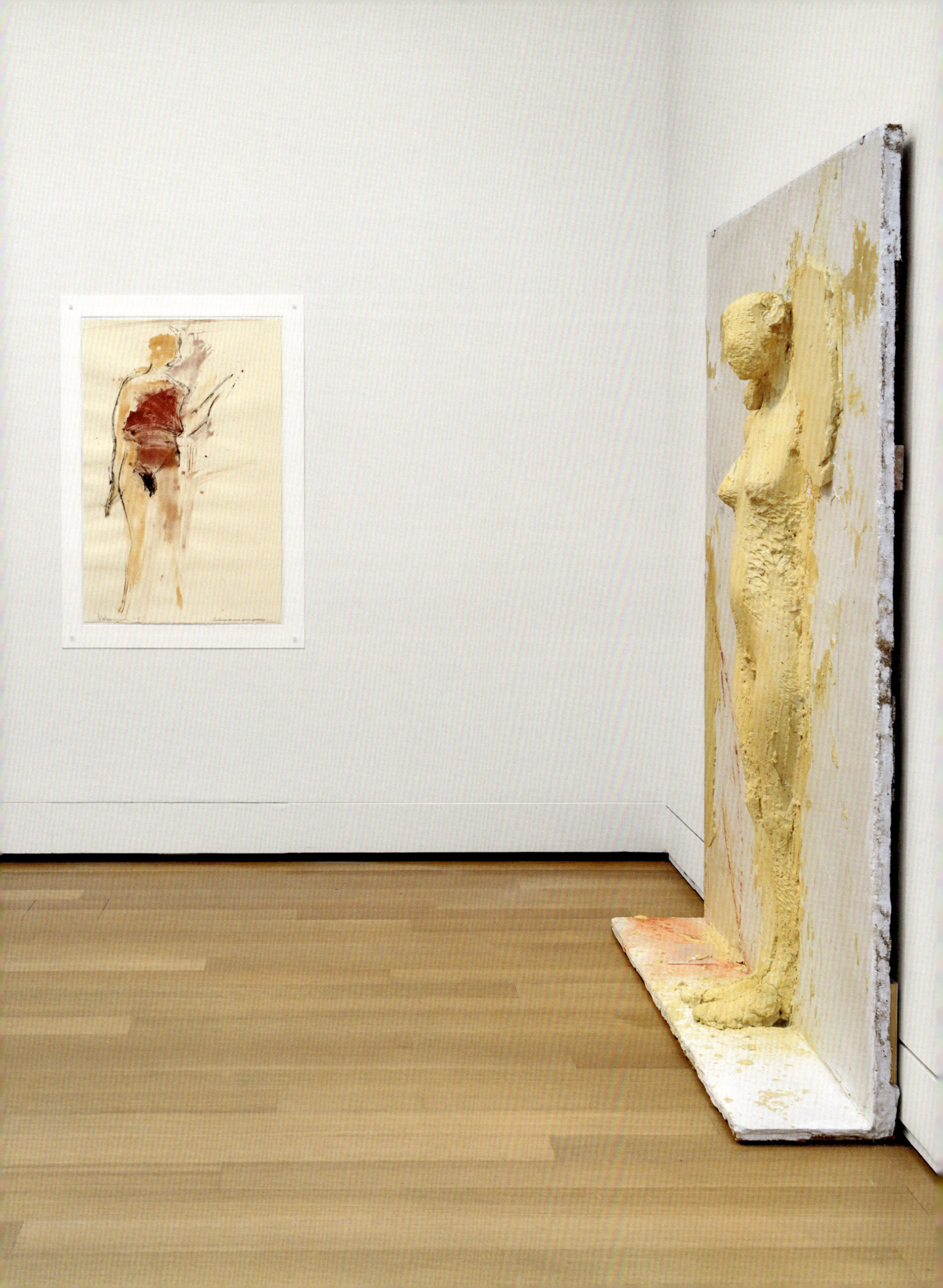

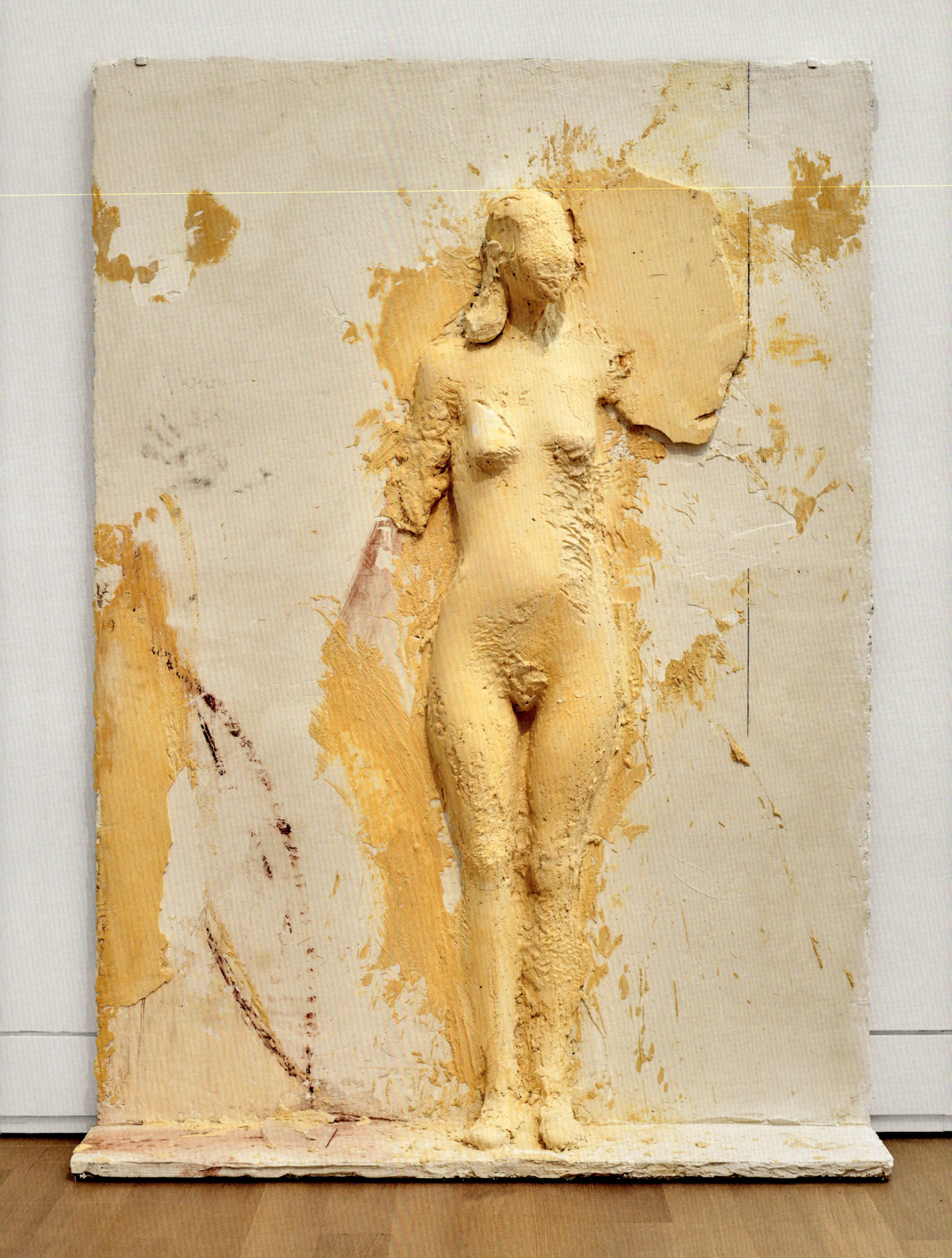

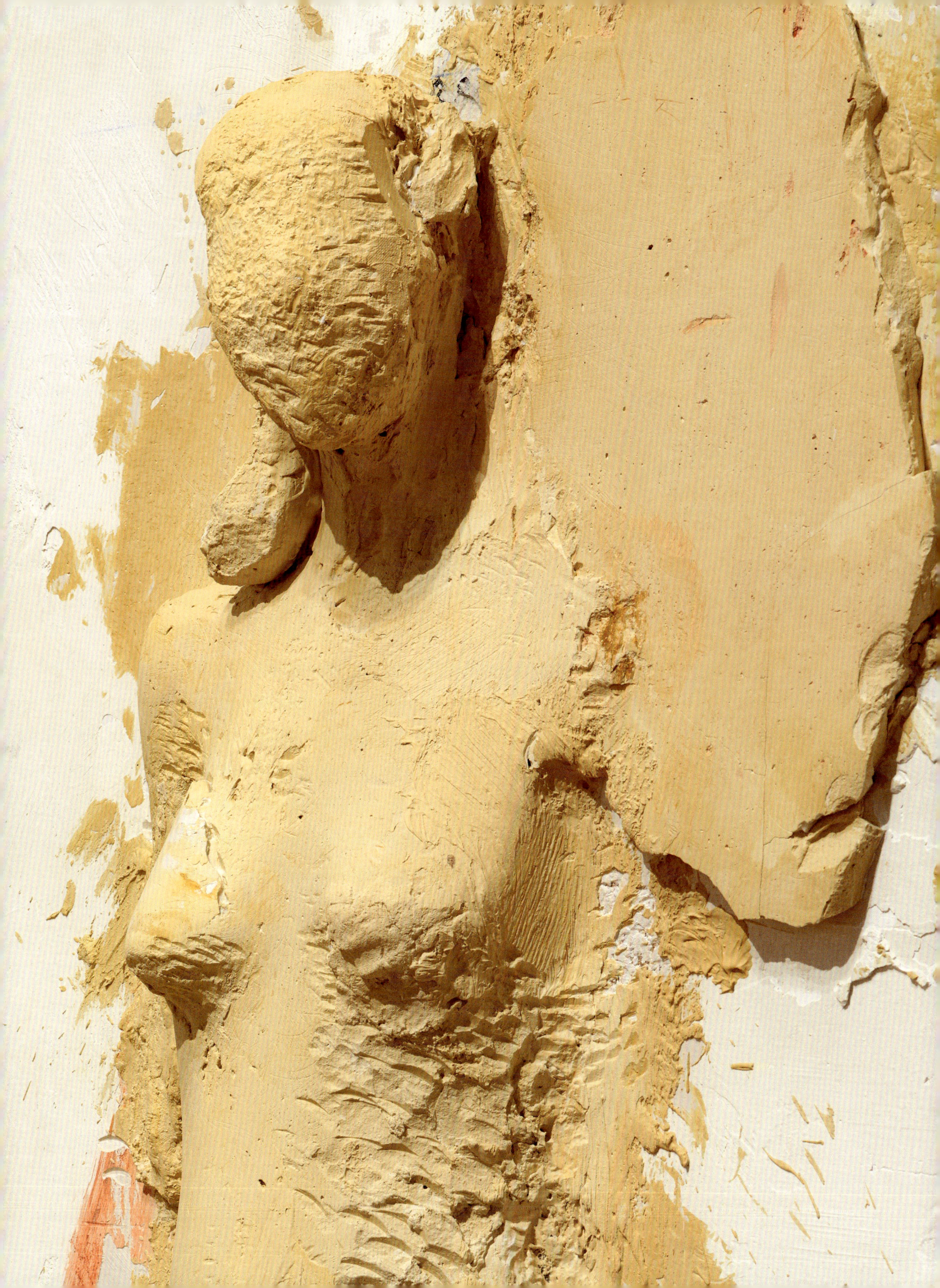

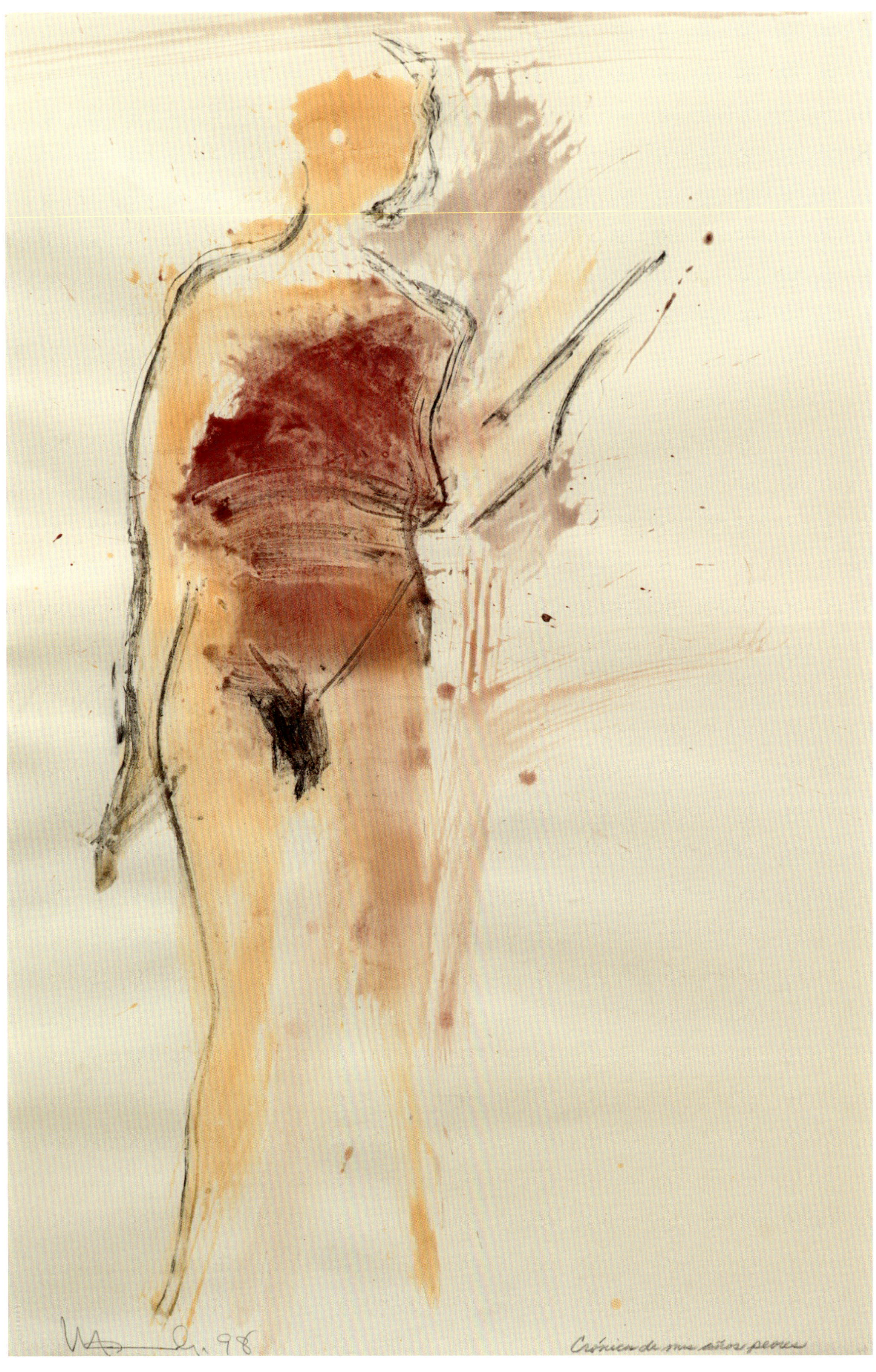
98
Crónica de mis años peores

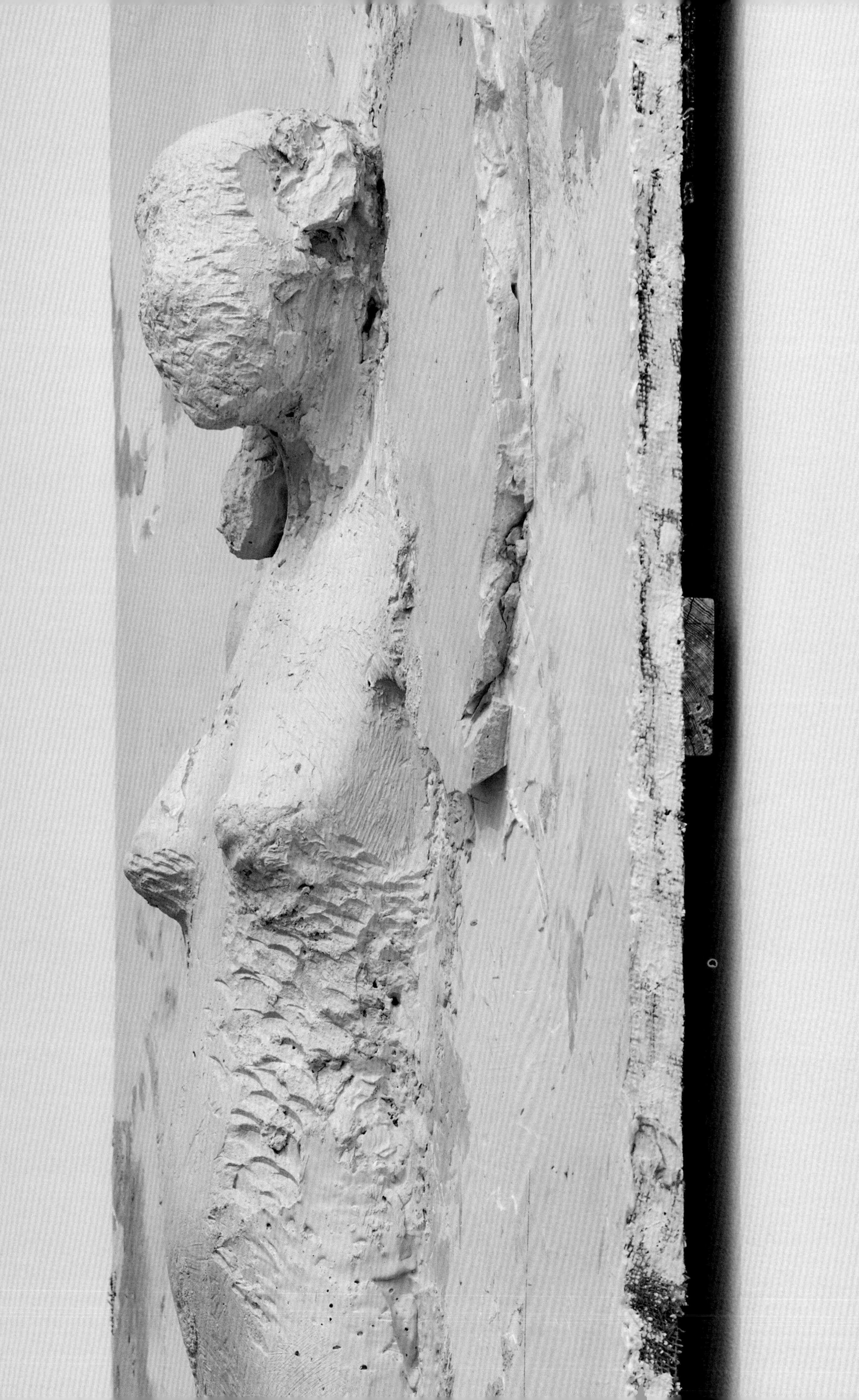

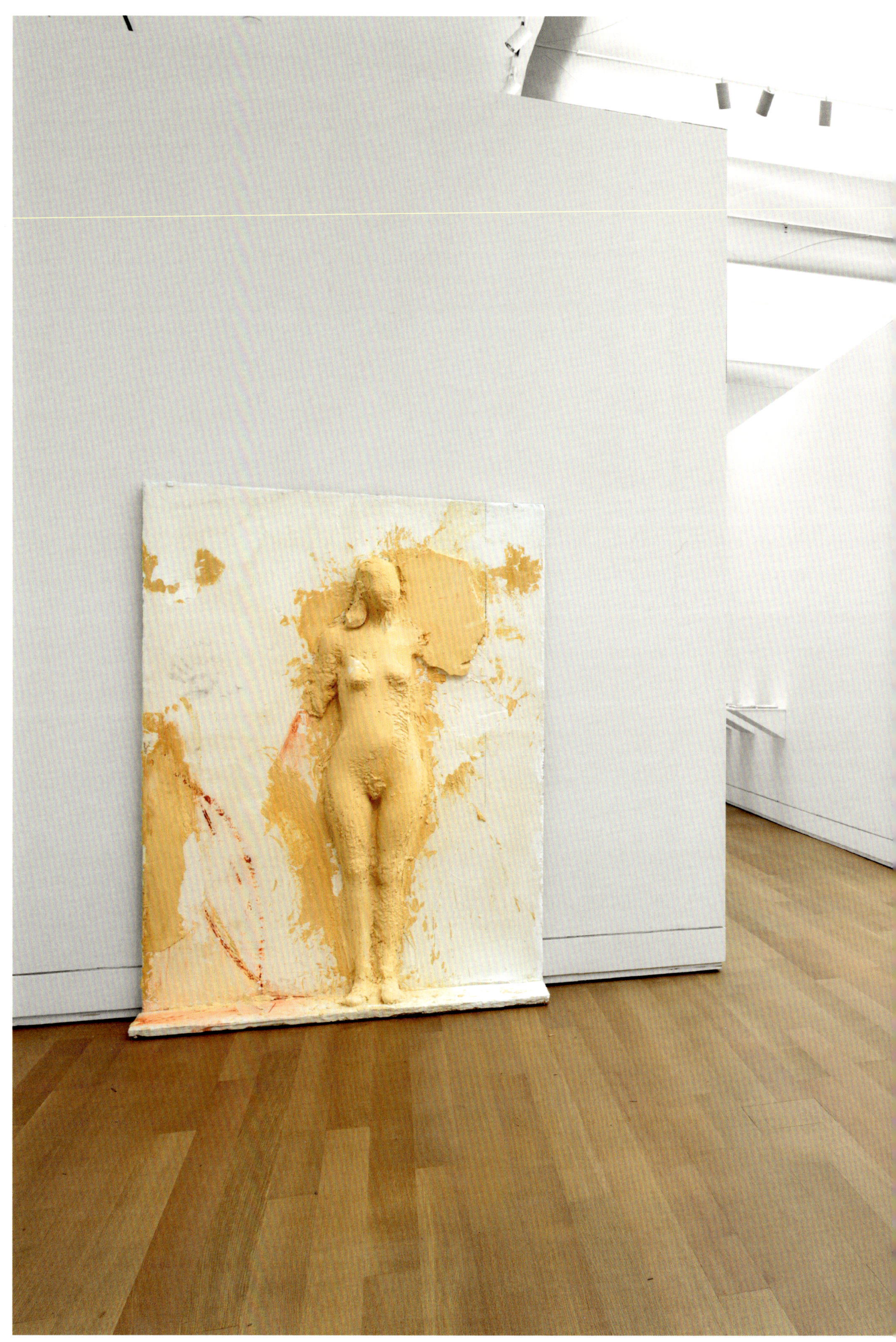

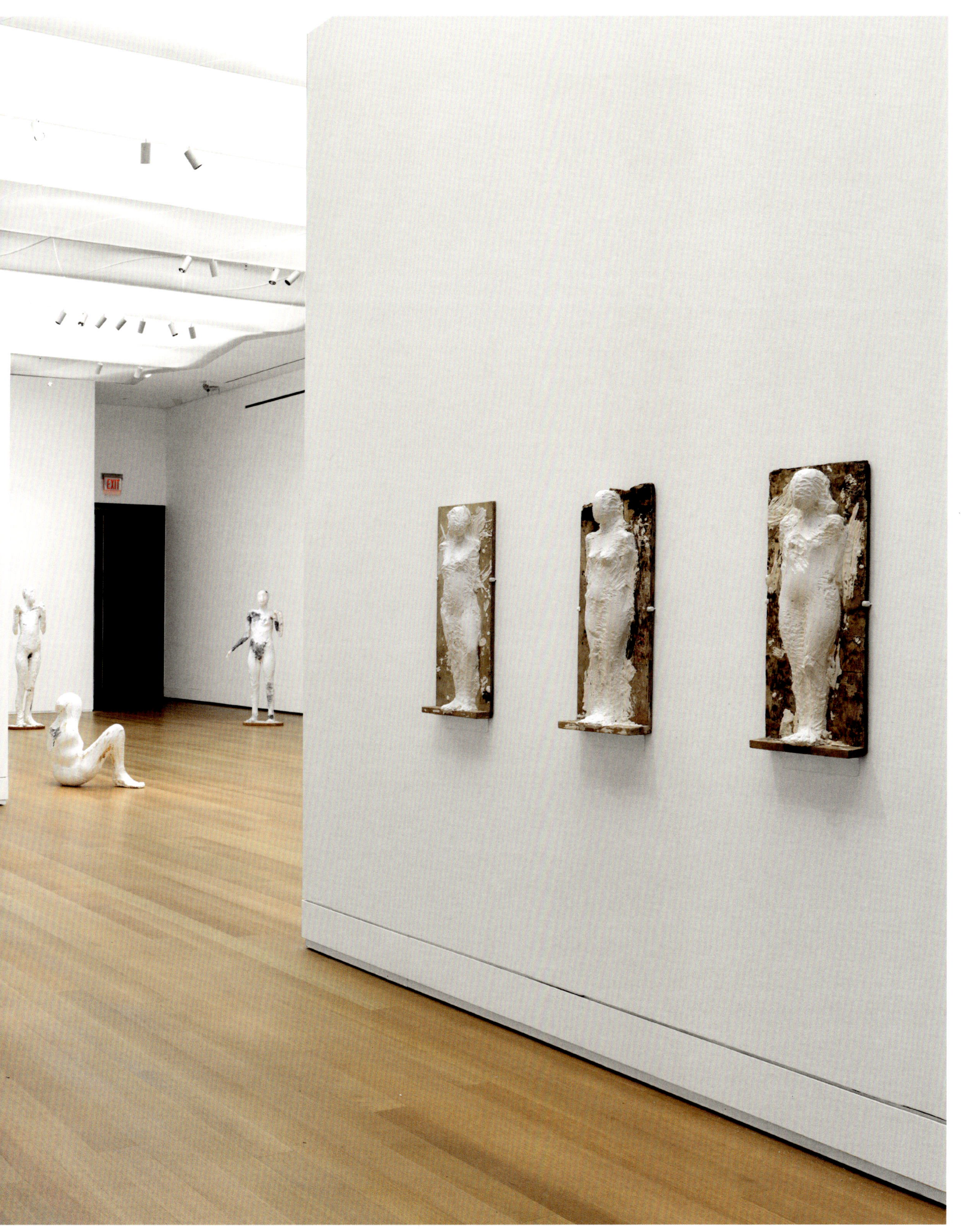

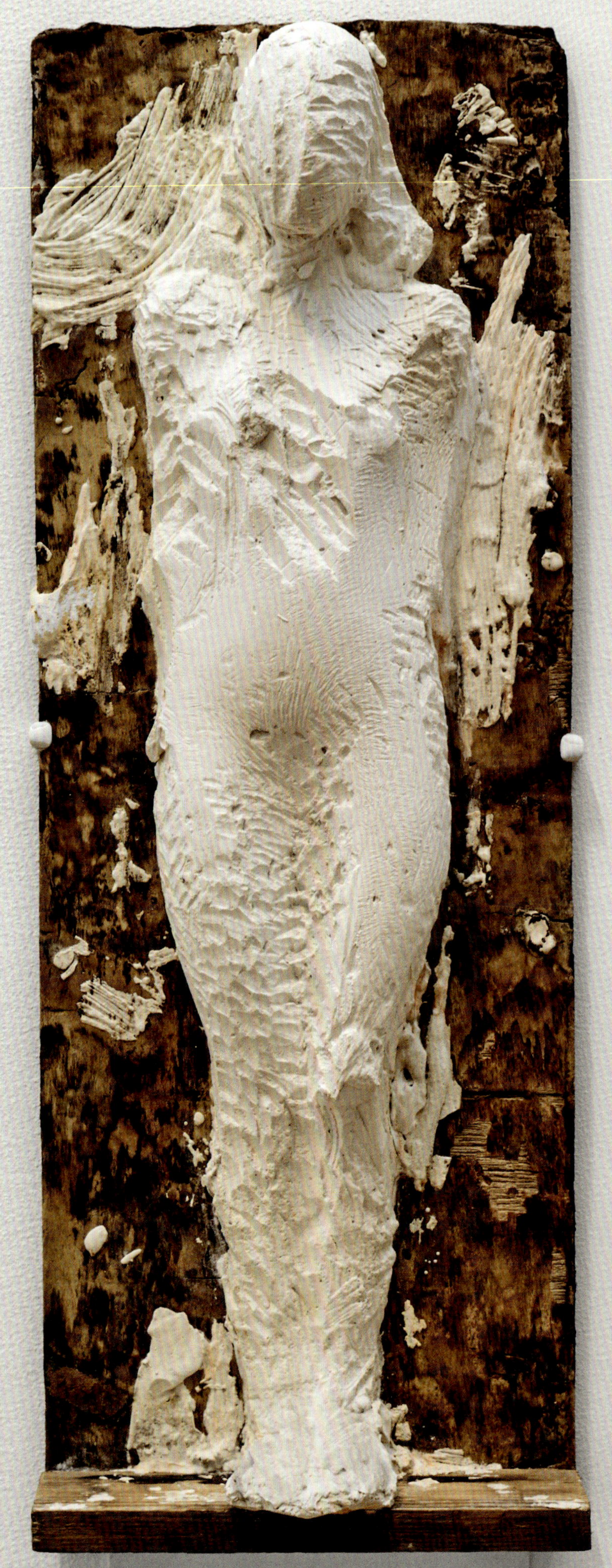

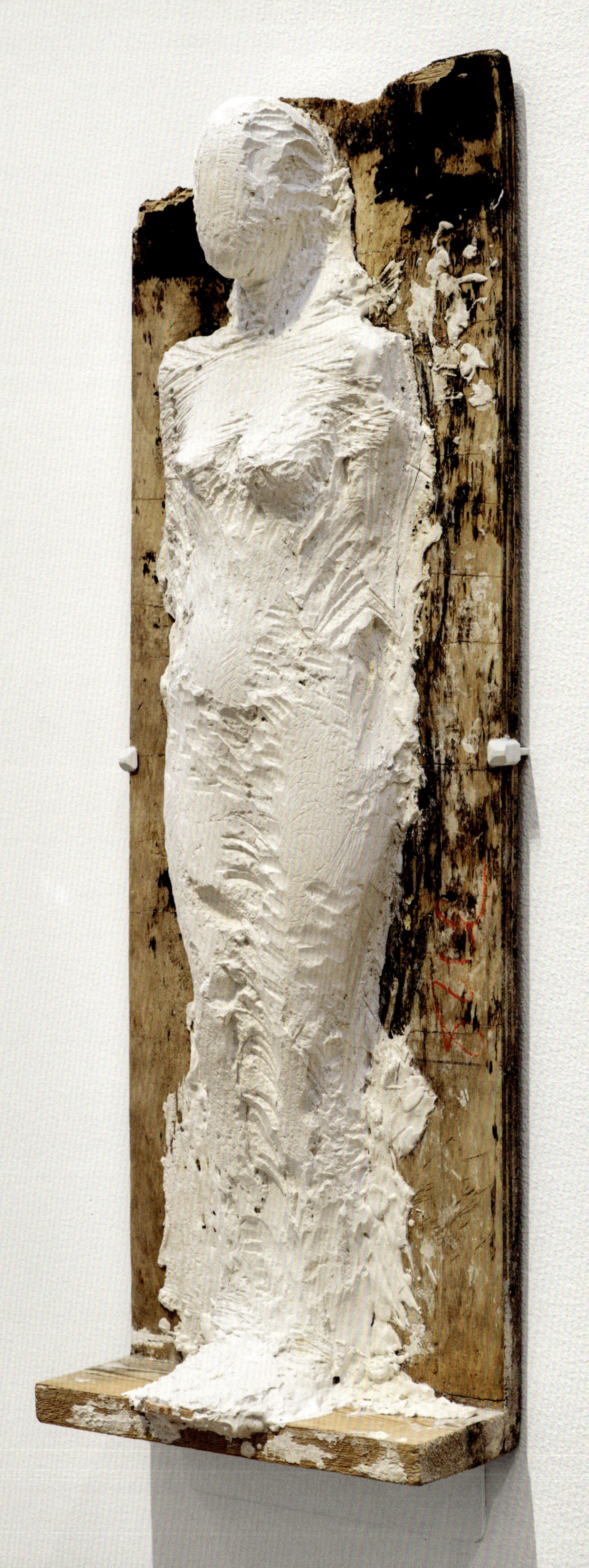

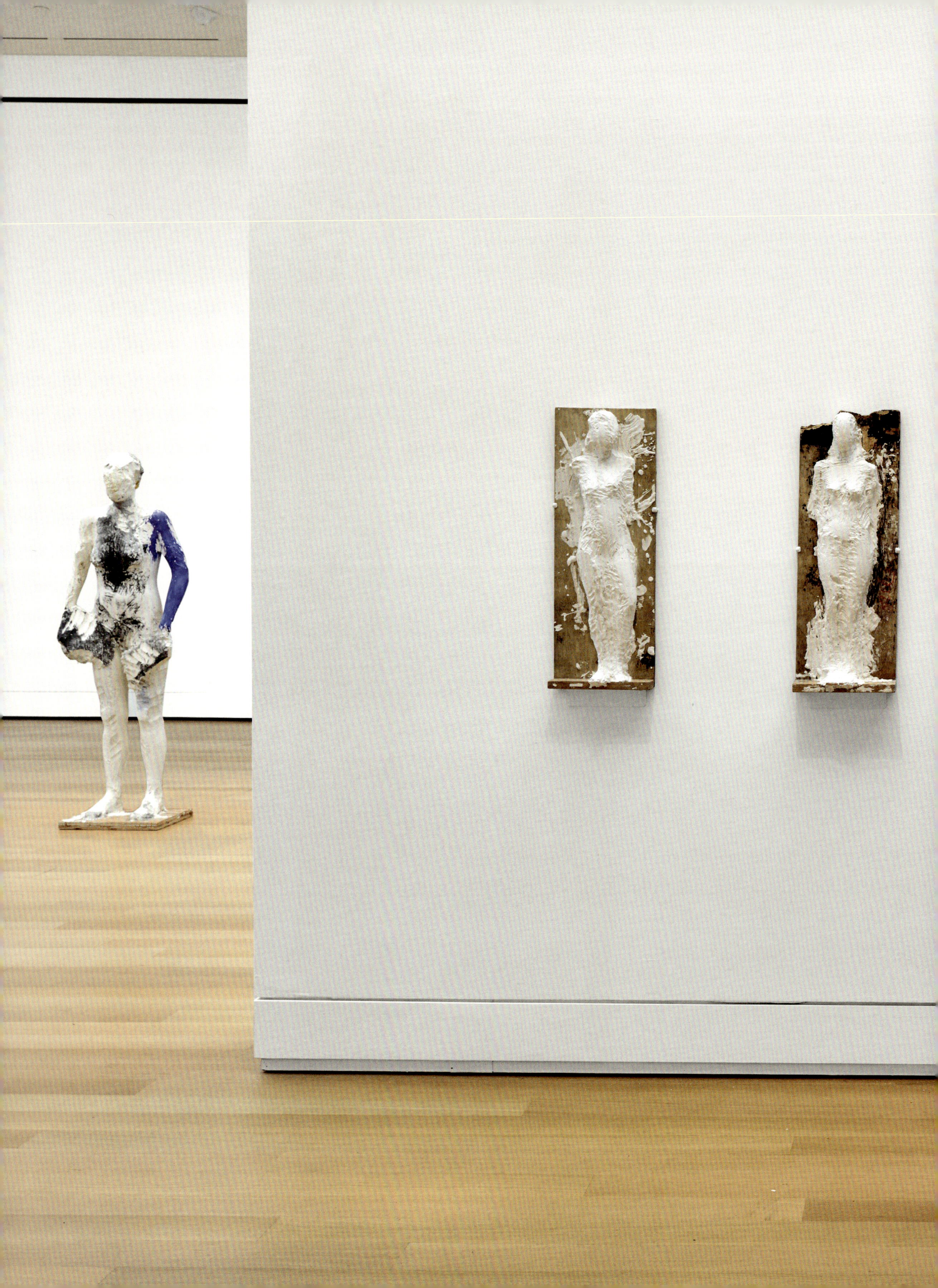

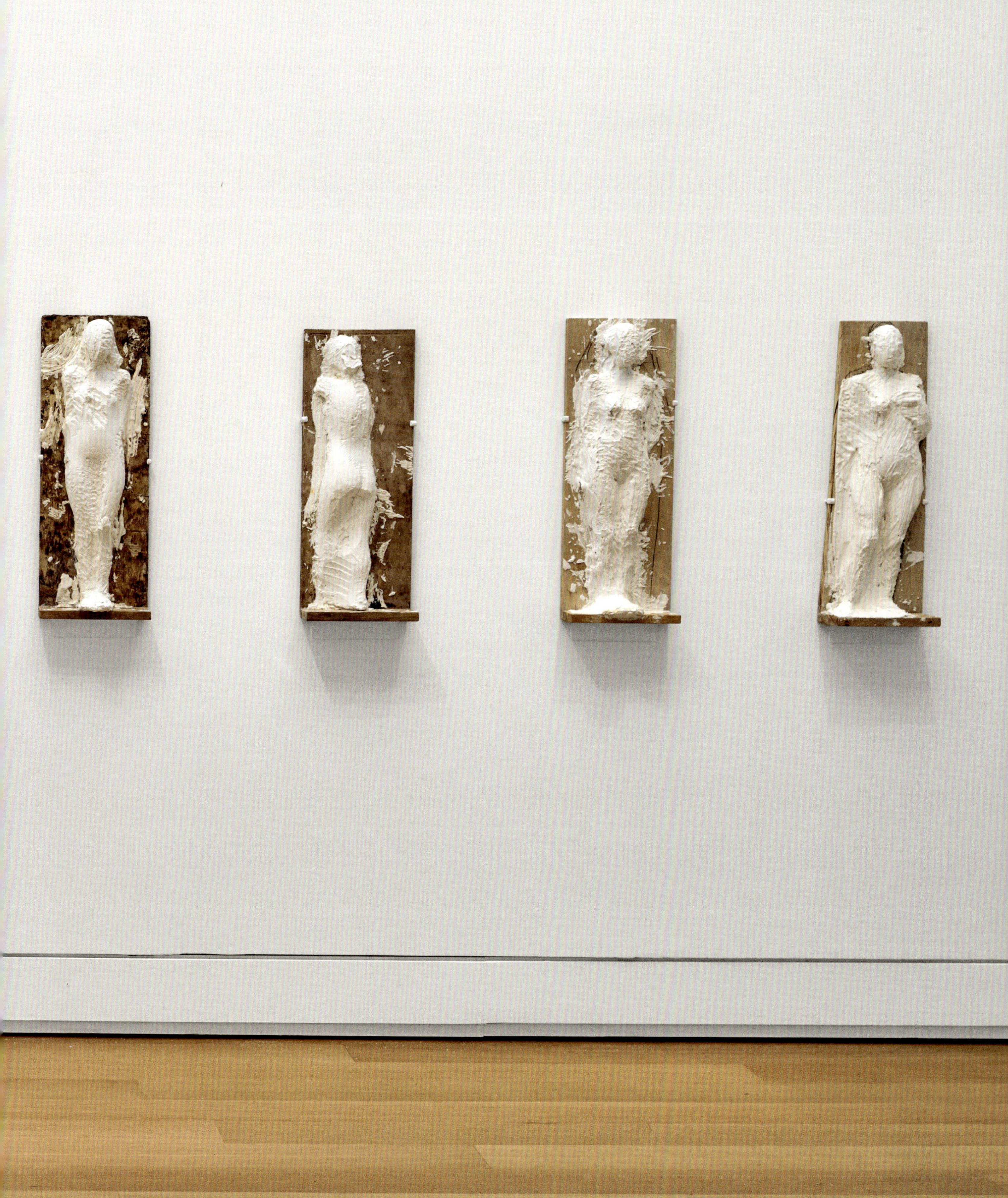

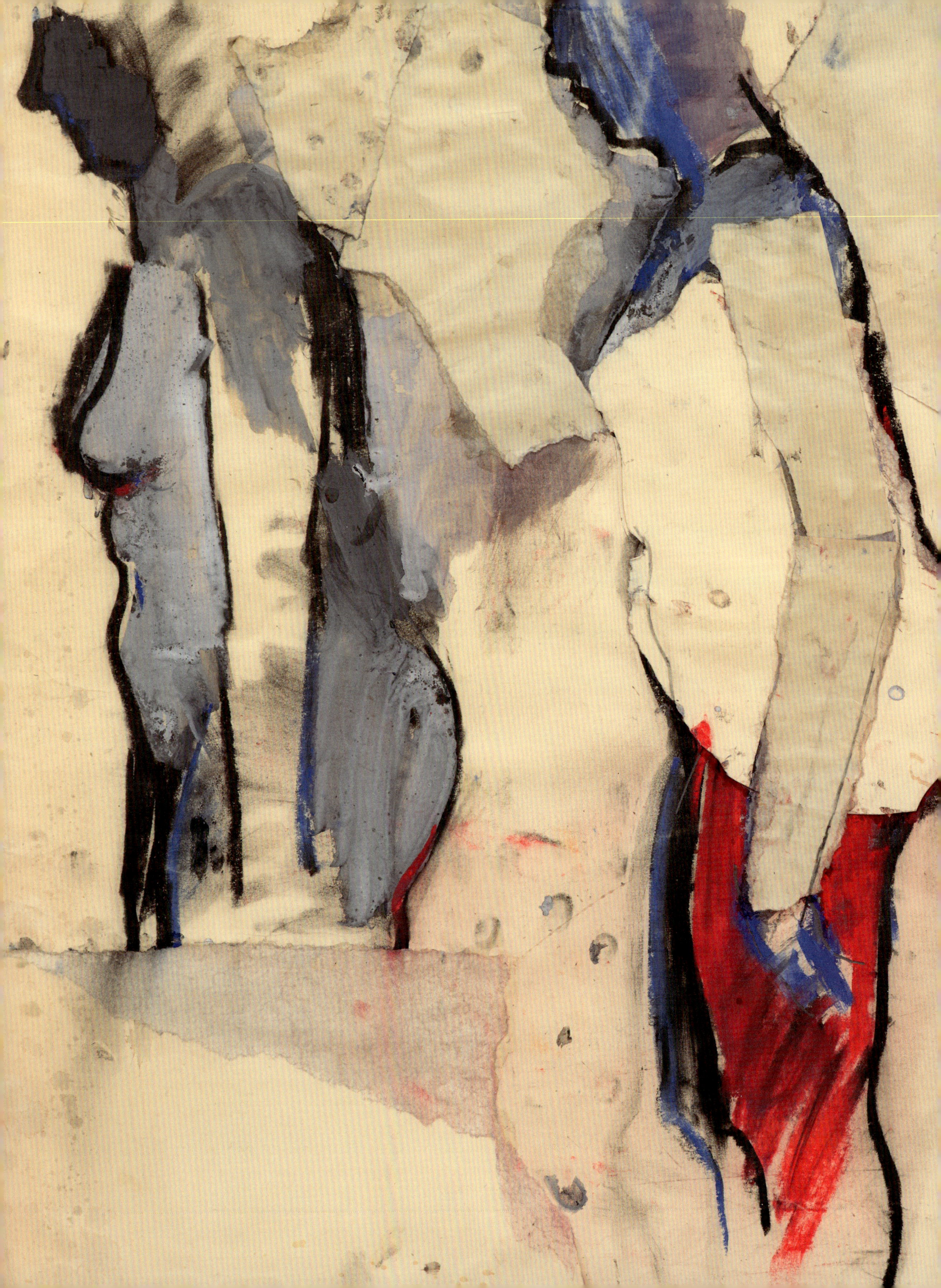

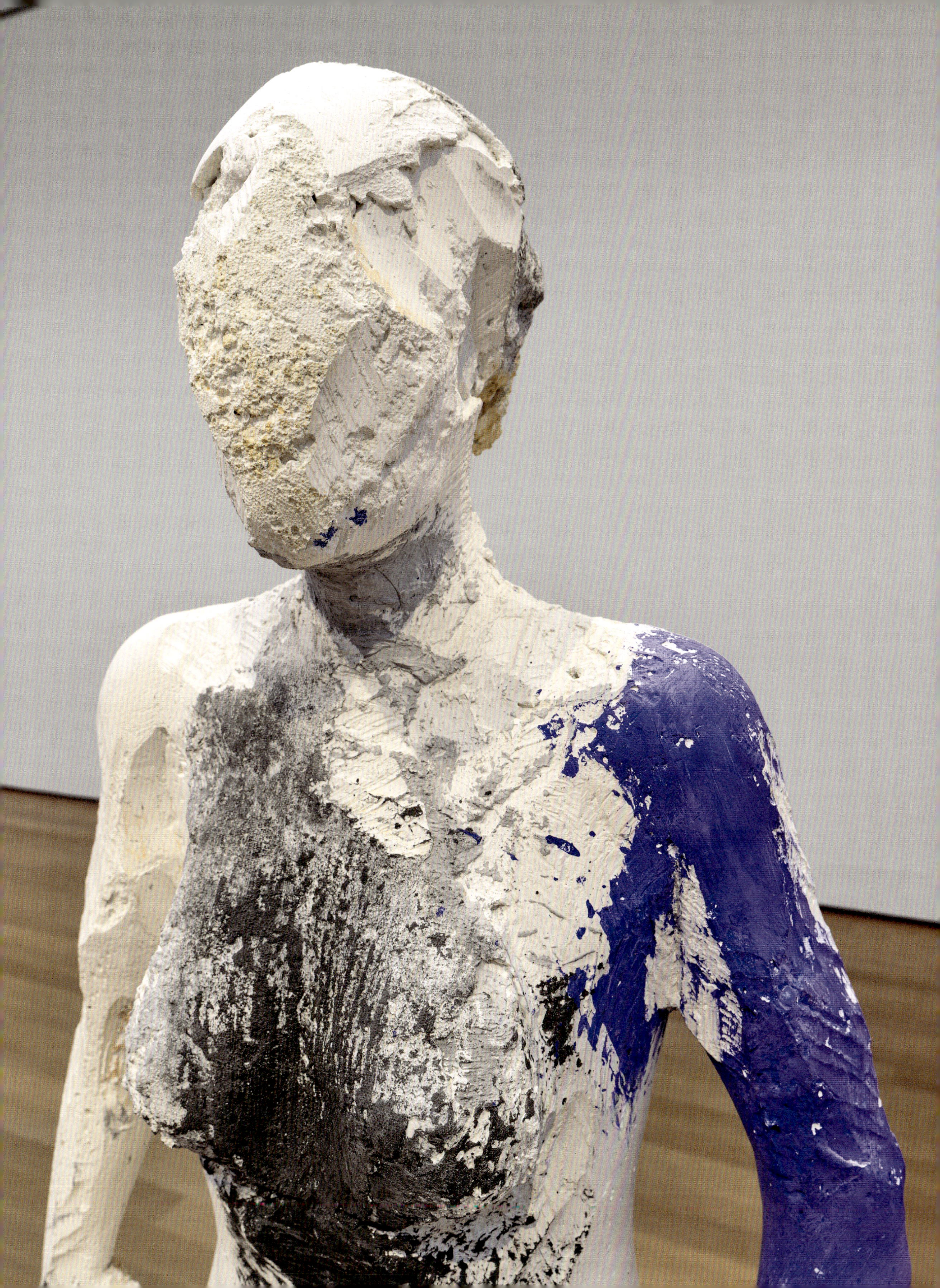

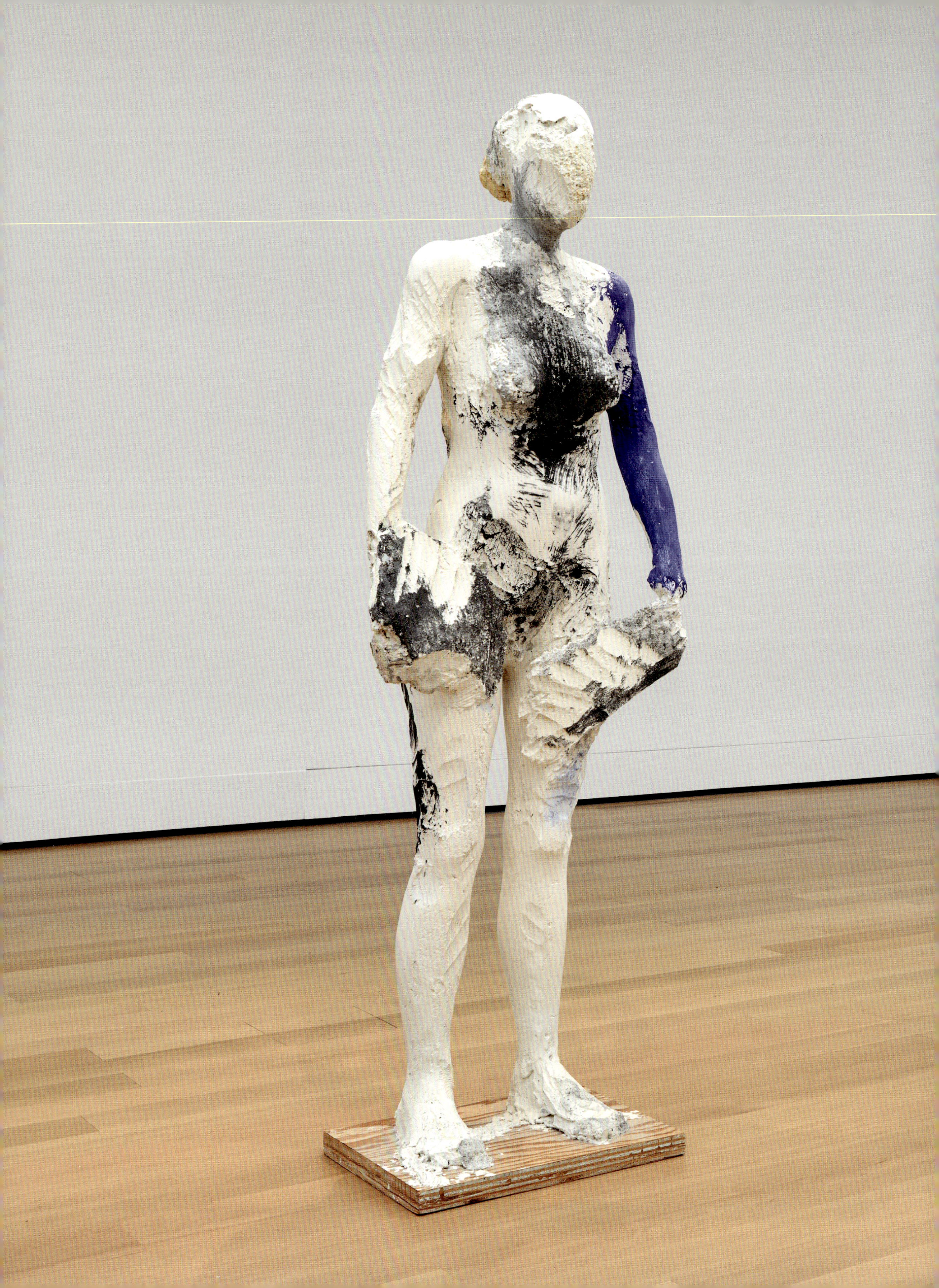

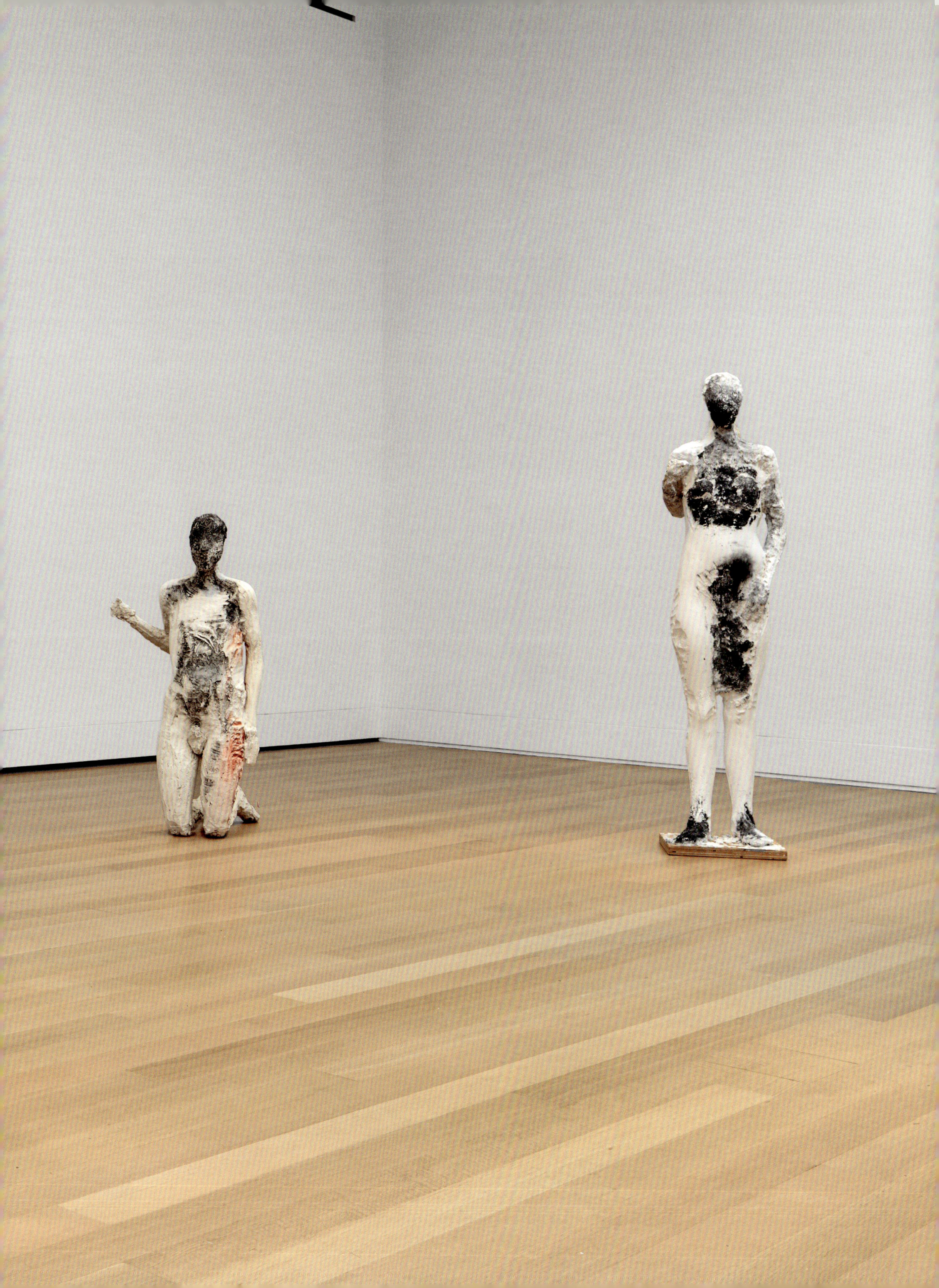

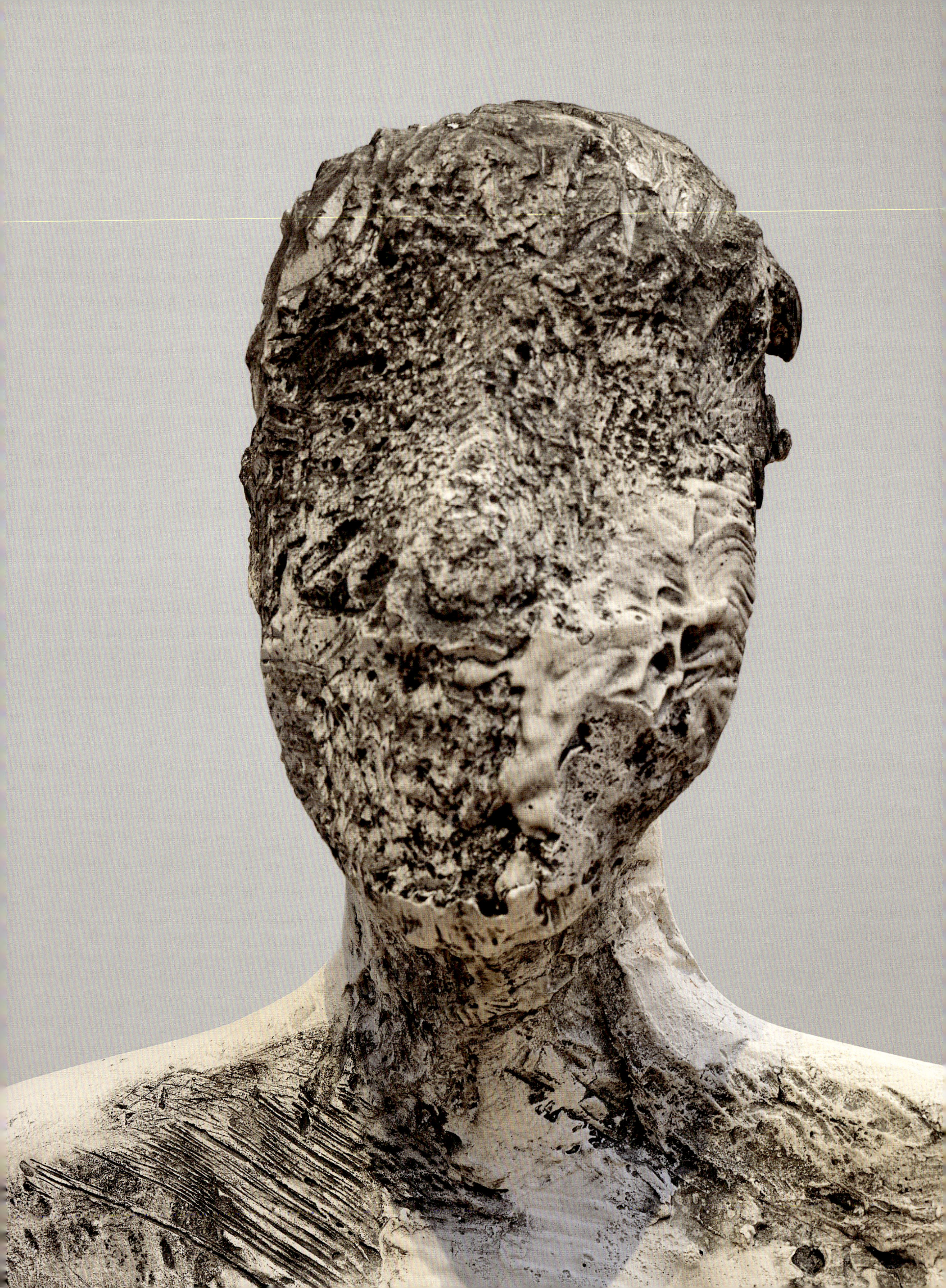

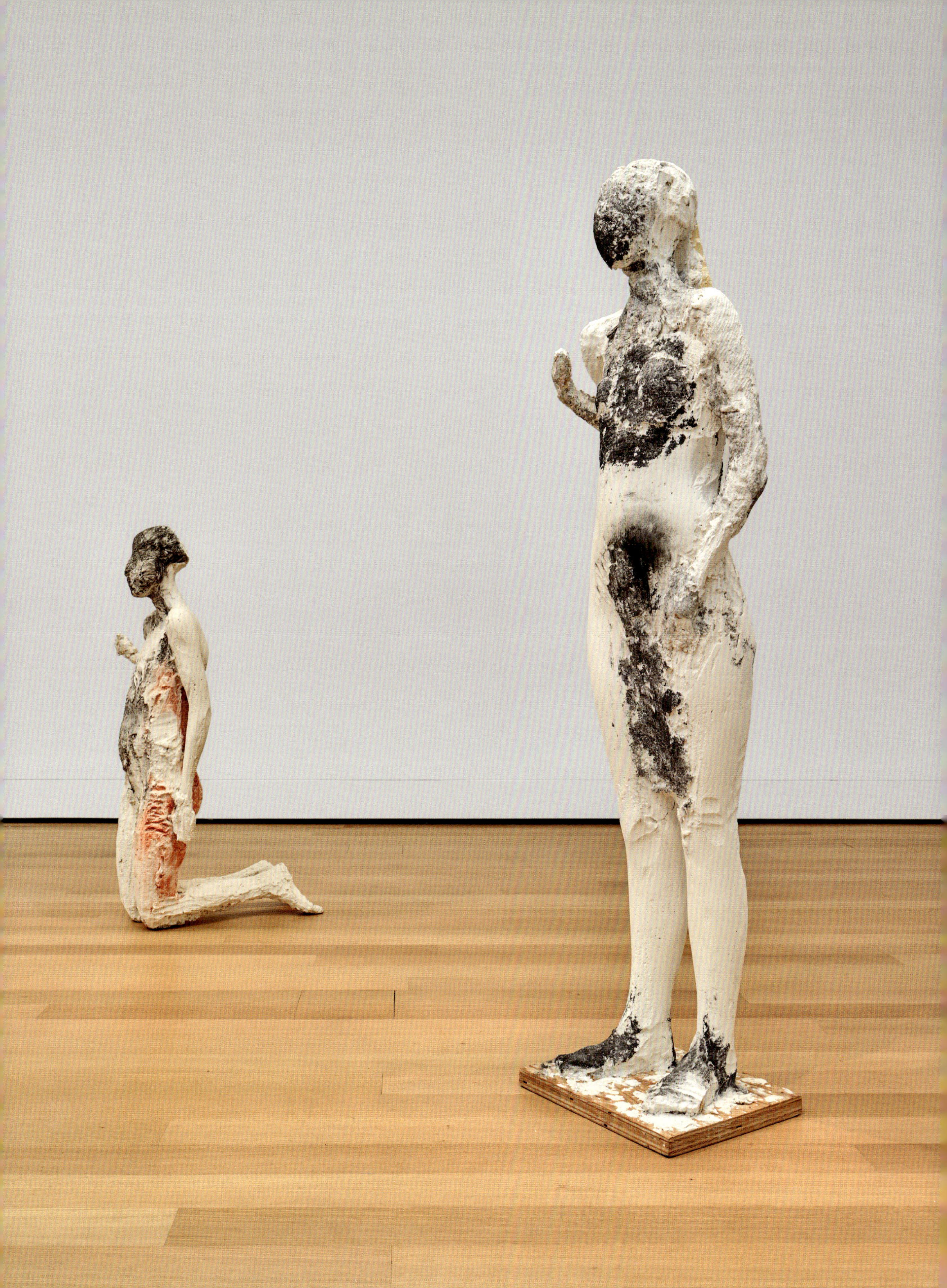

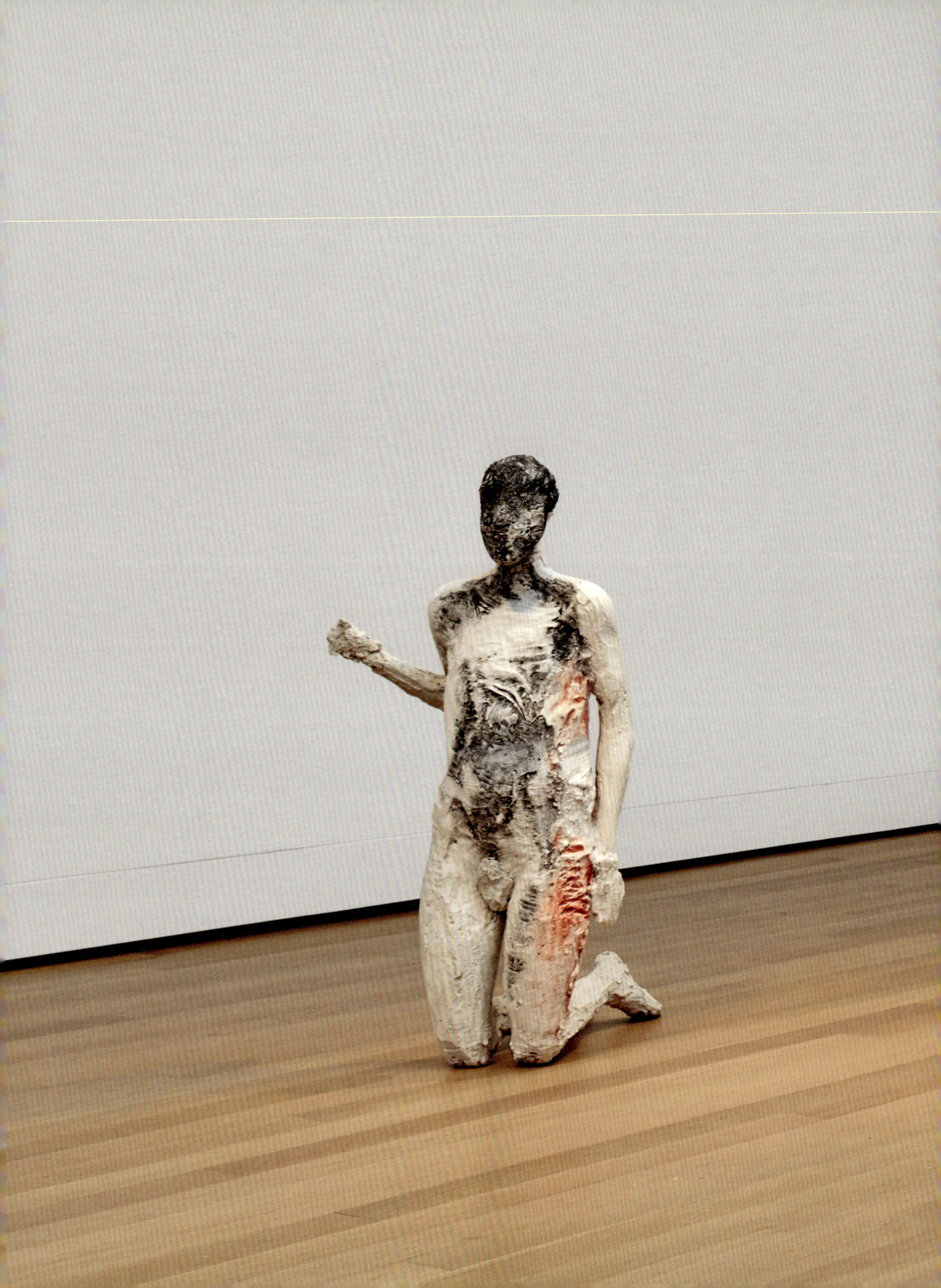

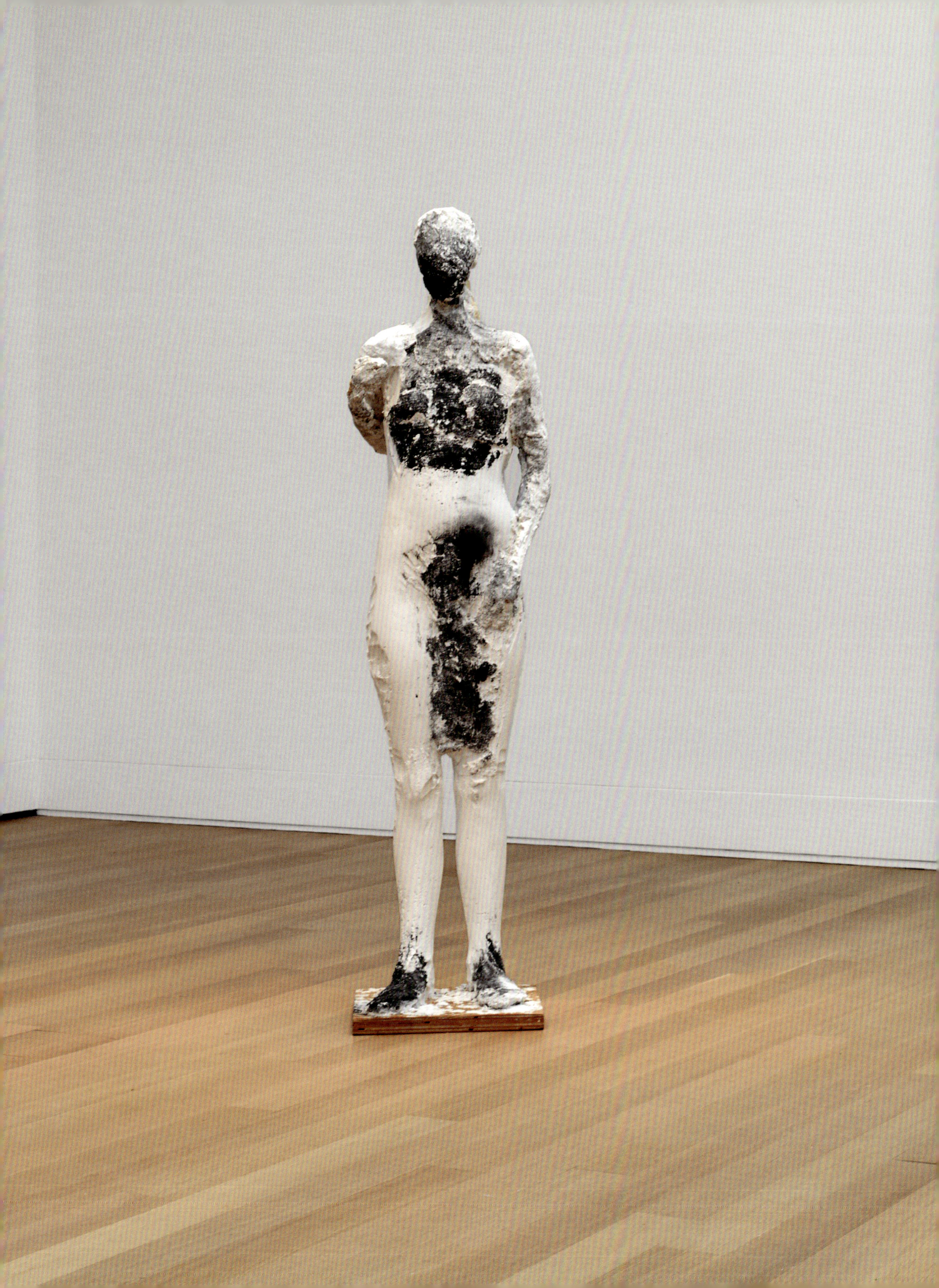

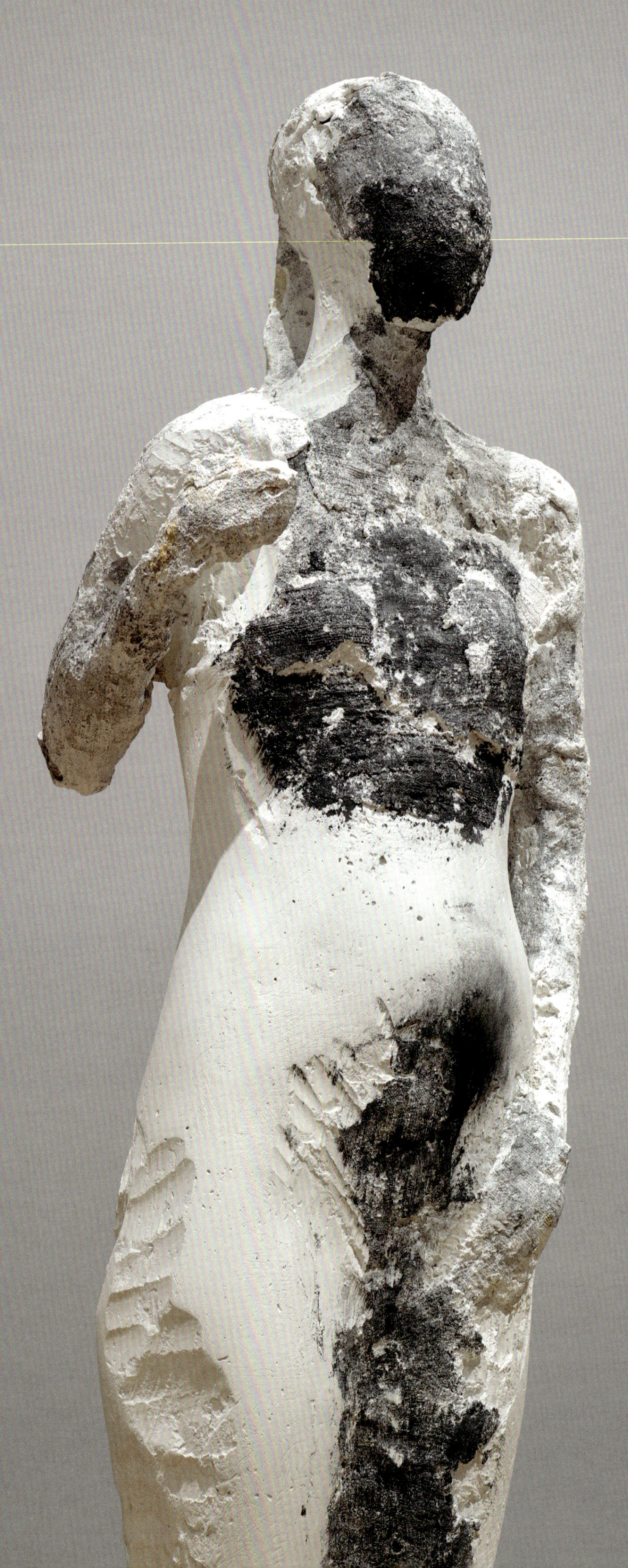

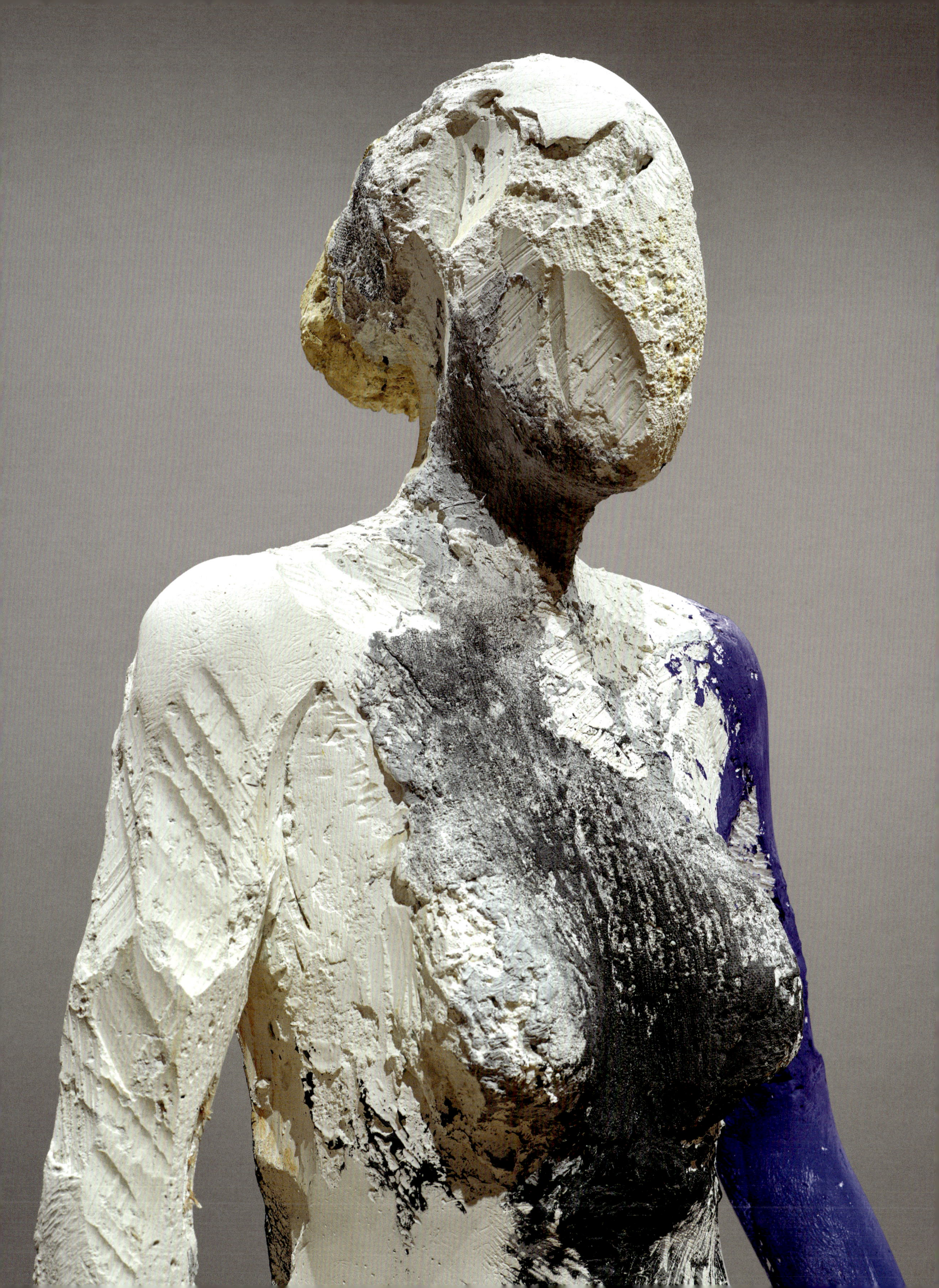

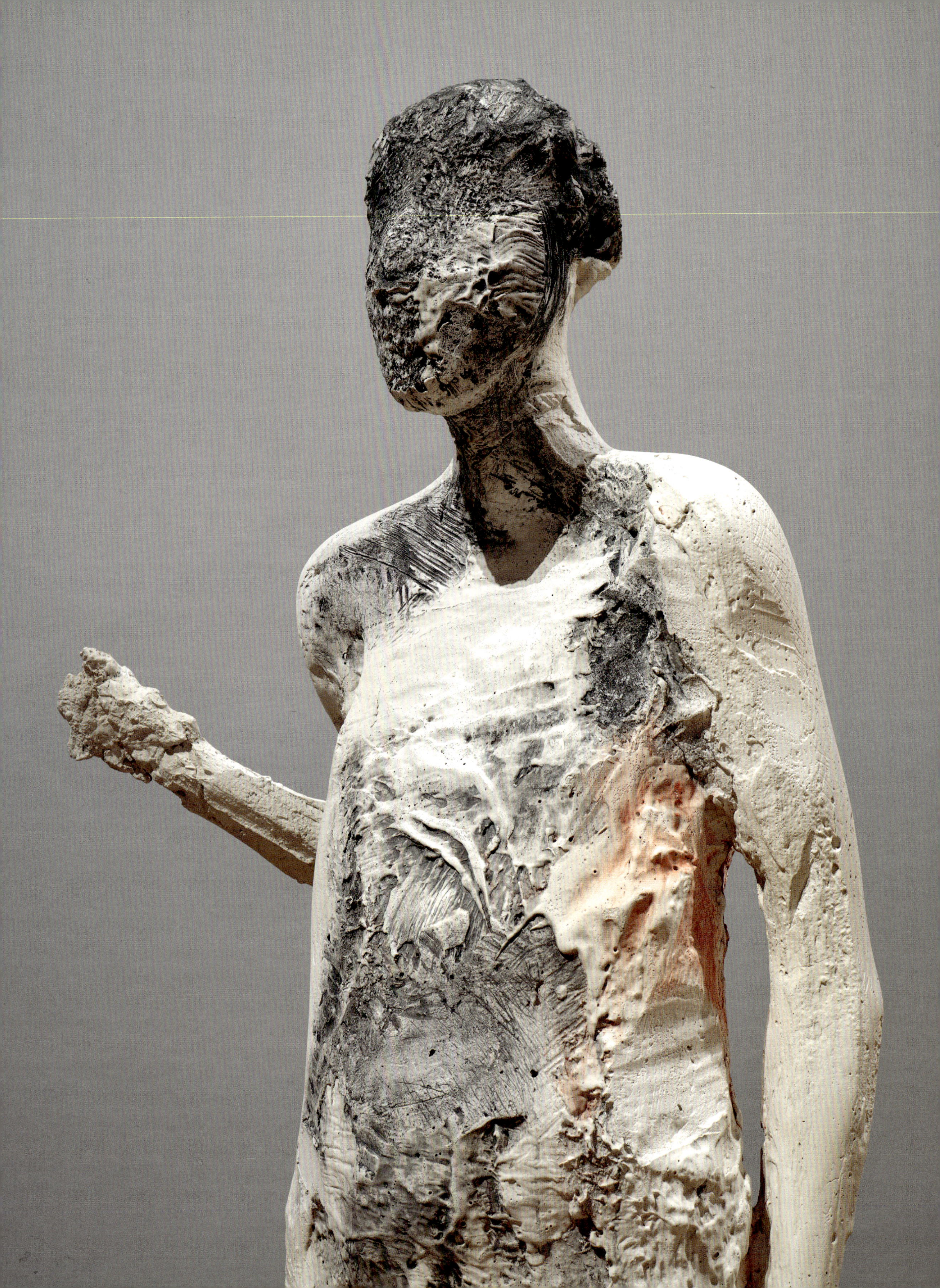

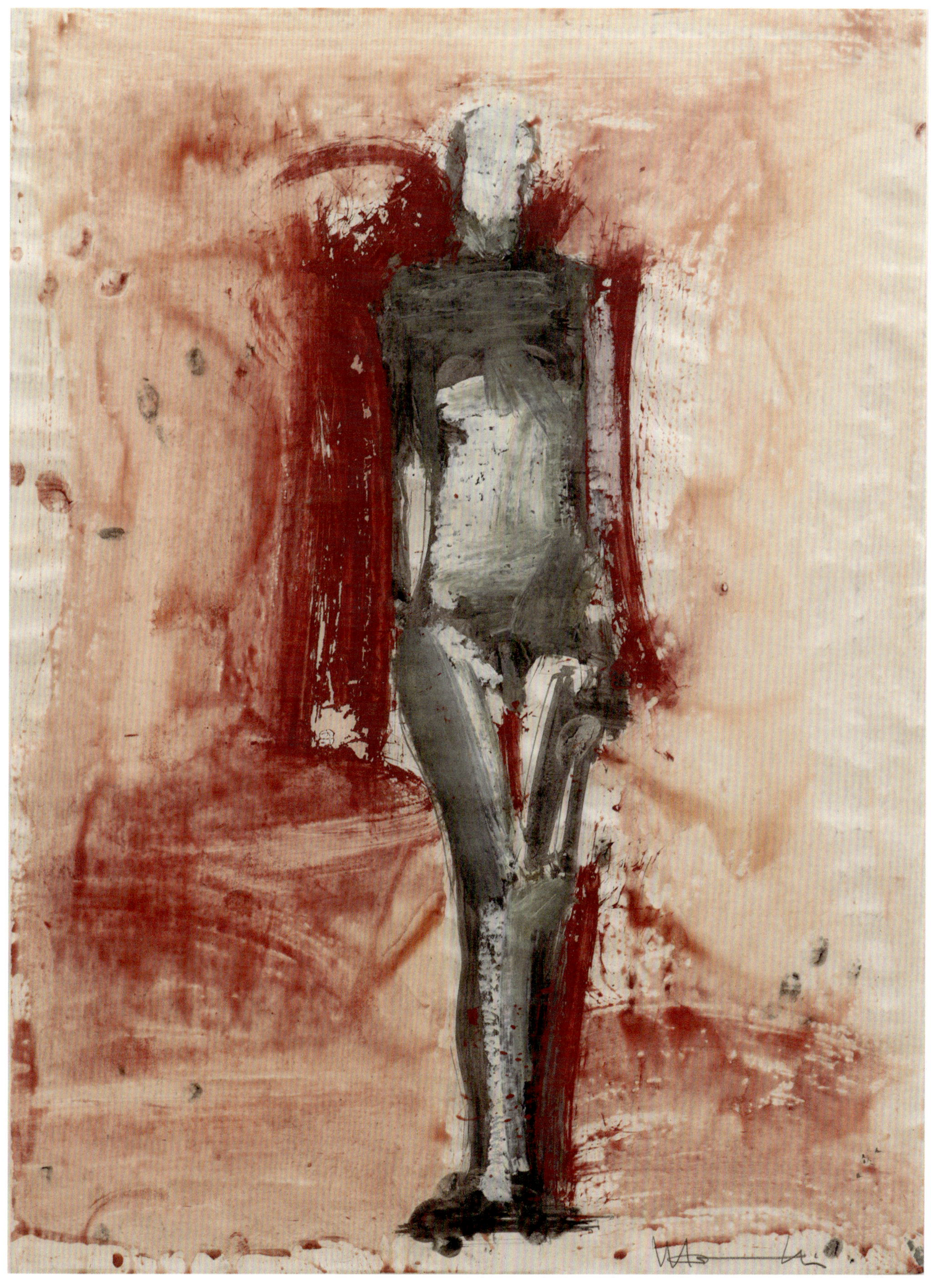

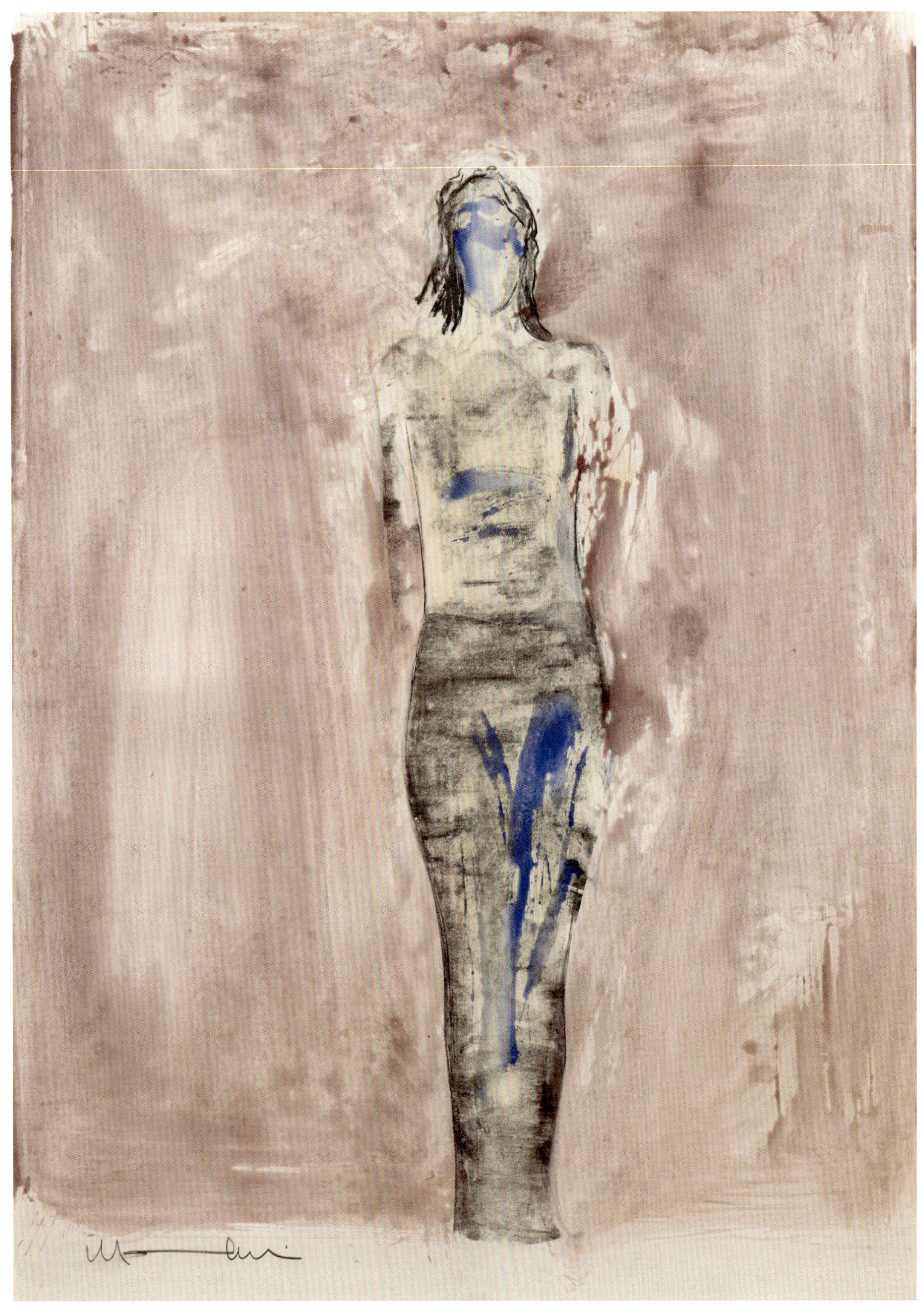

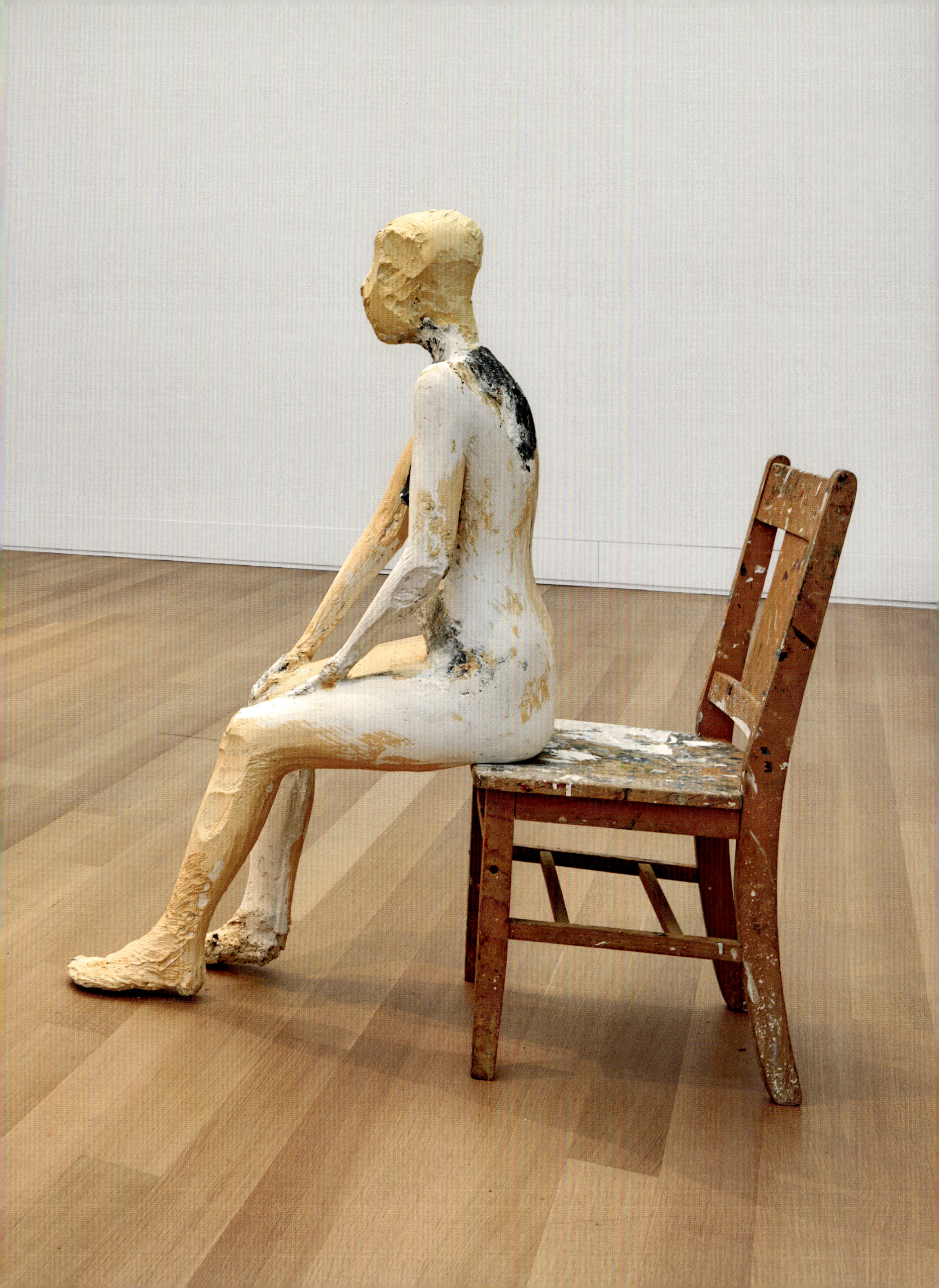

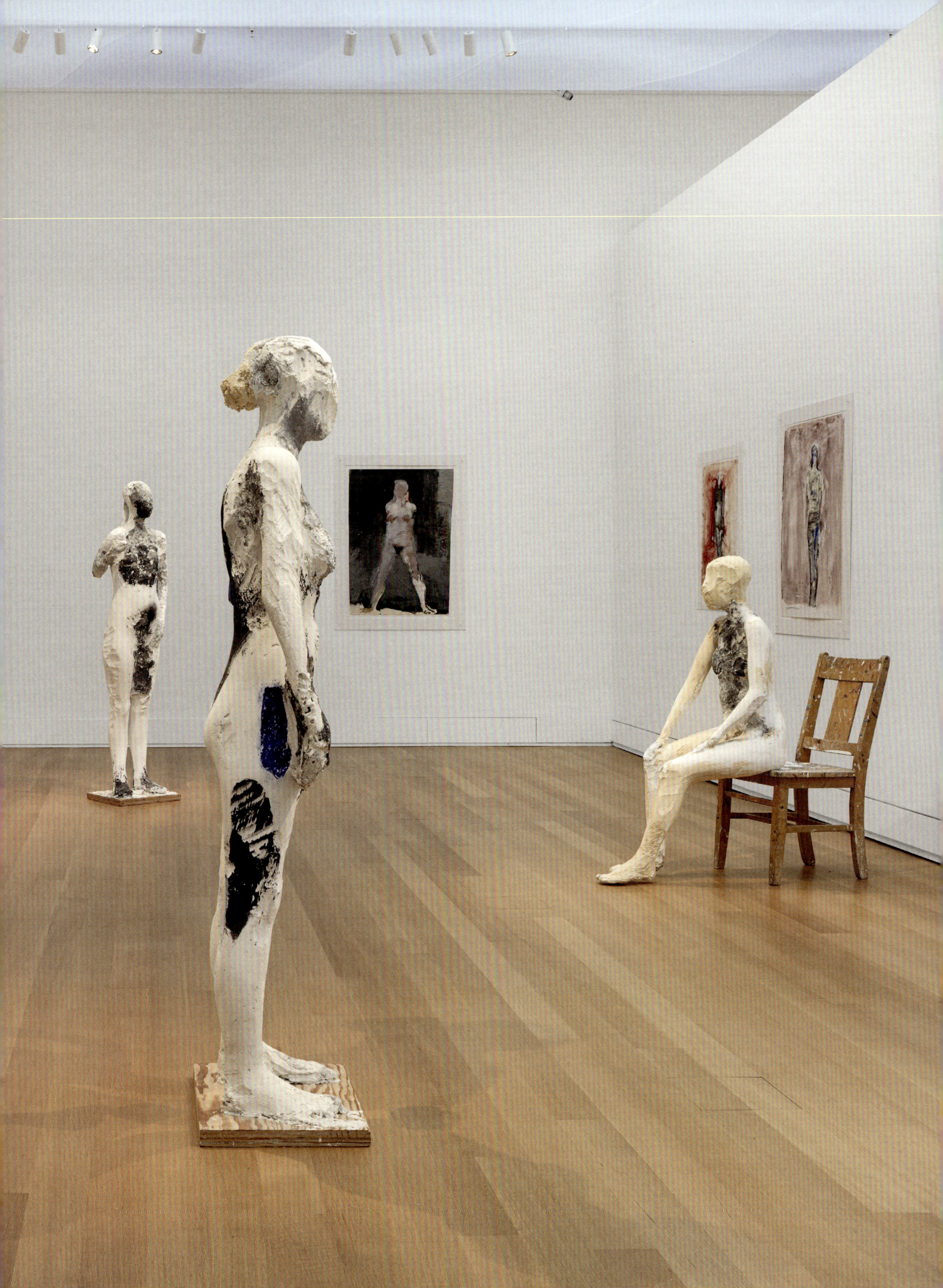

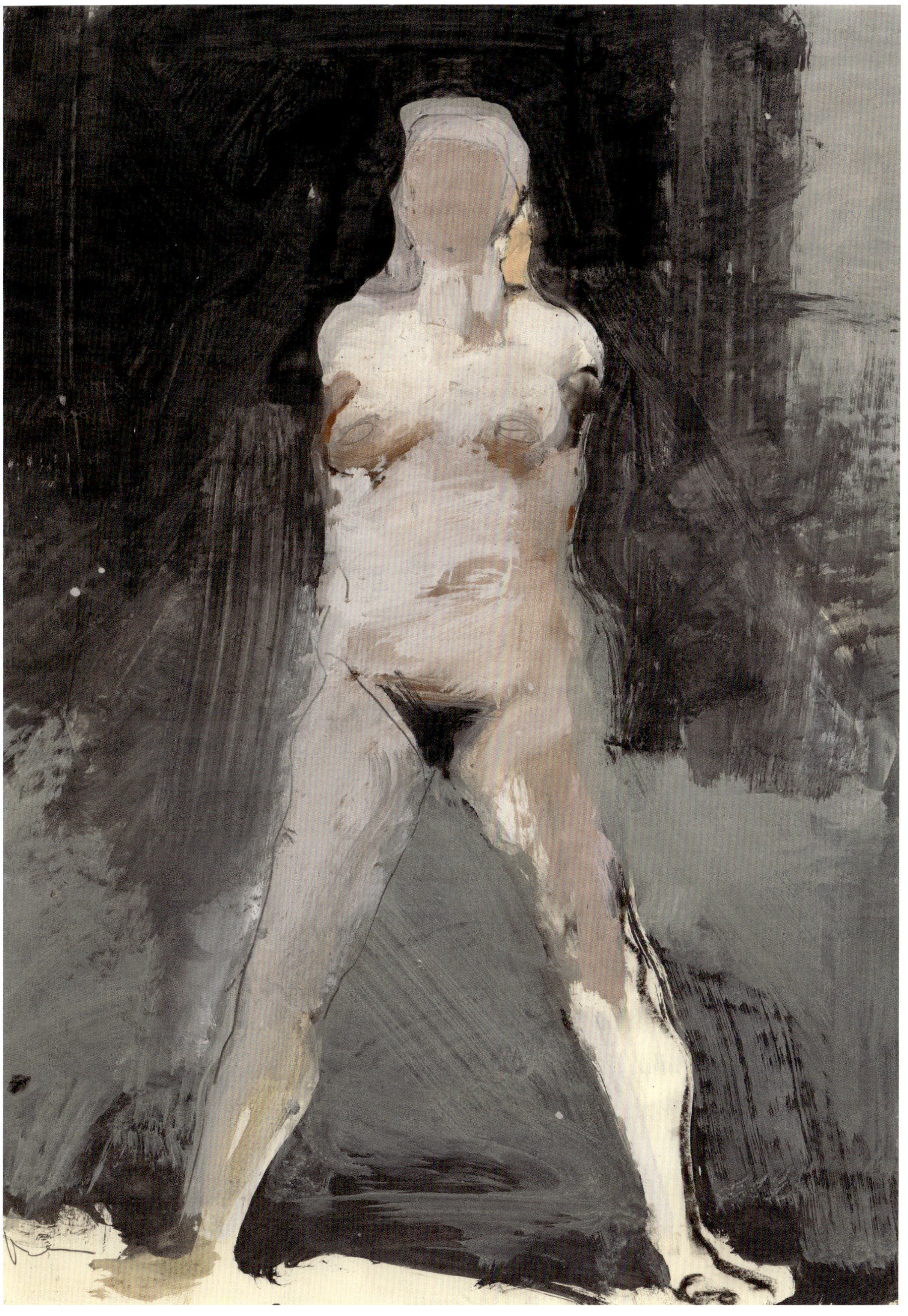

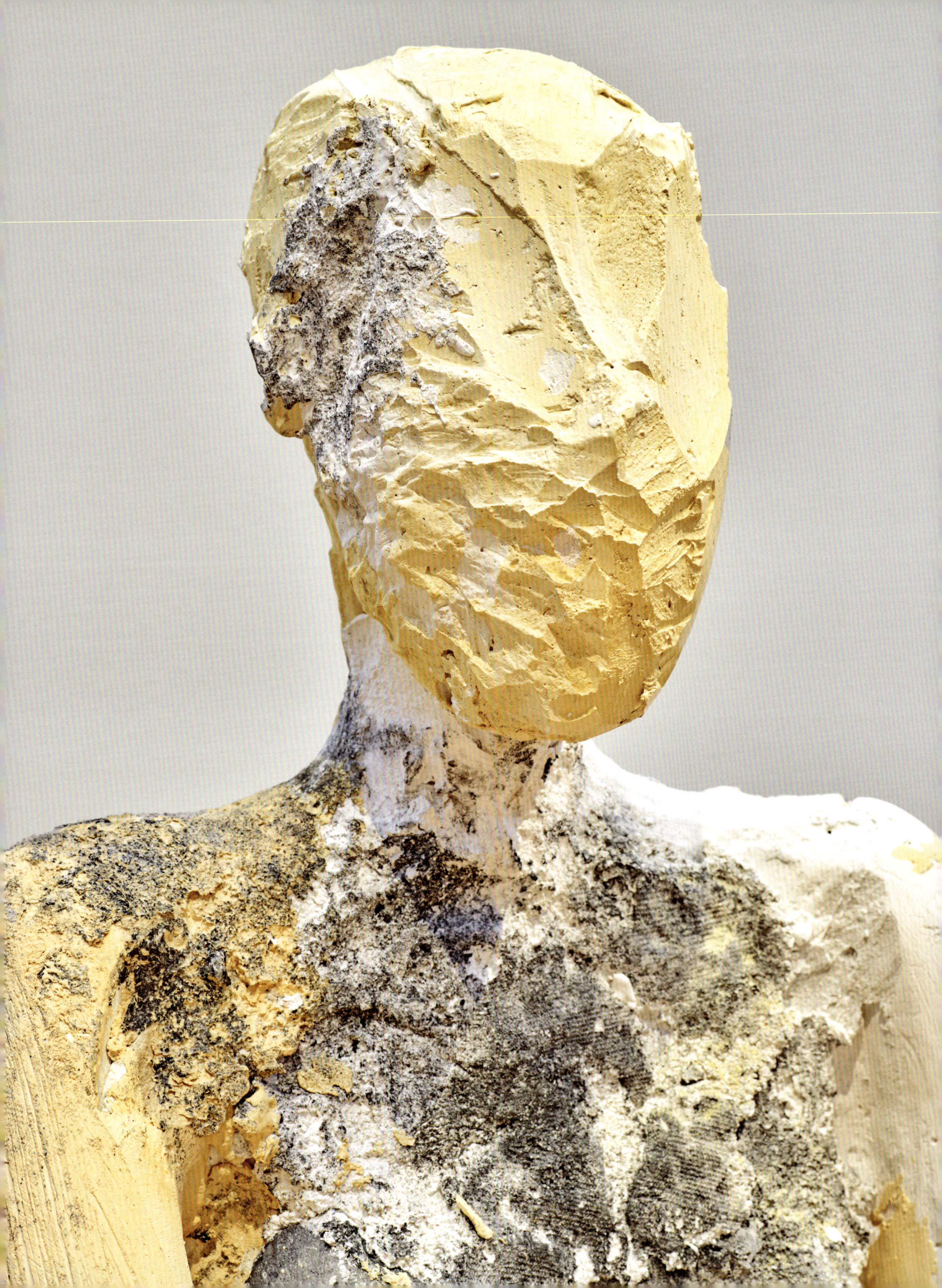

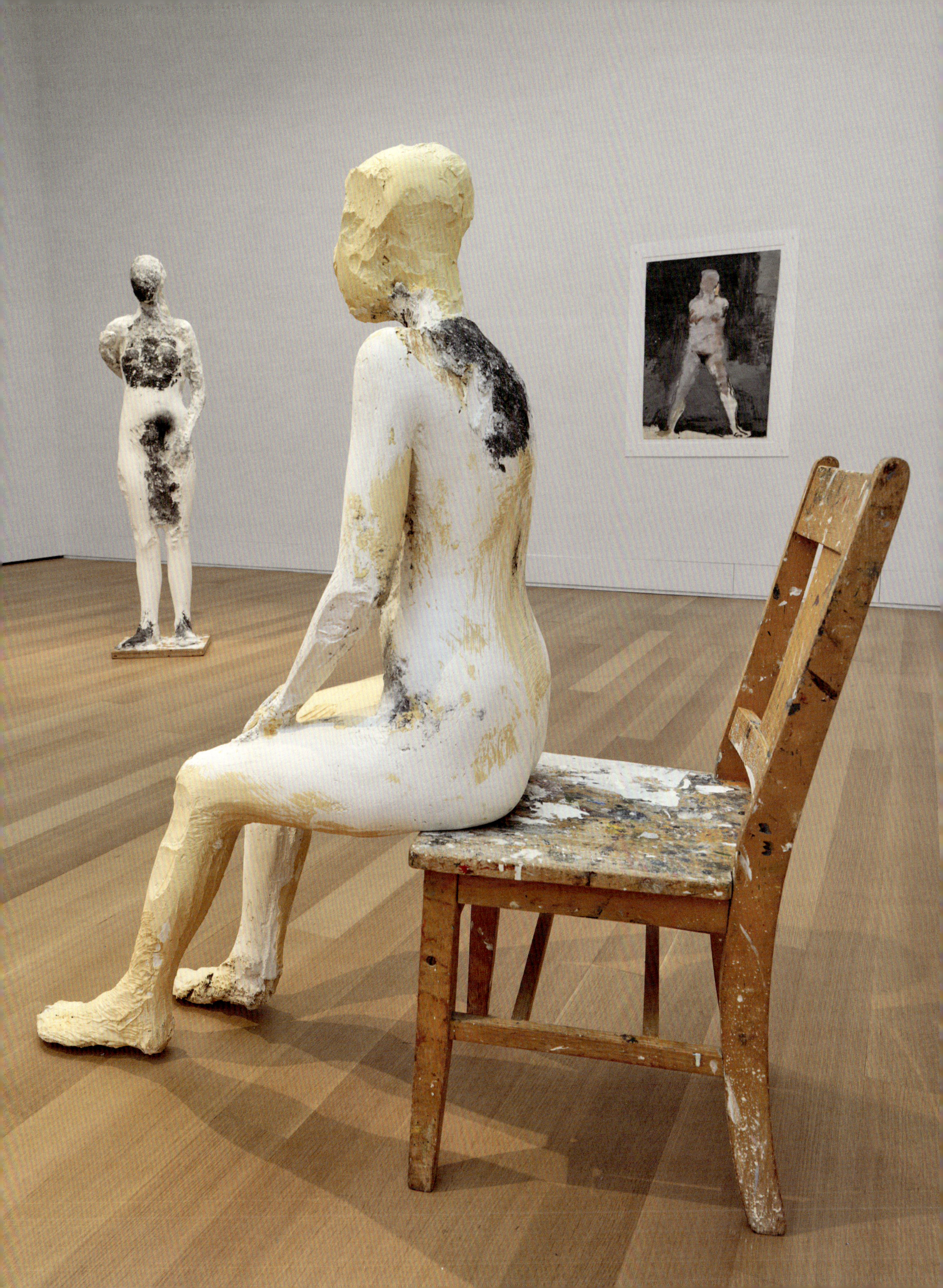

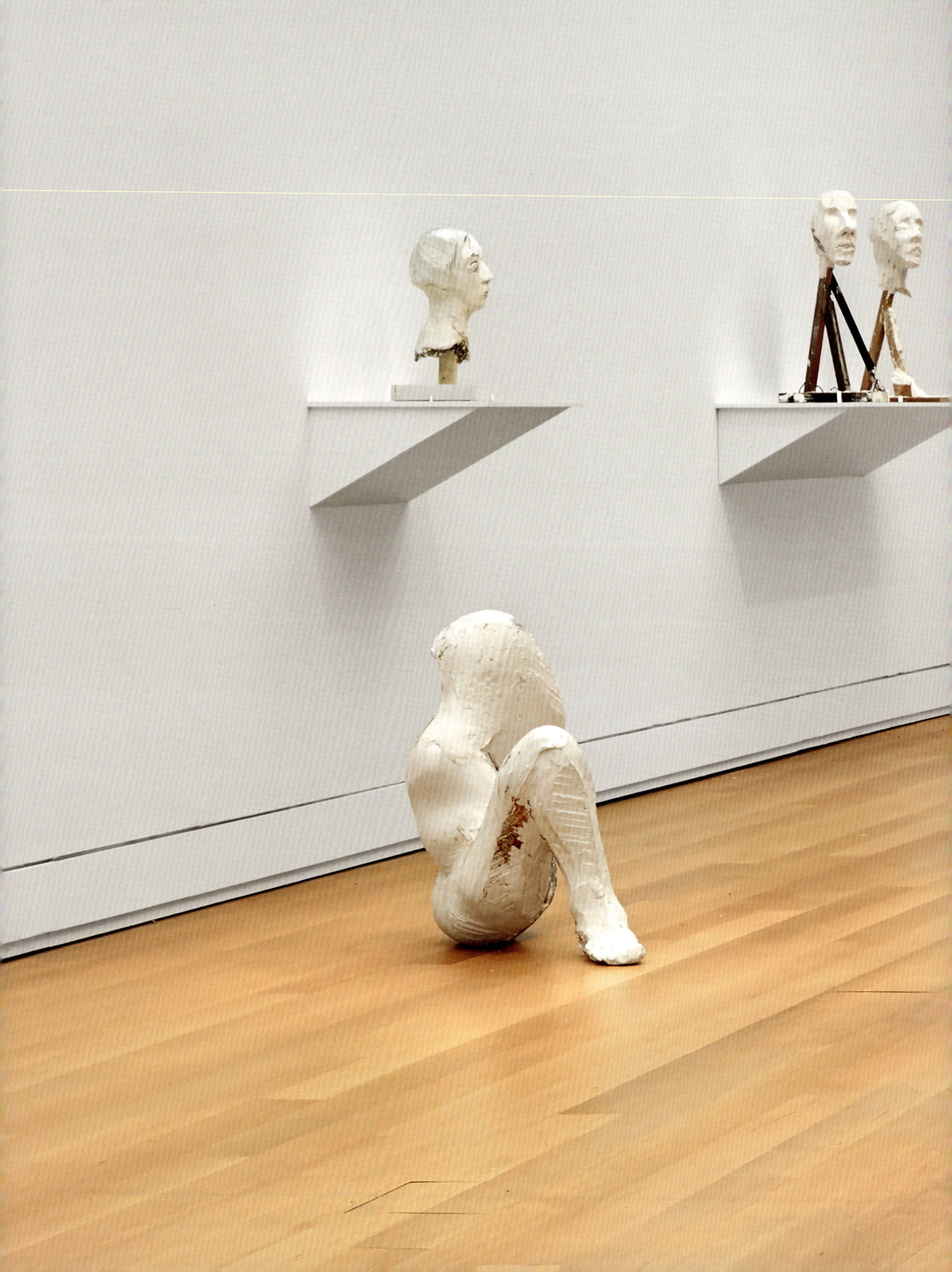

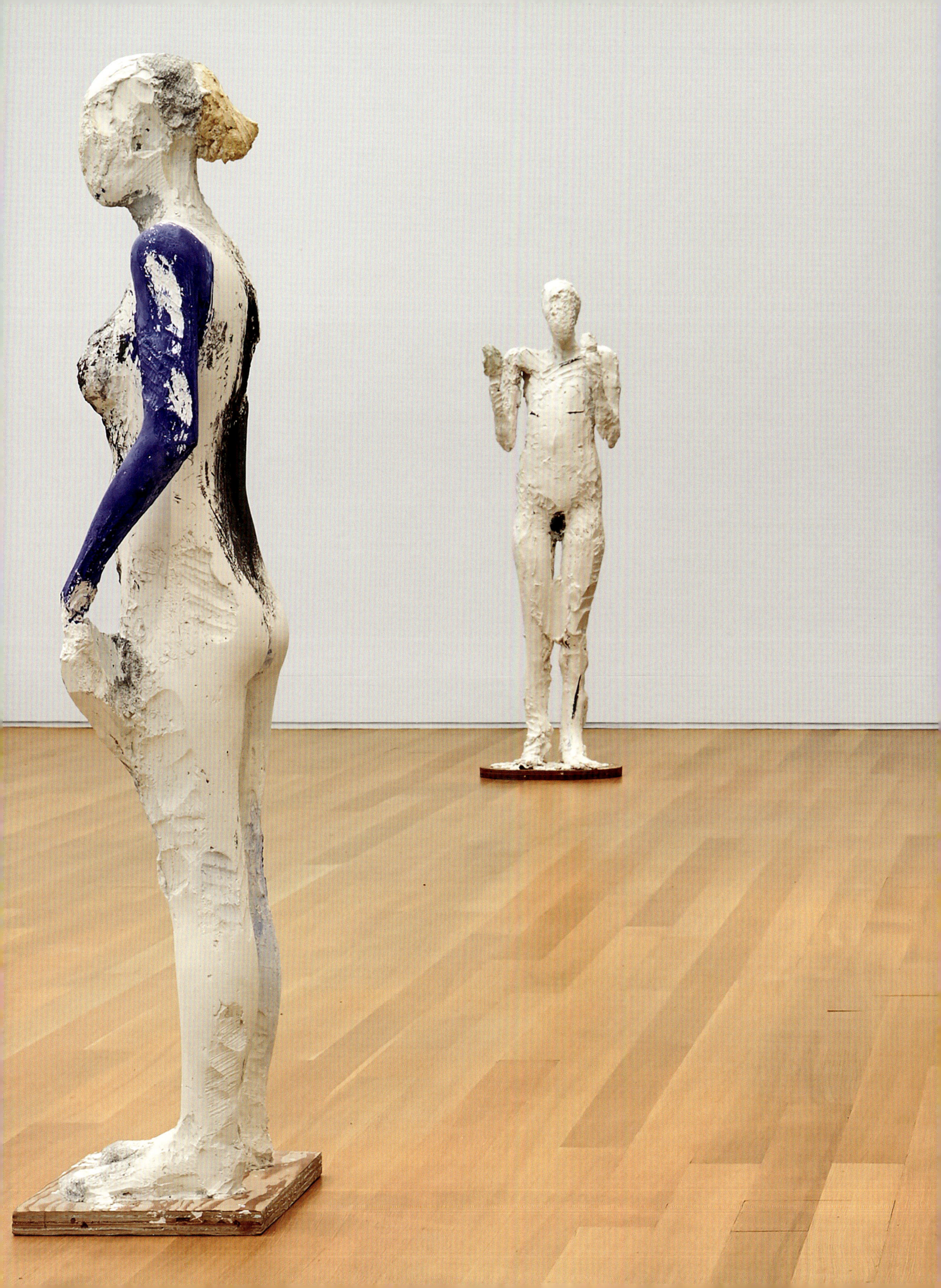

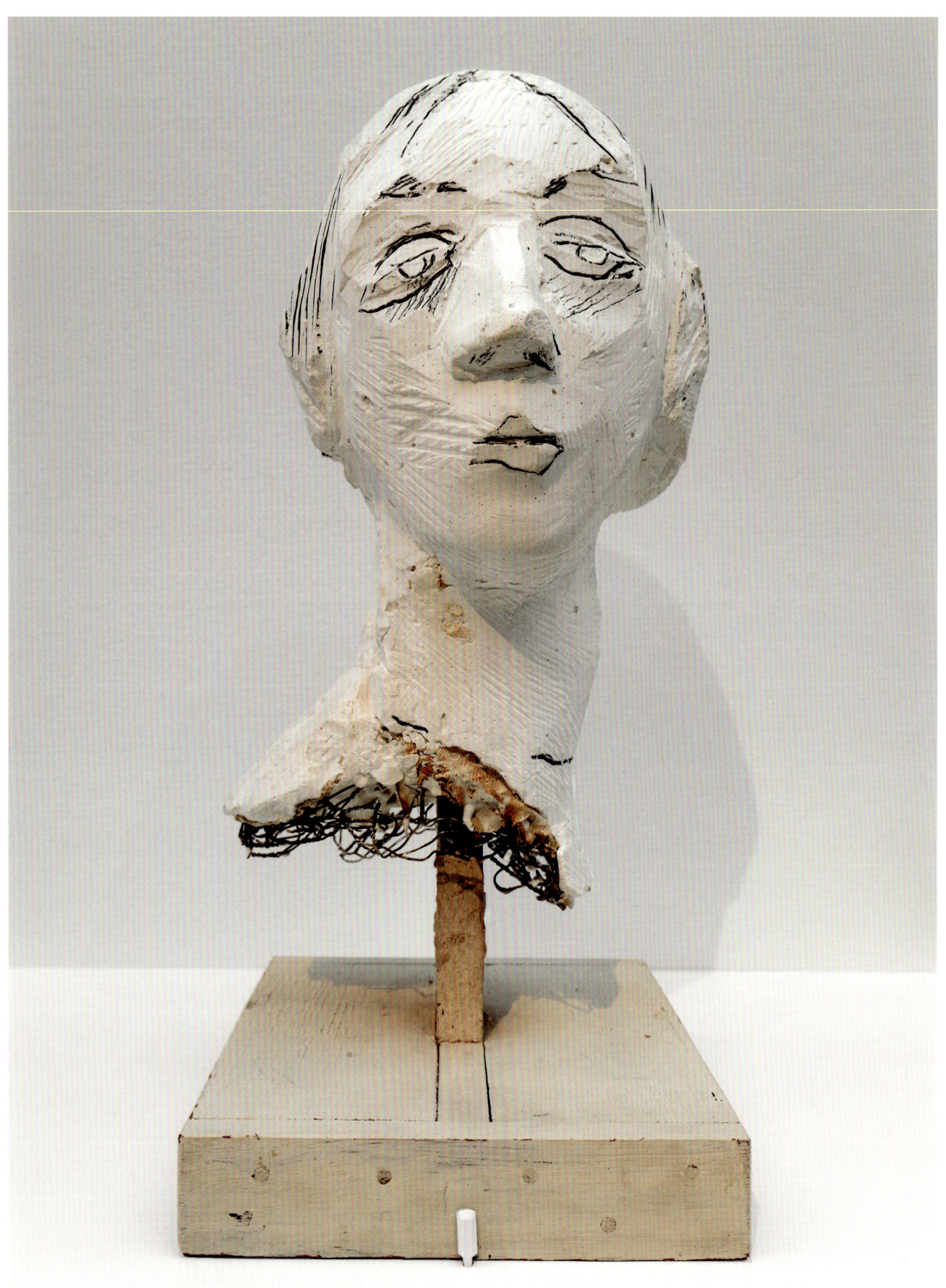

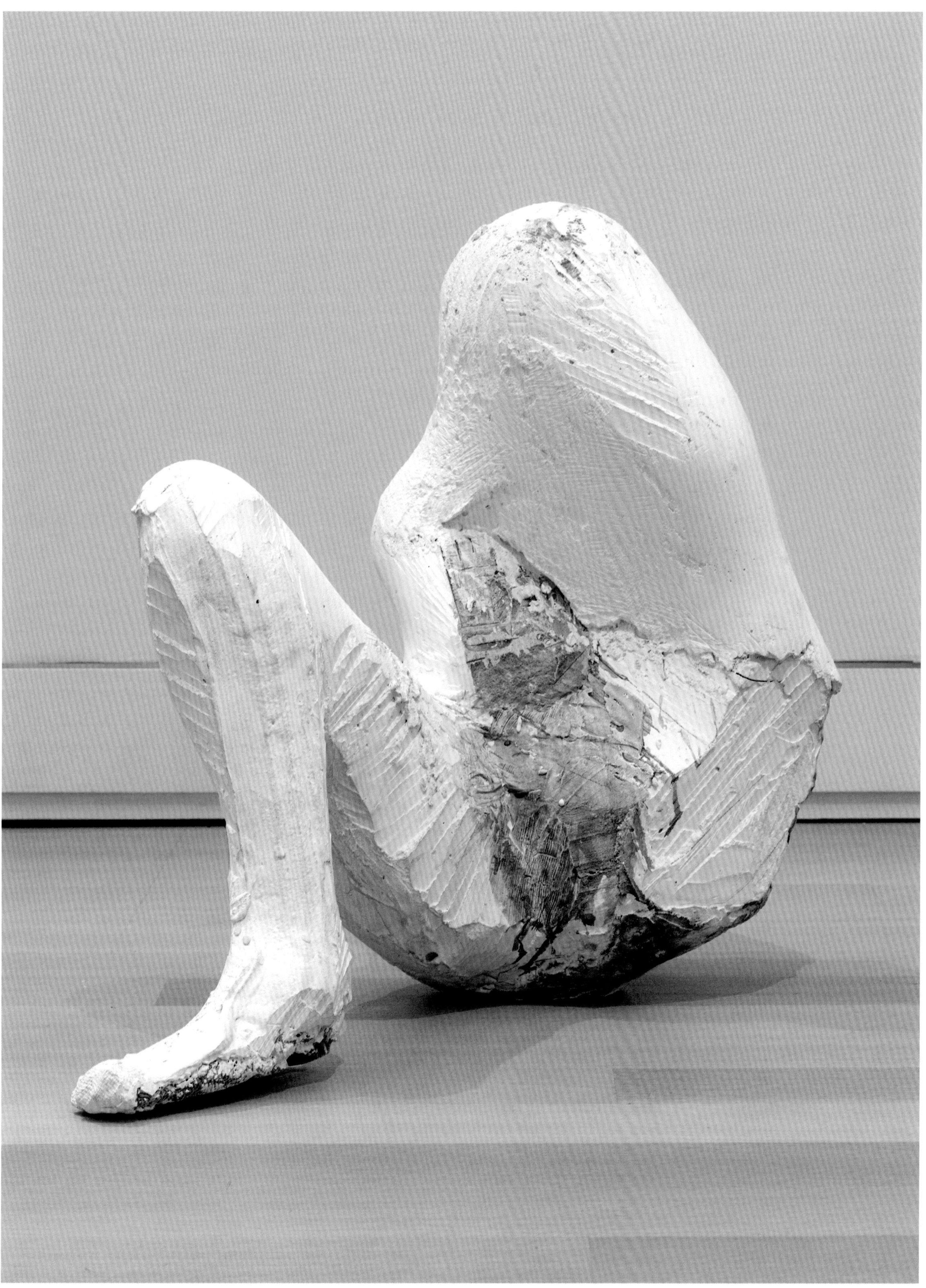

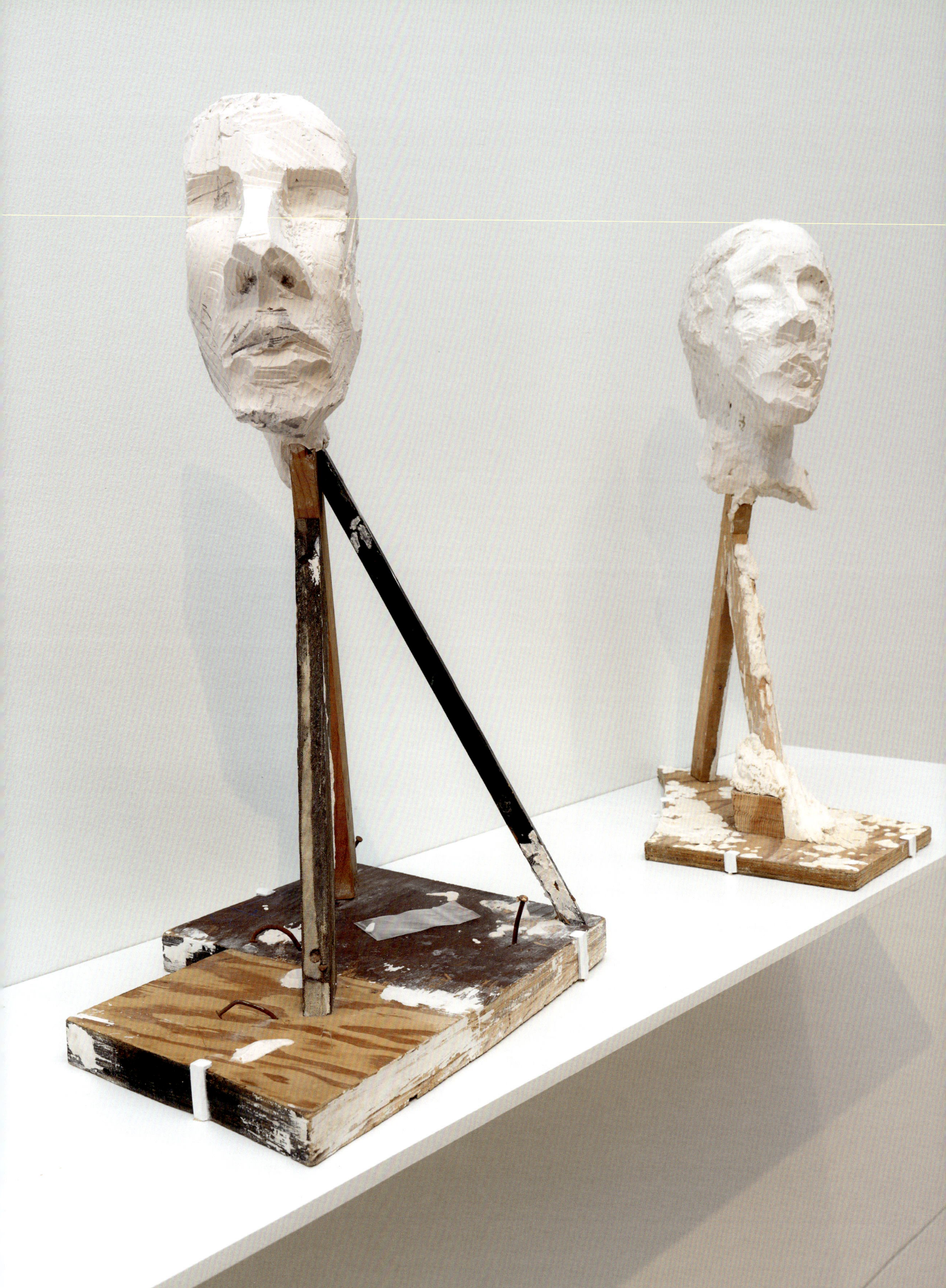

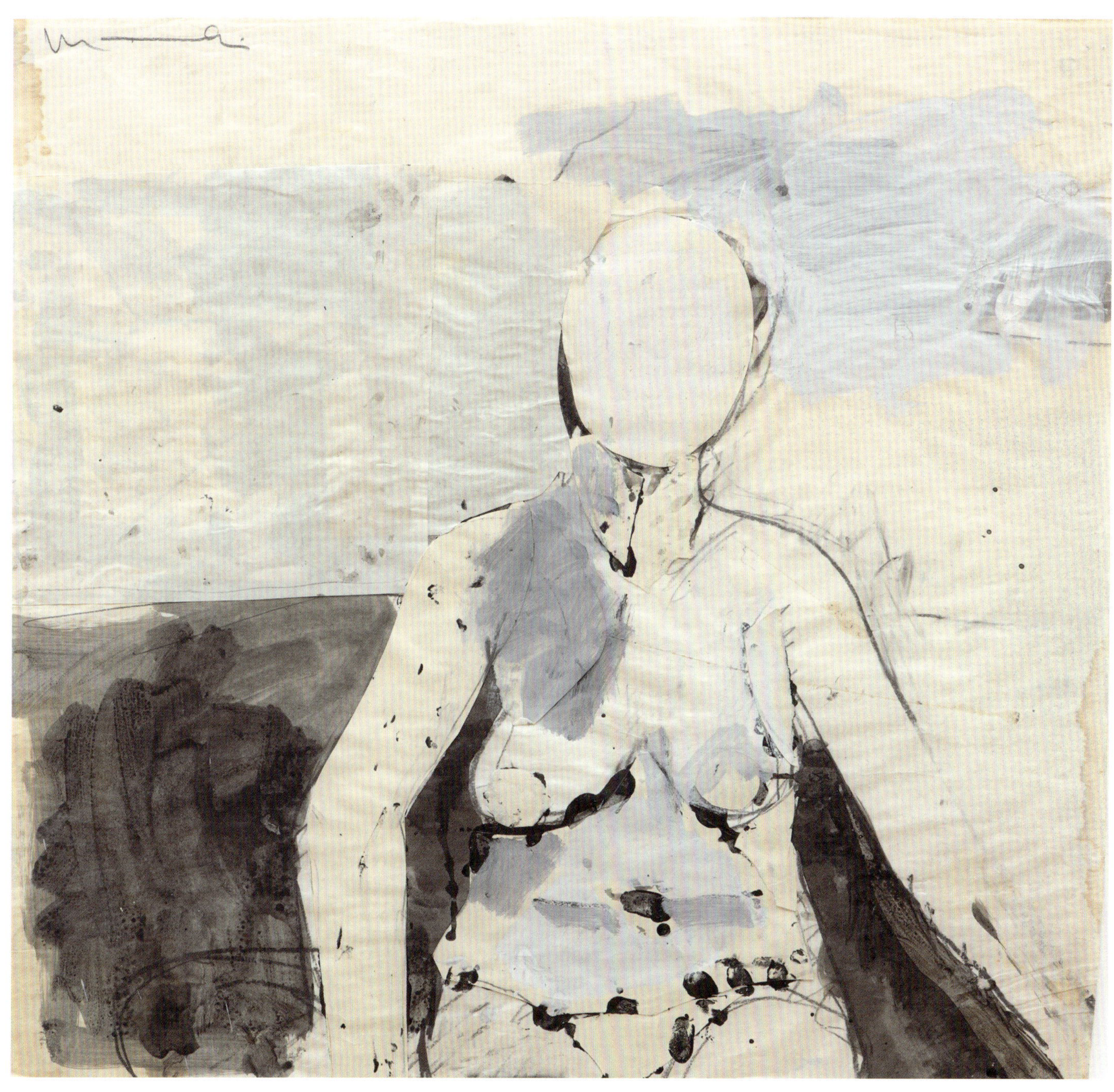

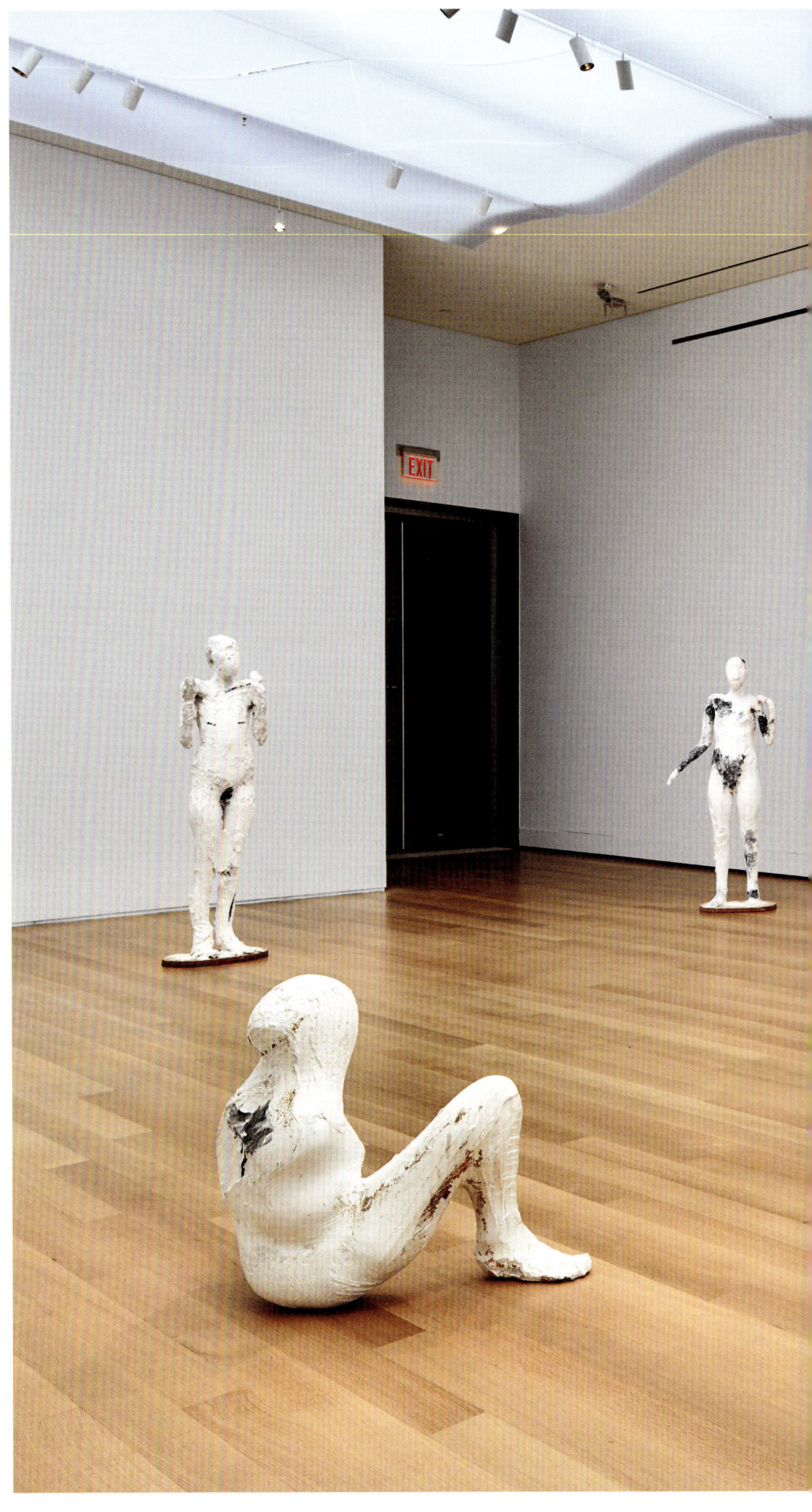

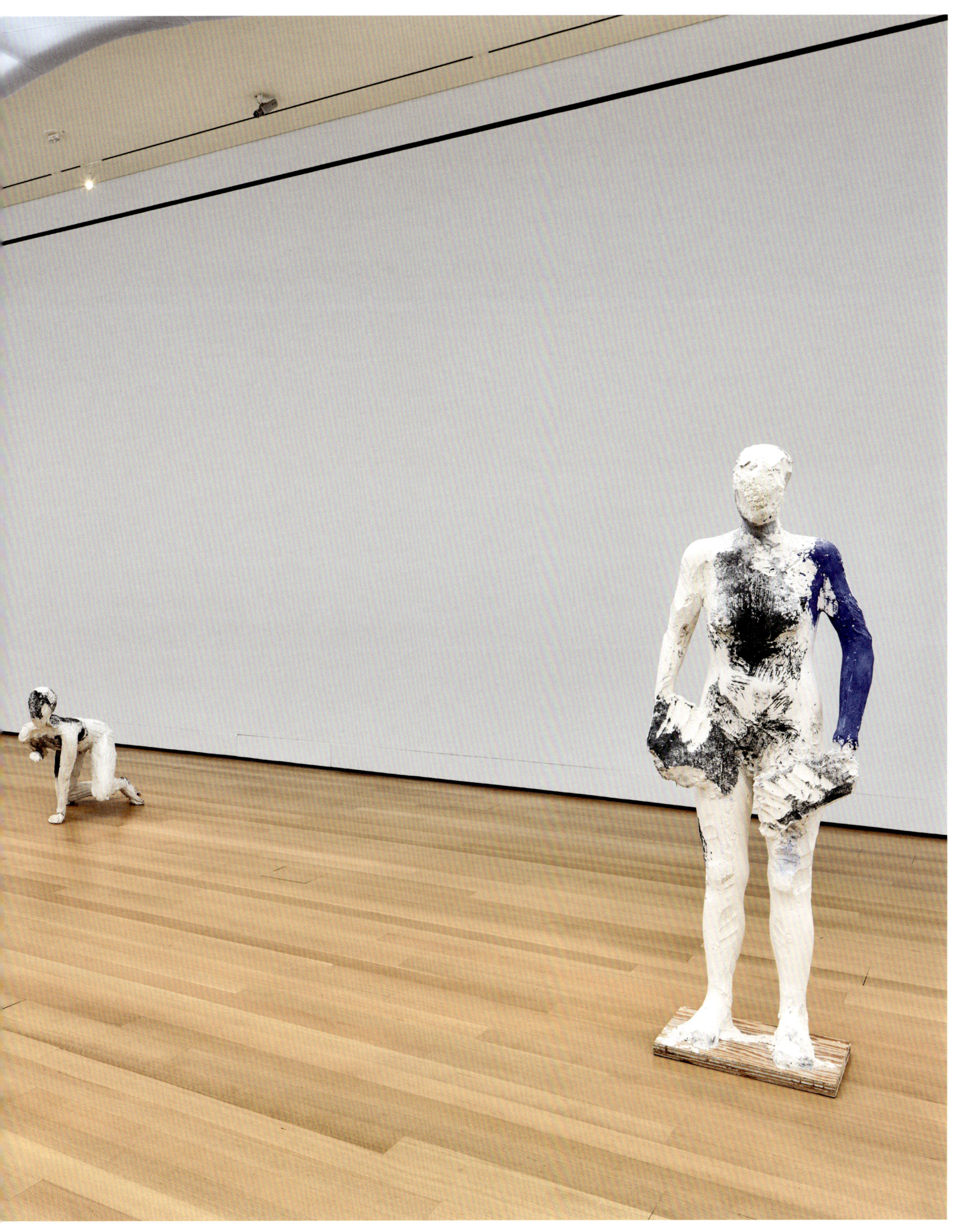

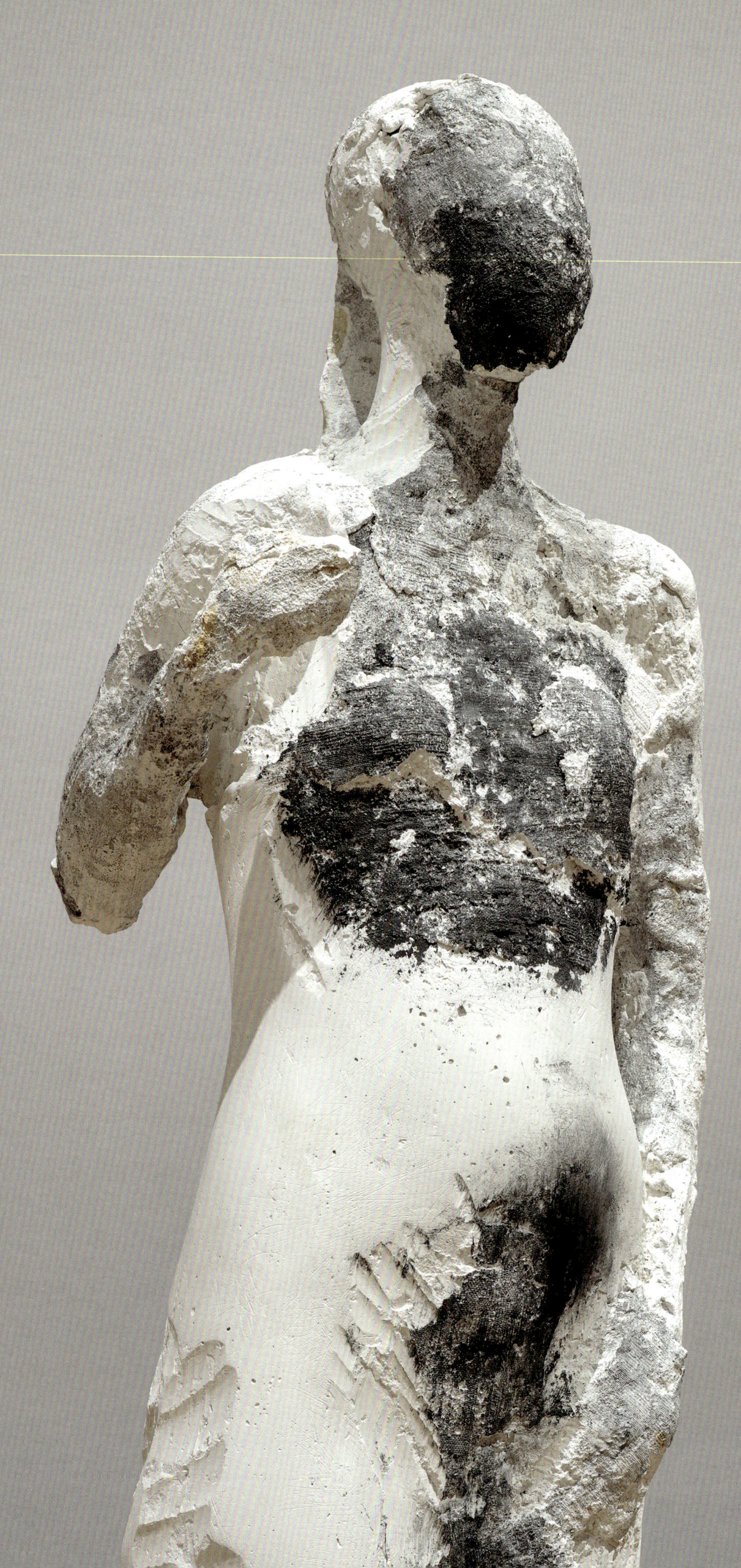

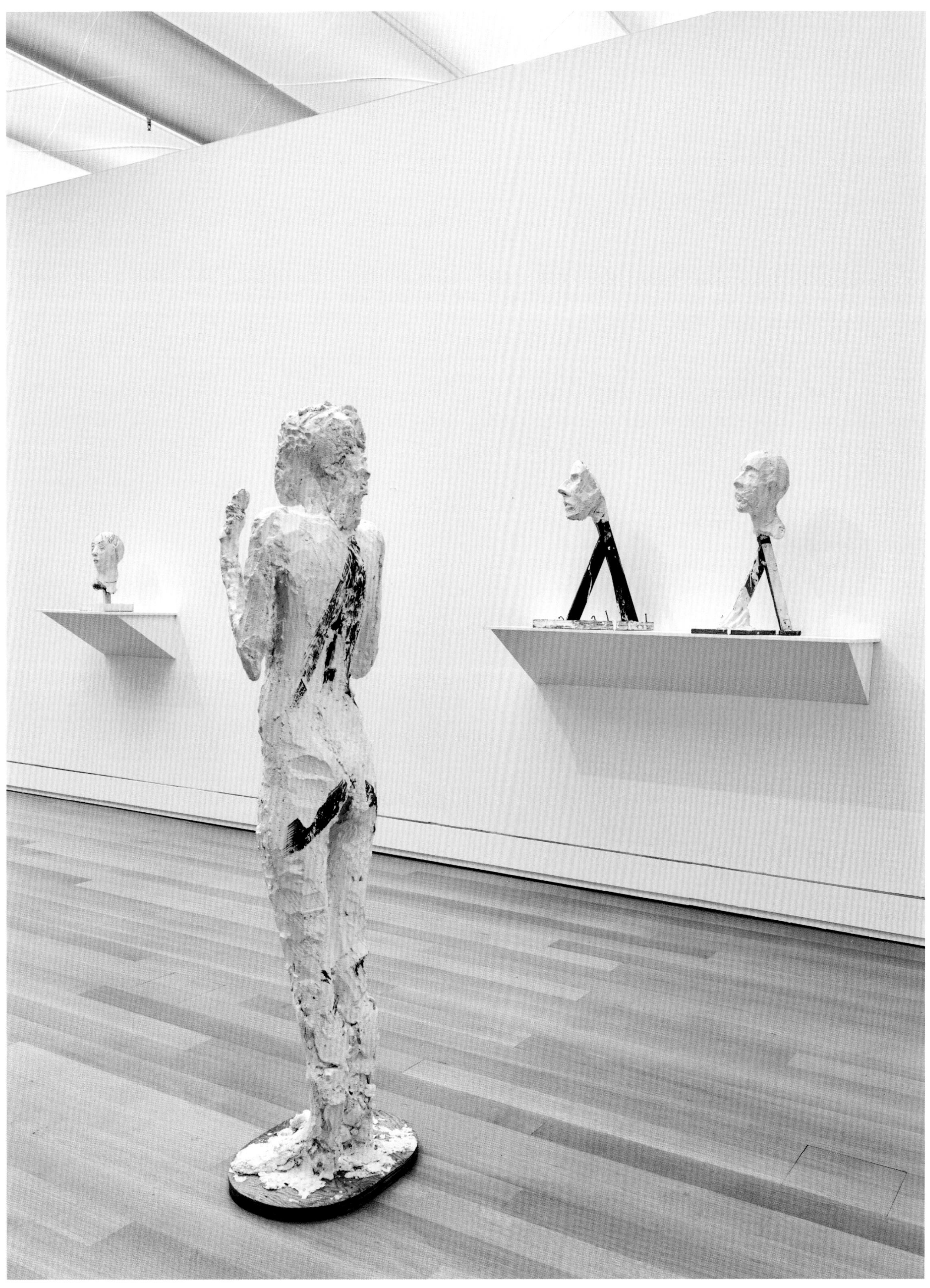

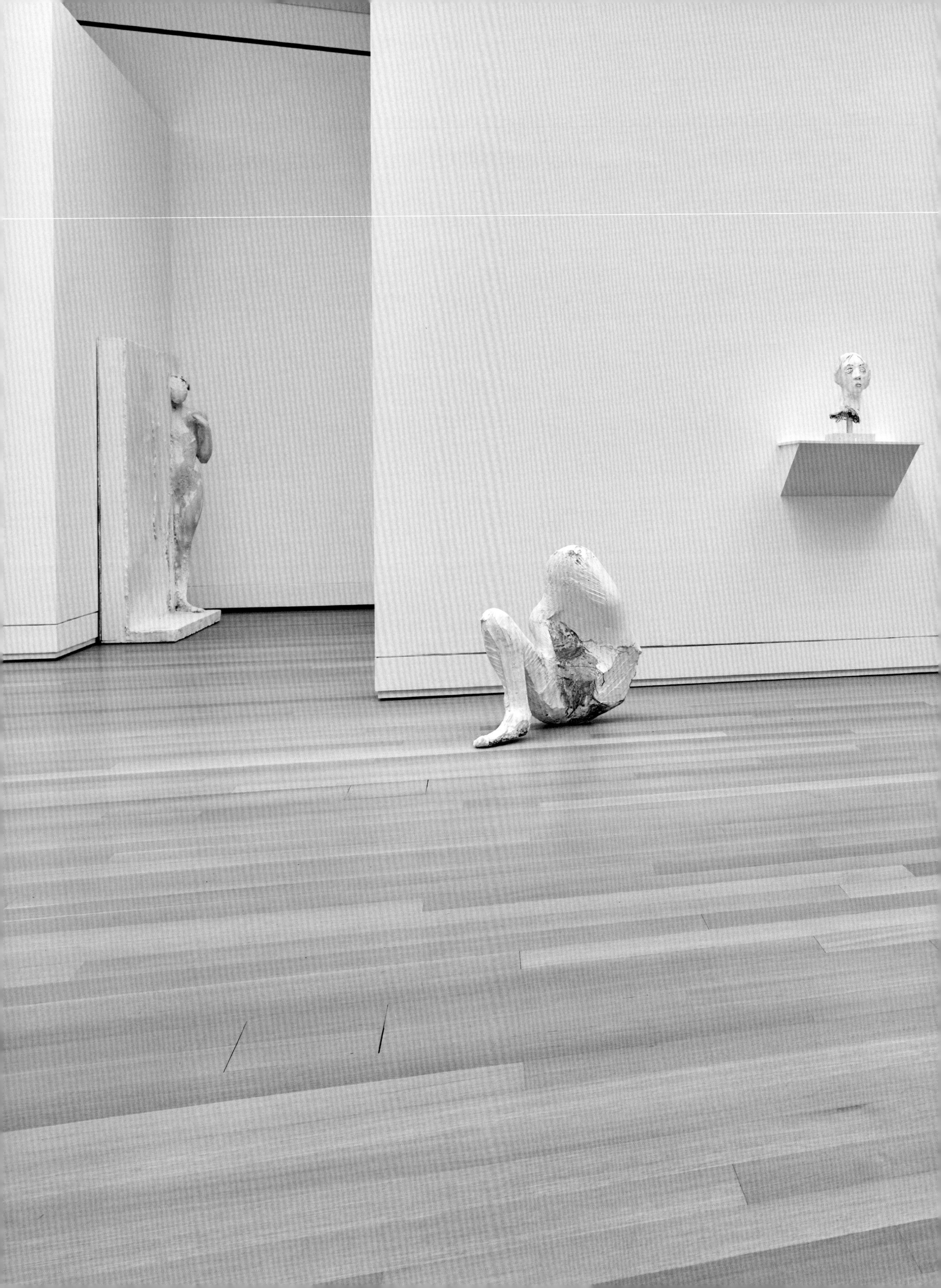

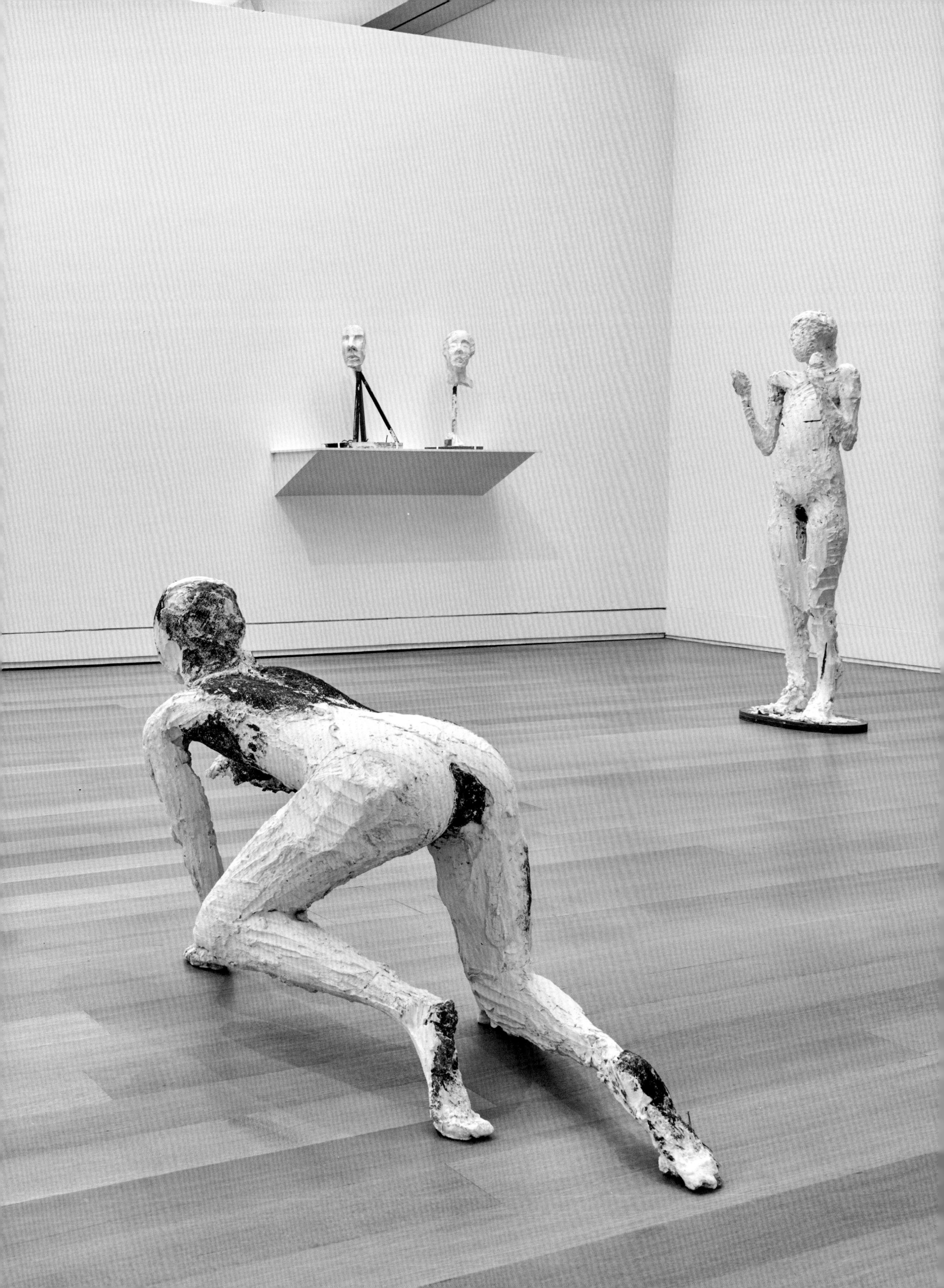

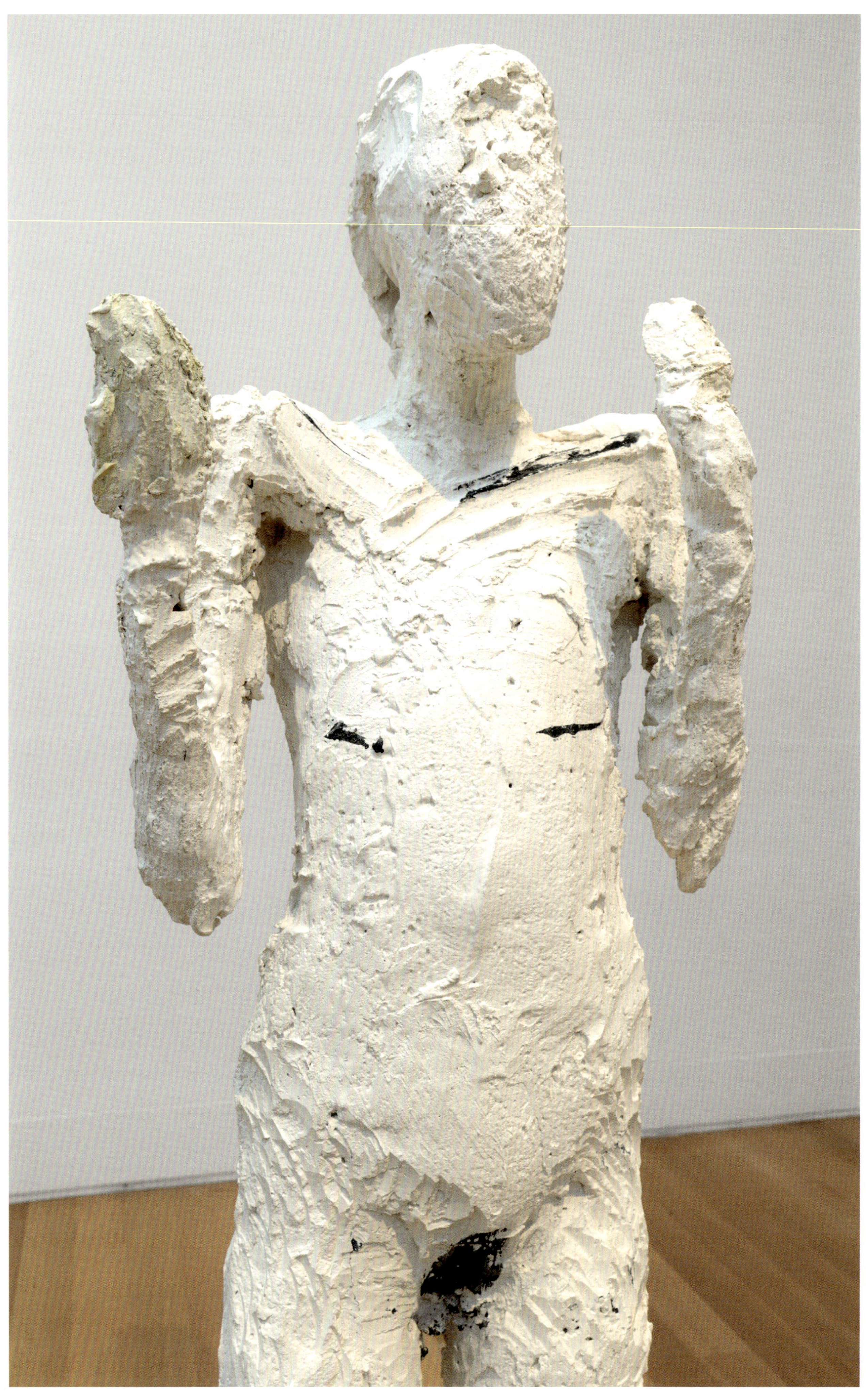

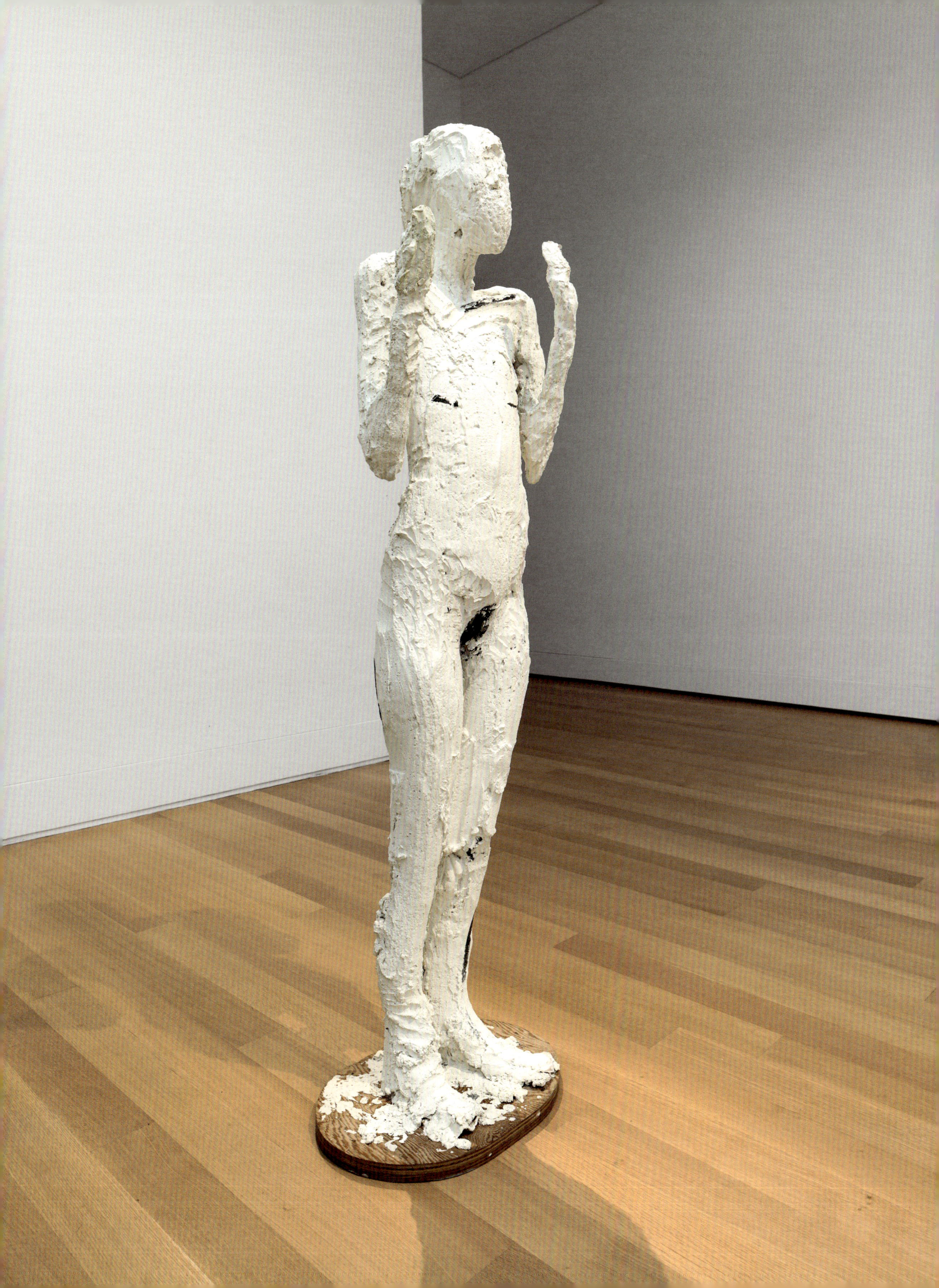

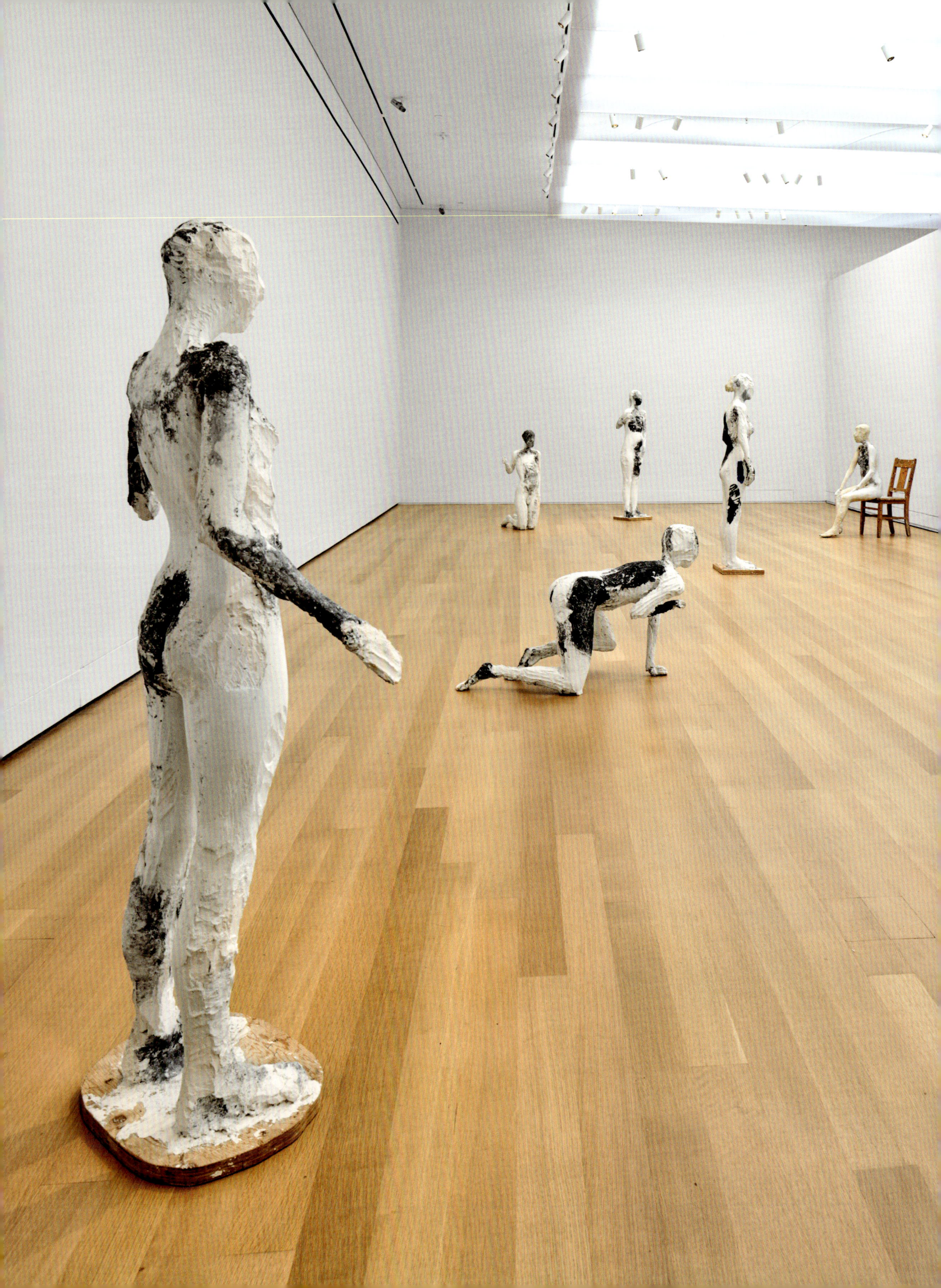

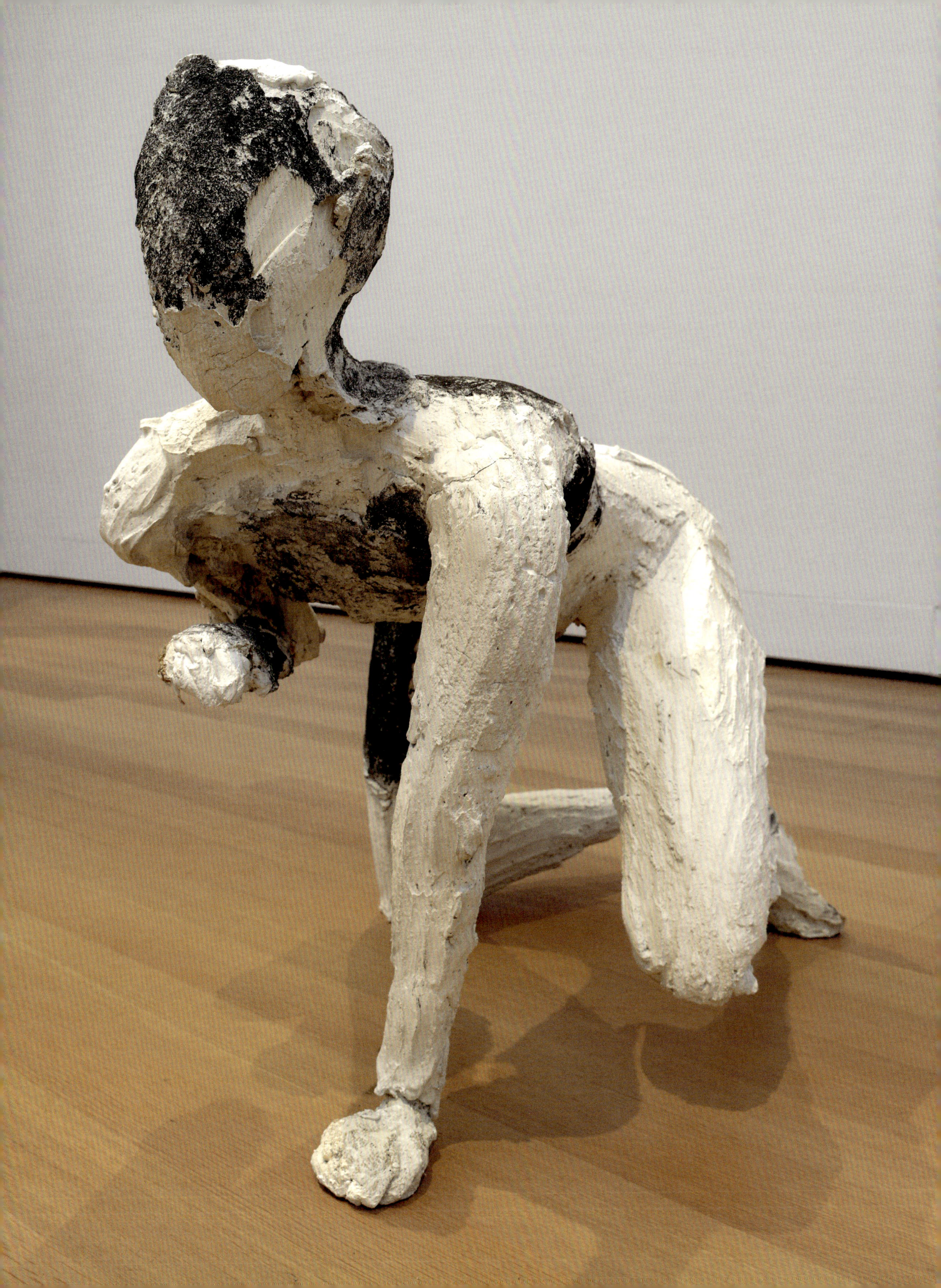

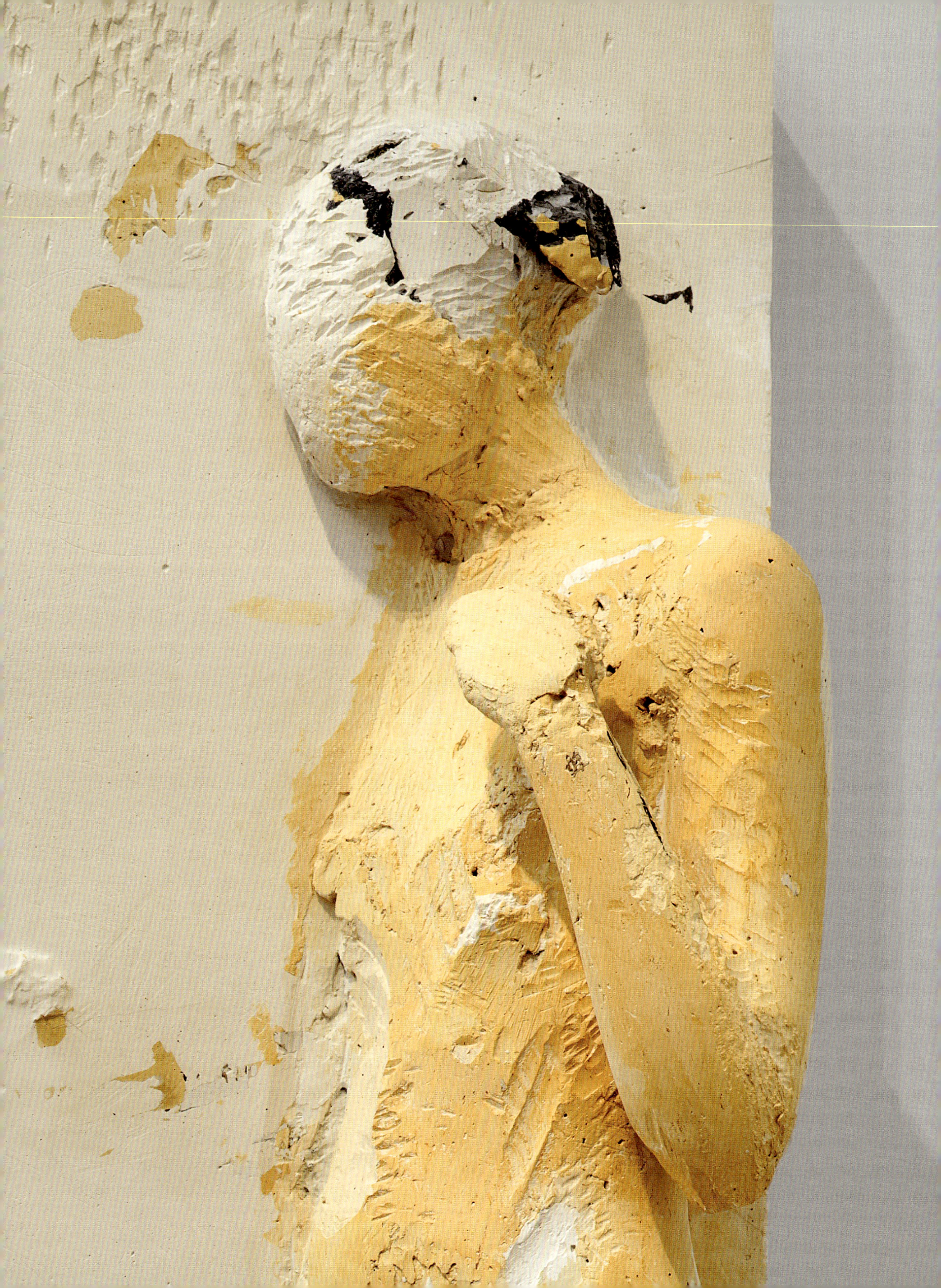

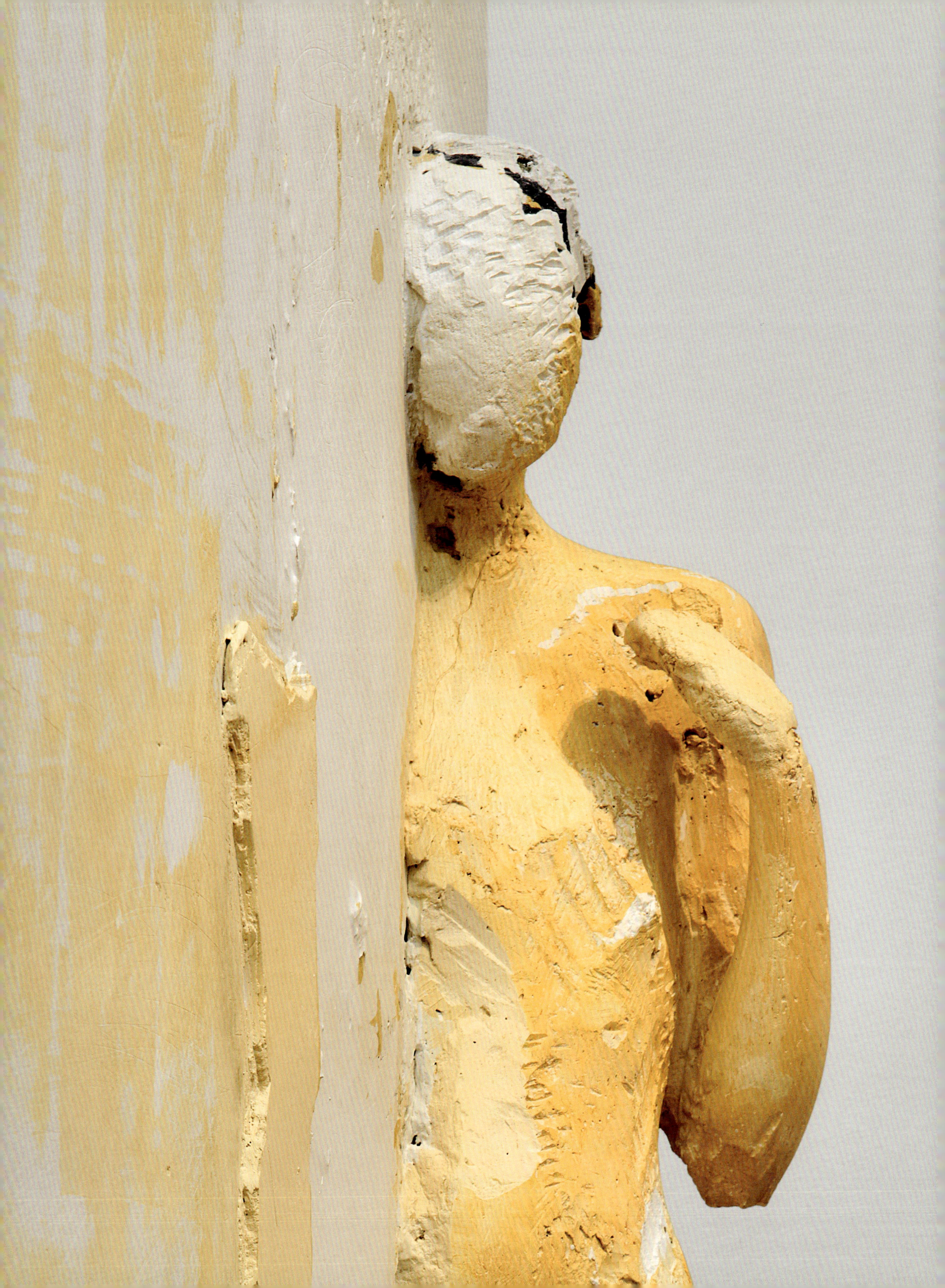

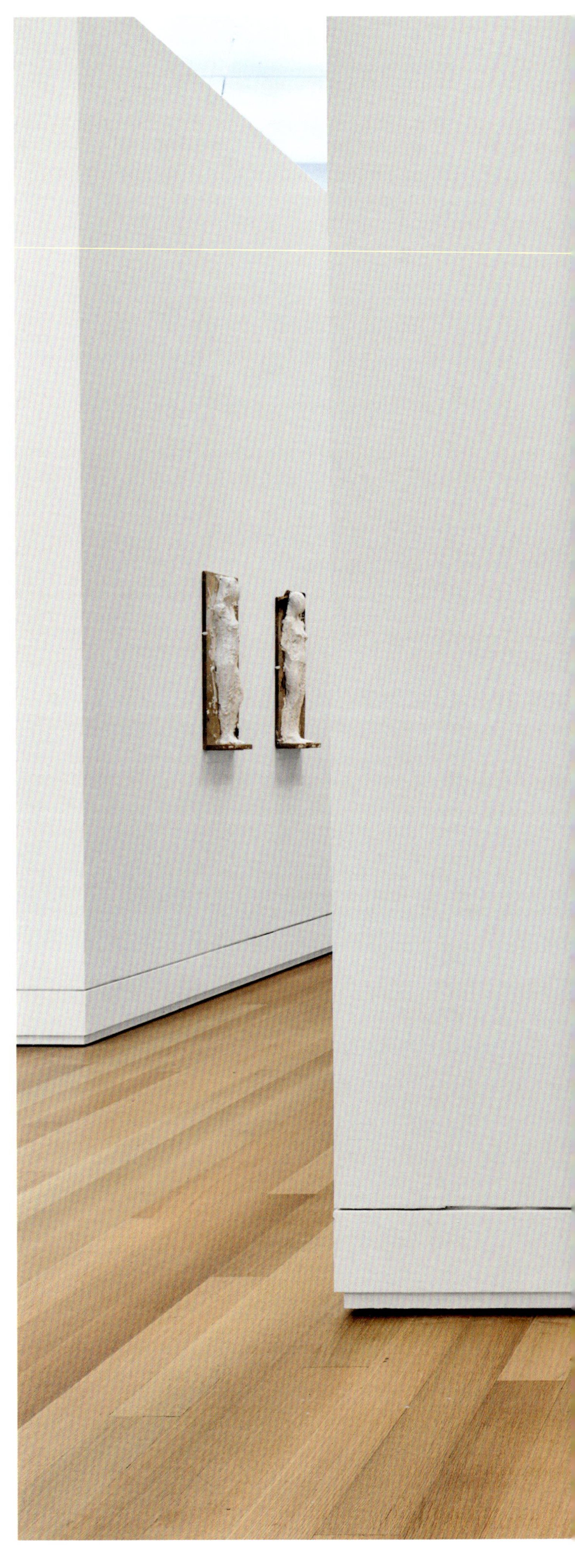

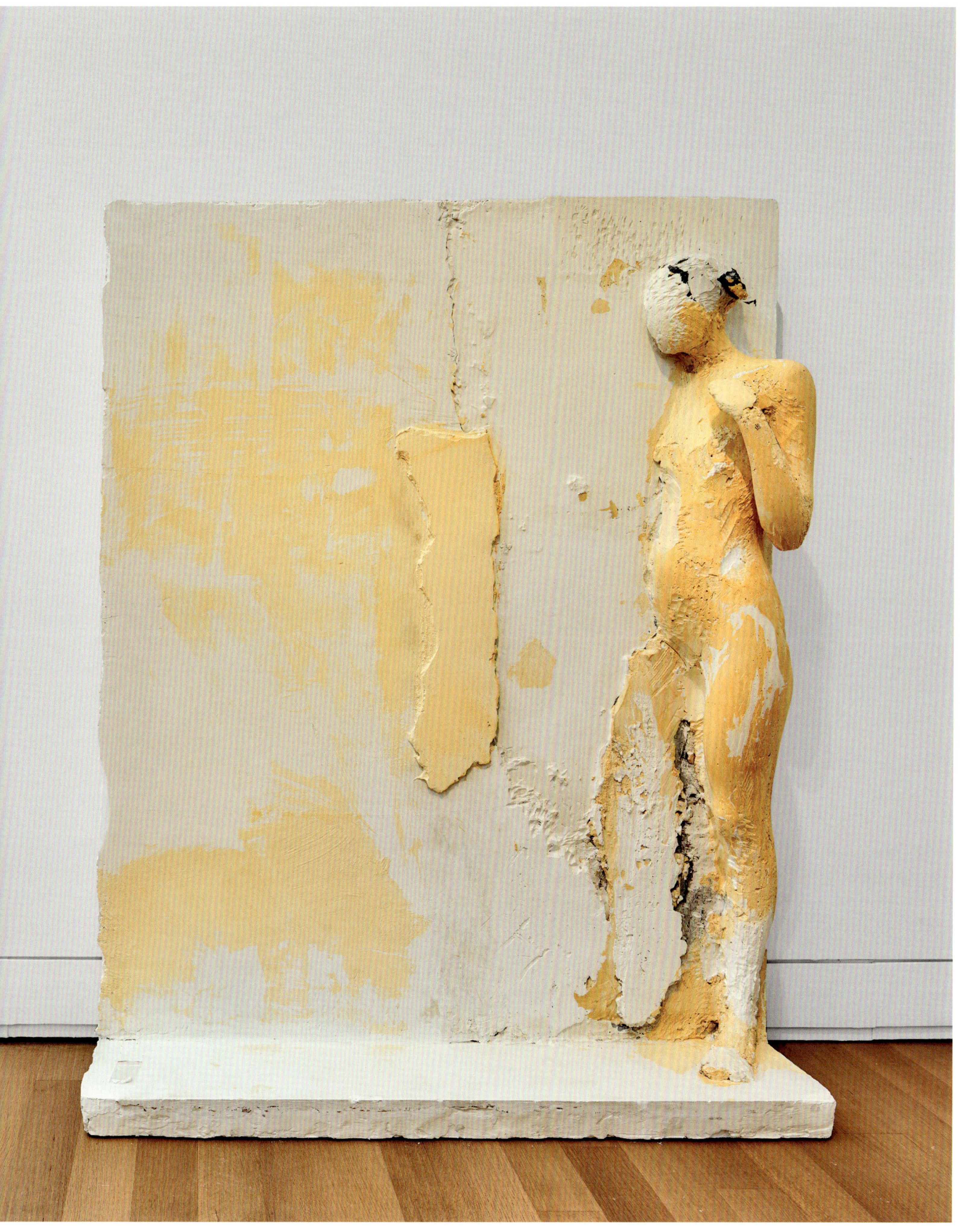

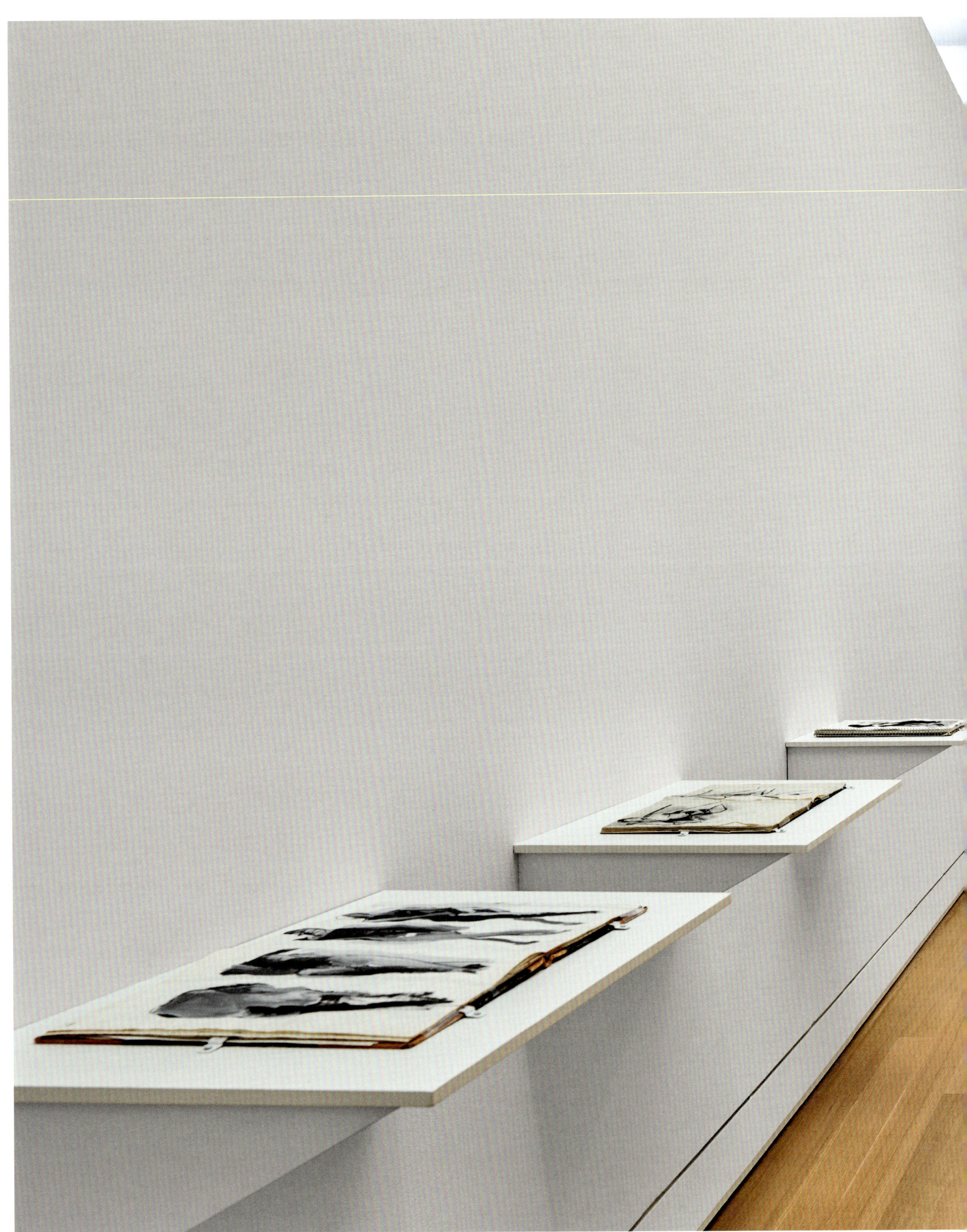

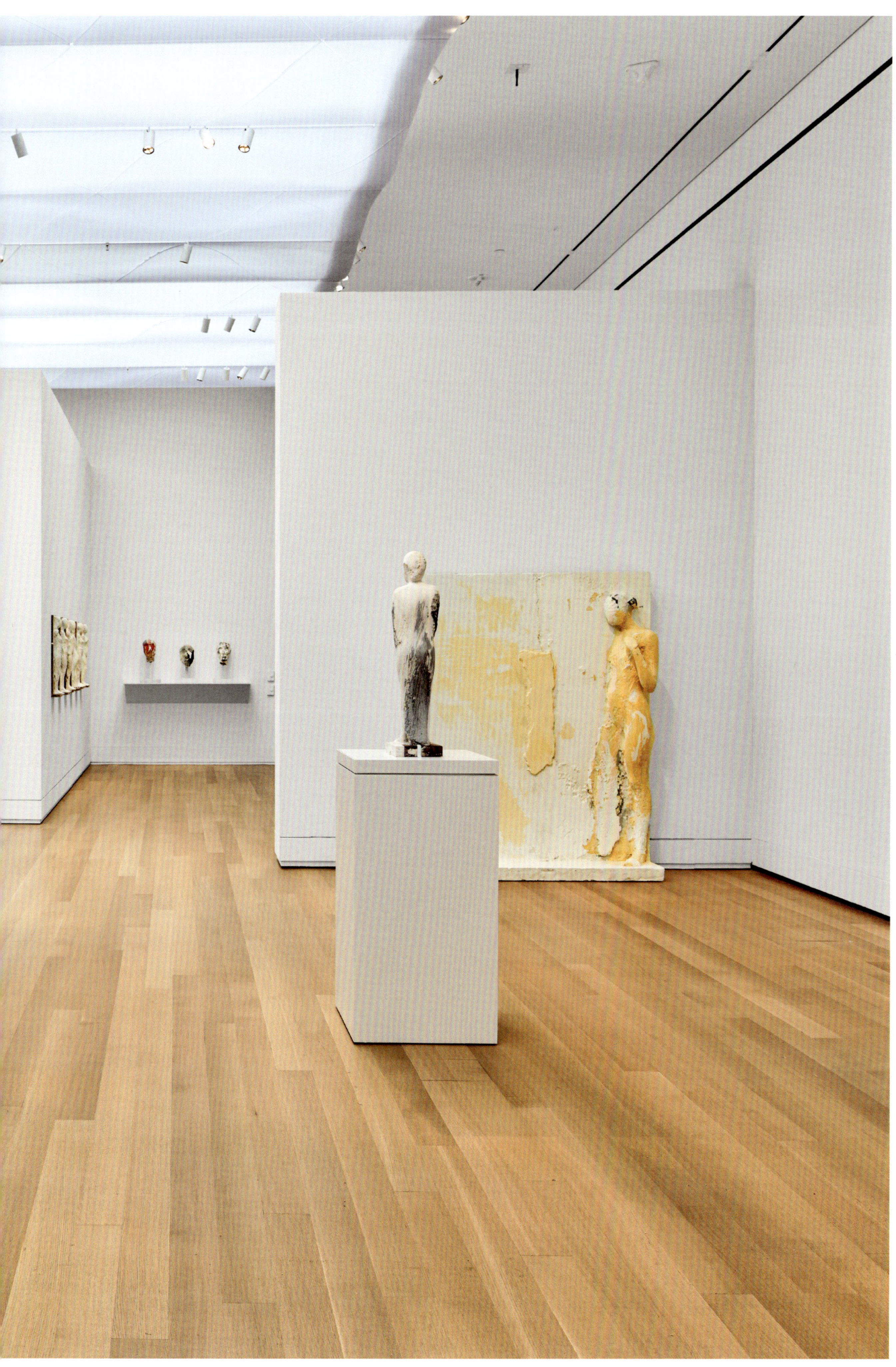

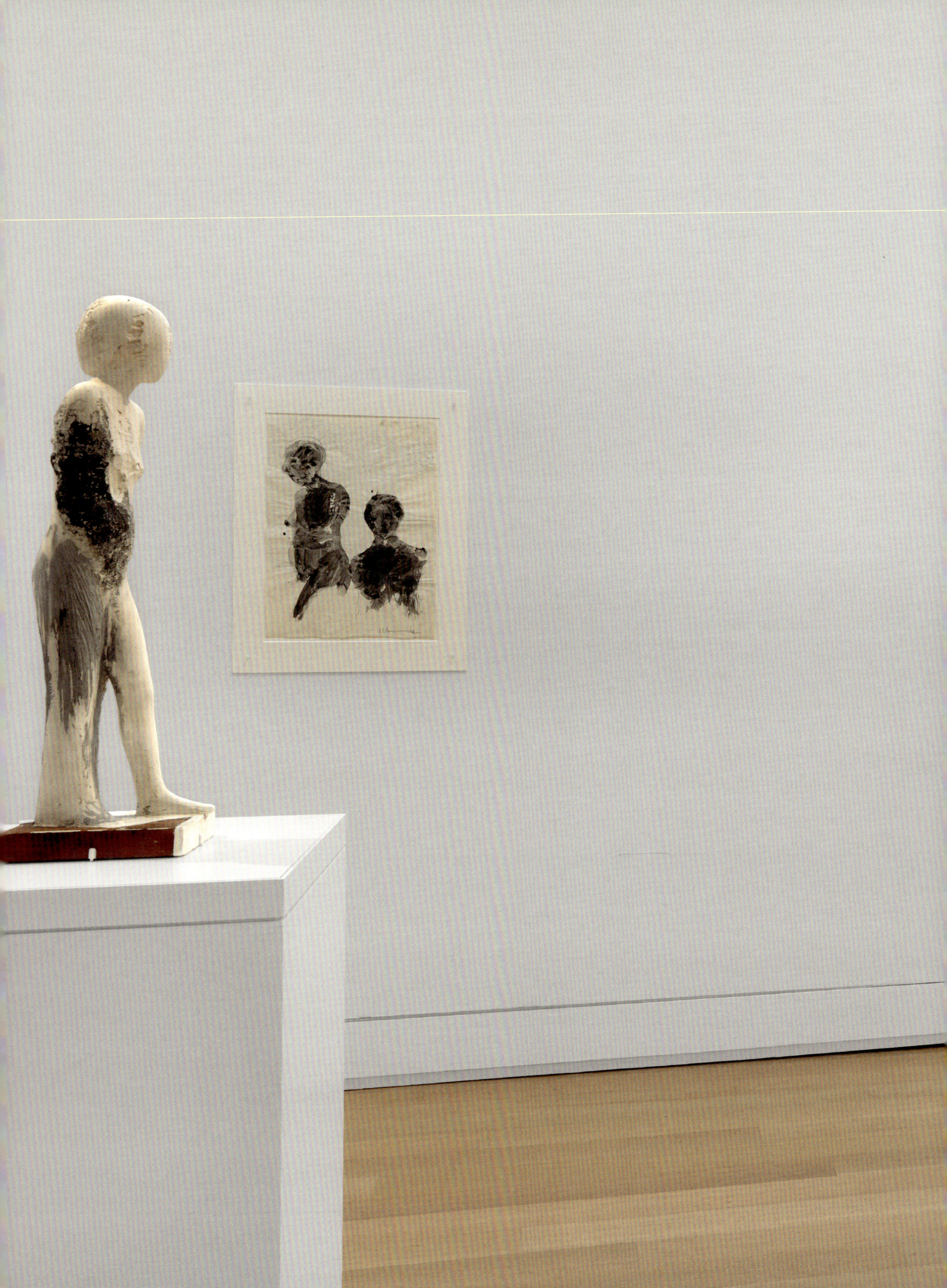

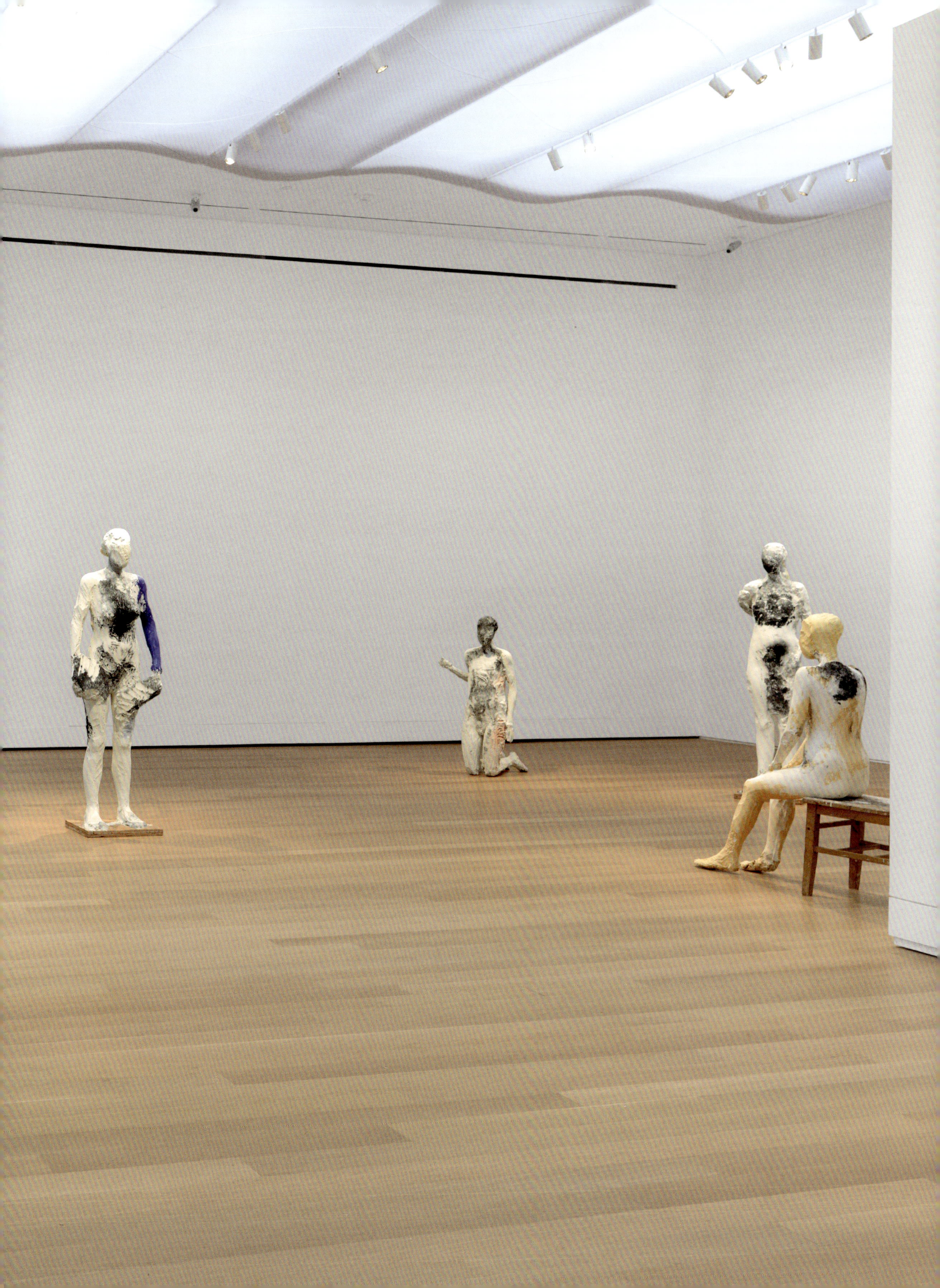

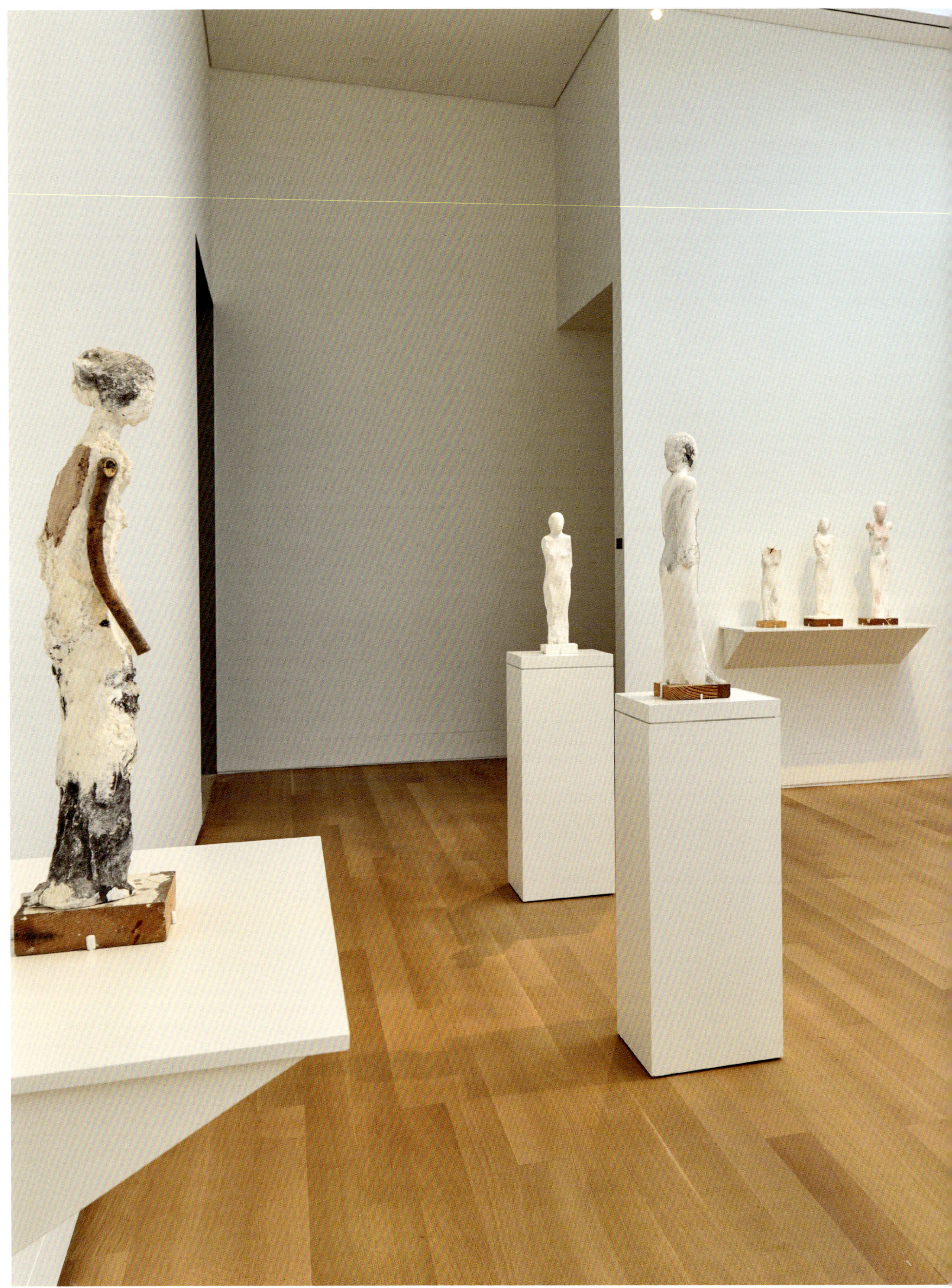

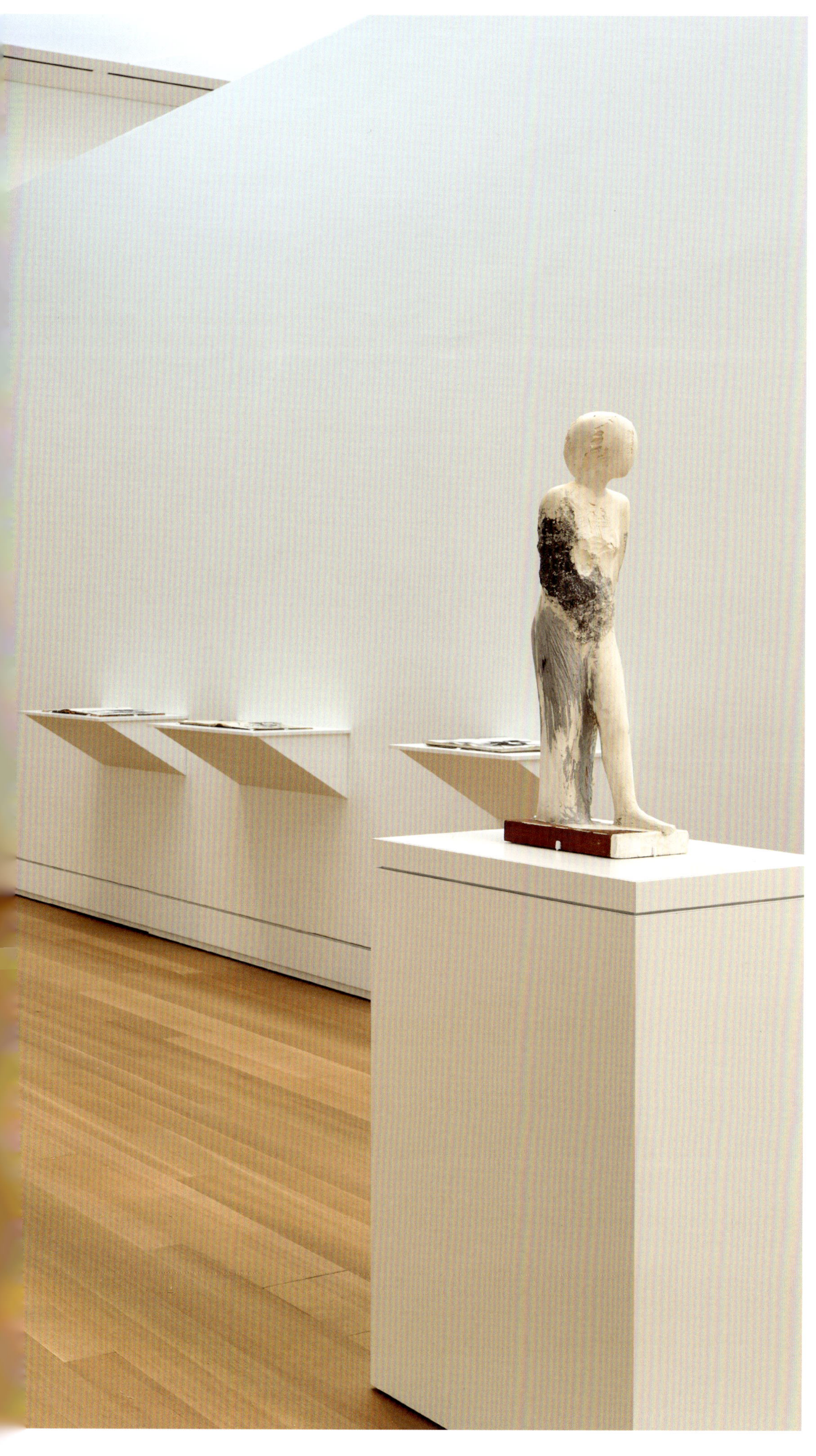

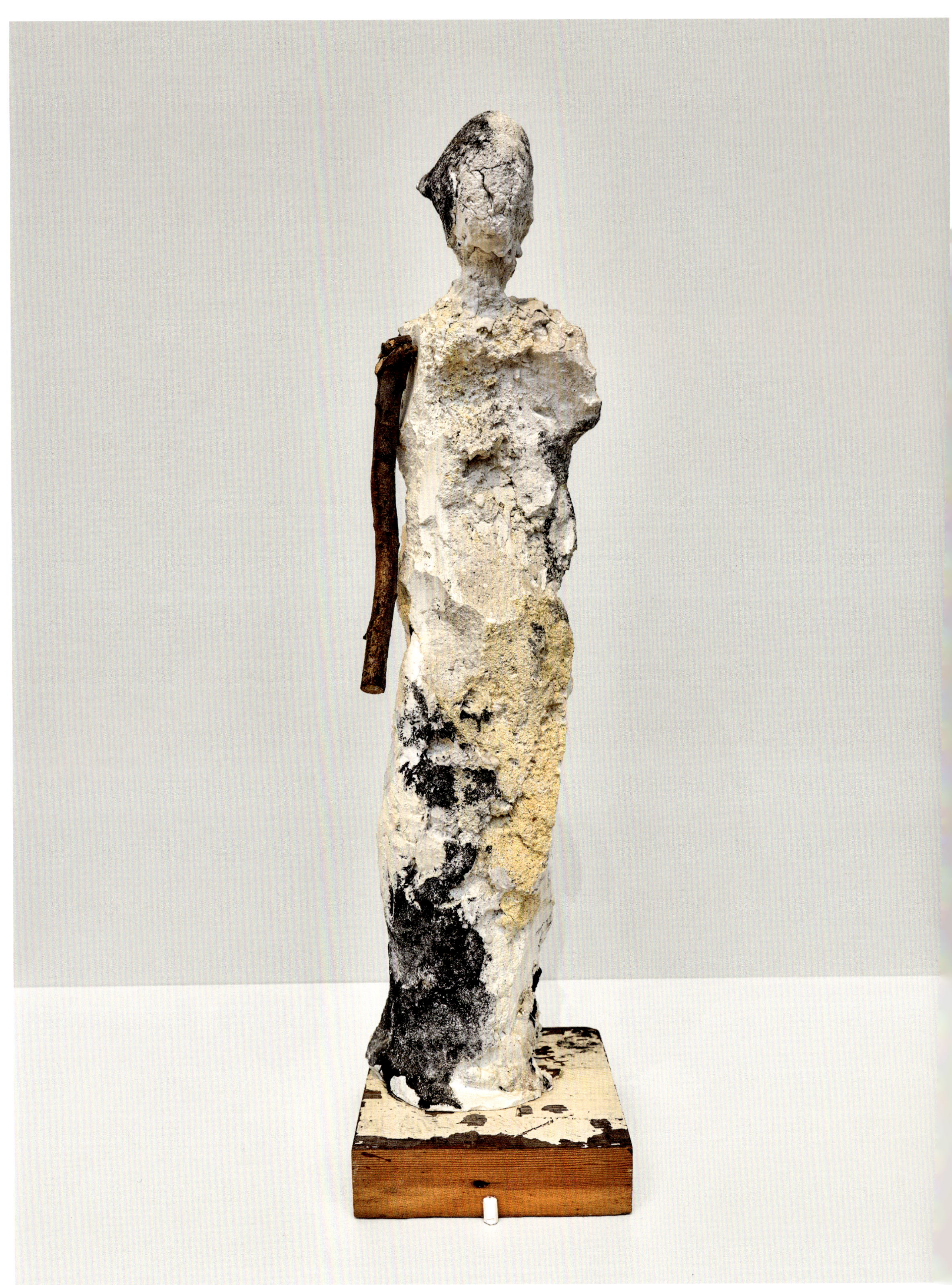

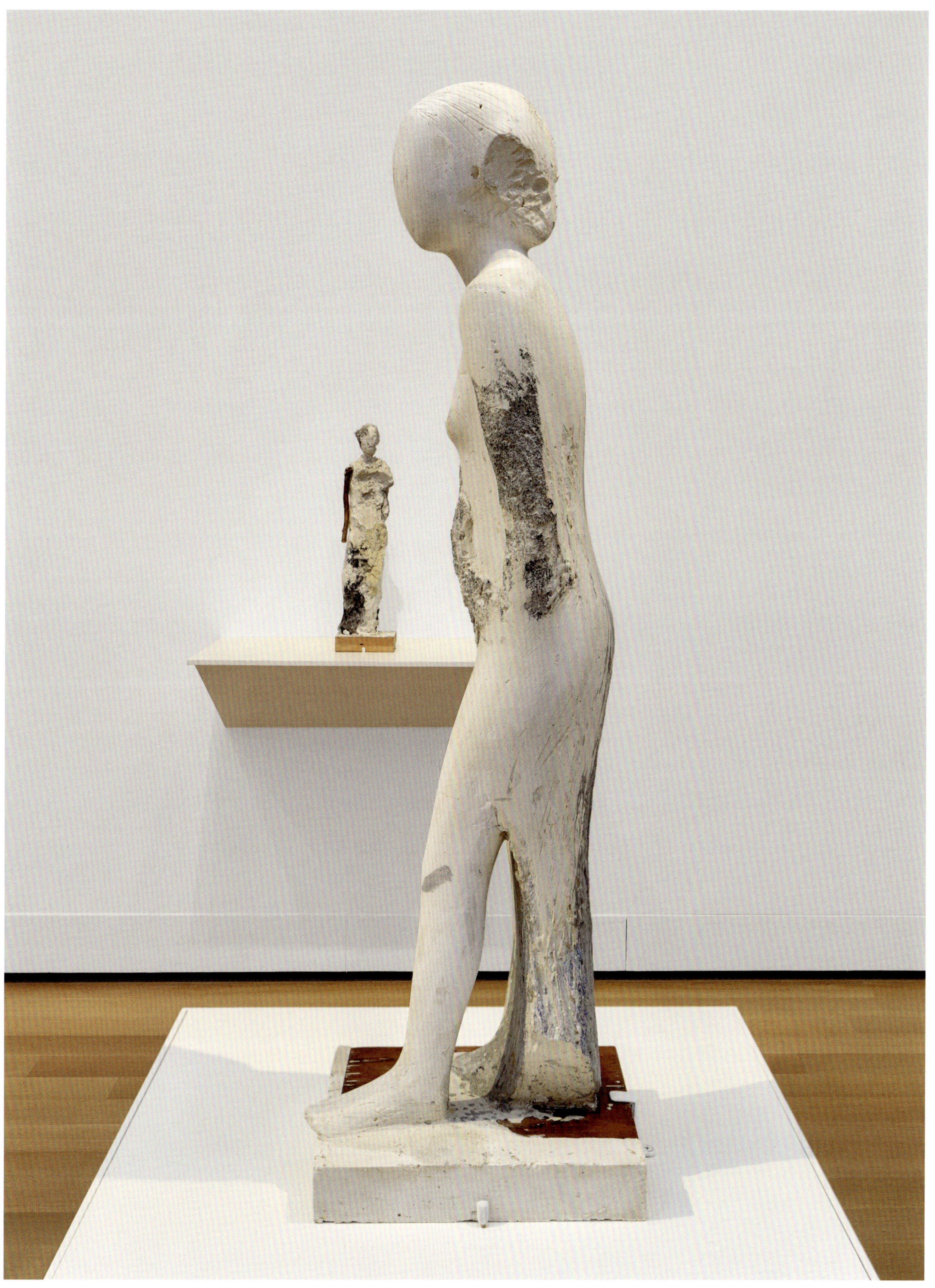

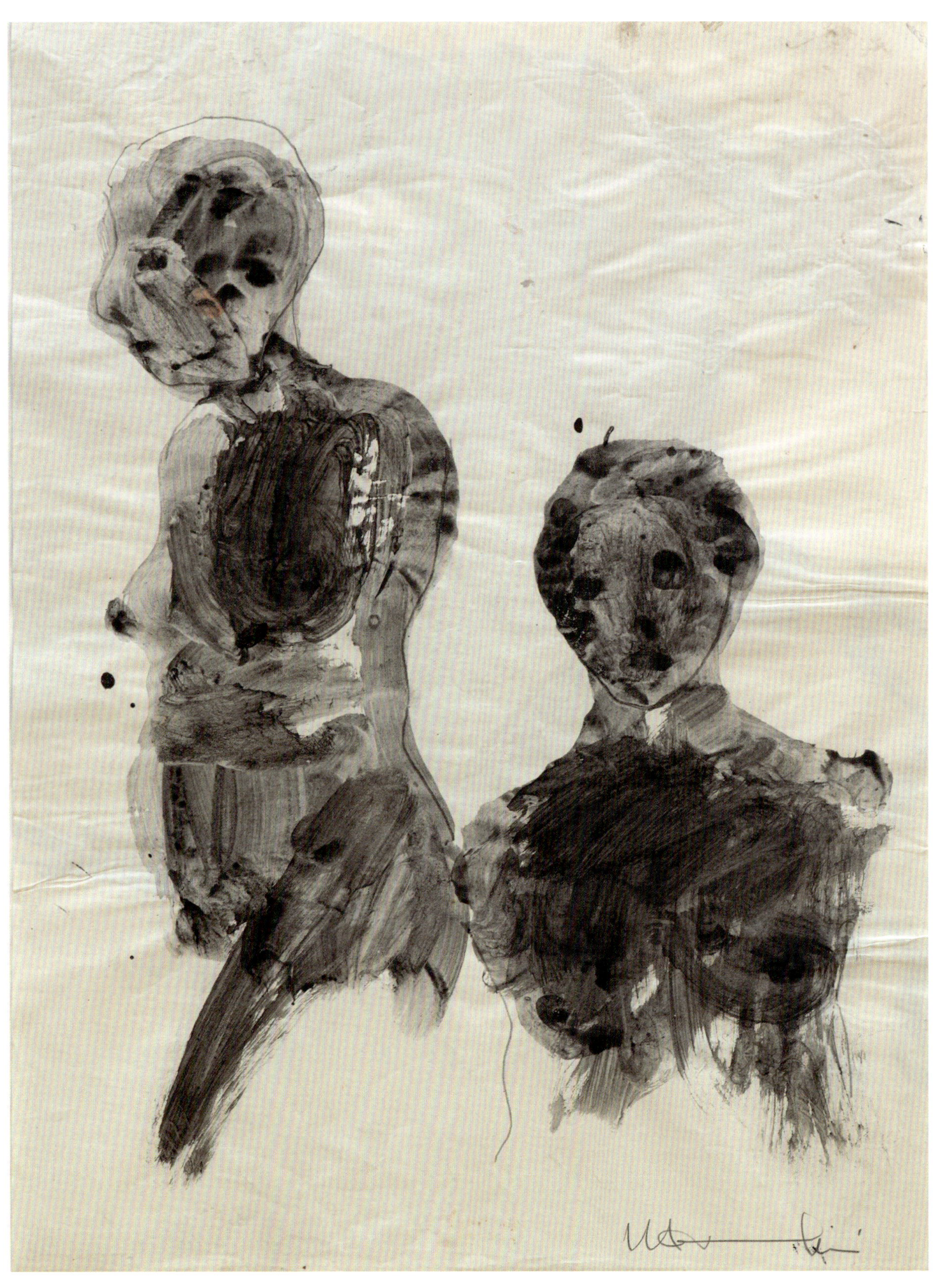

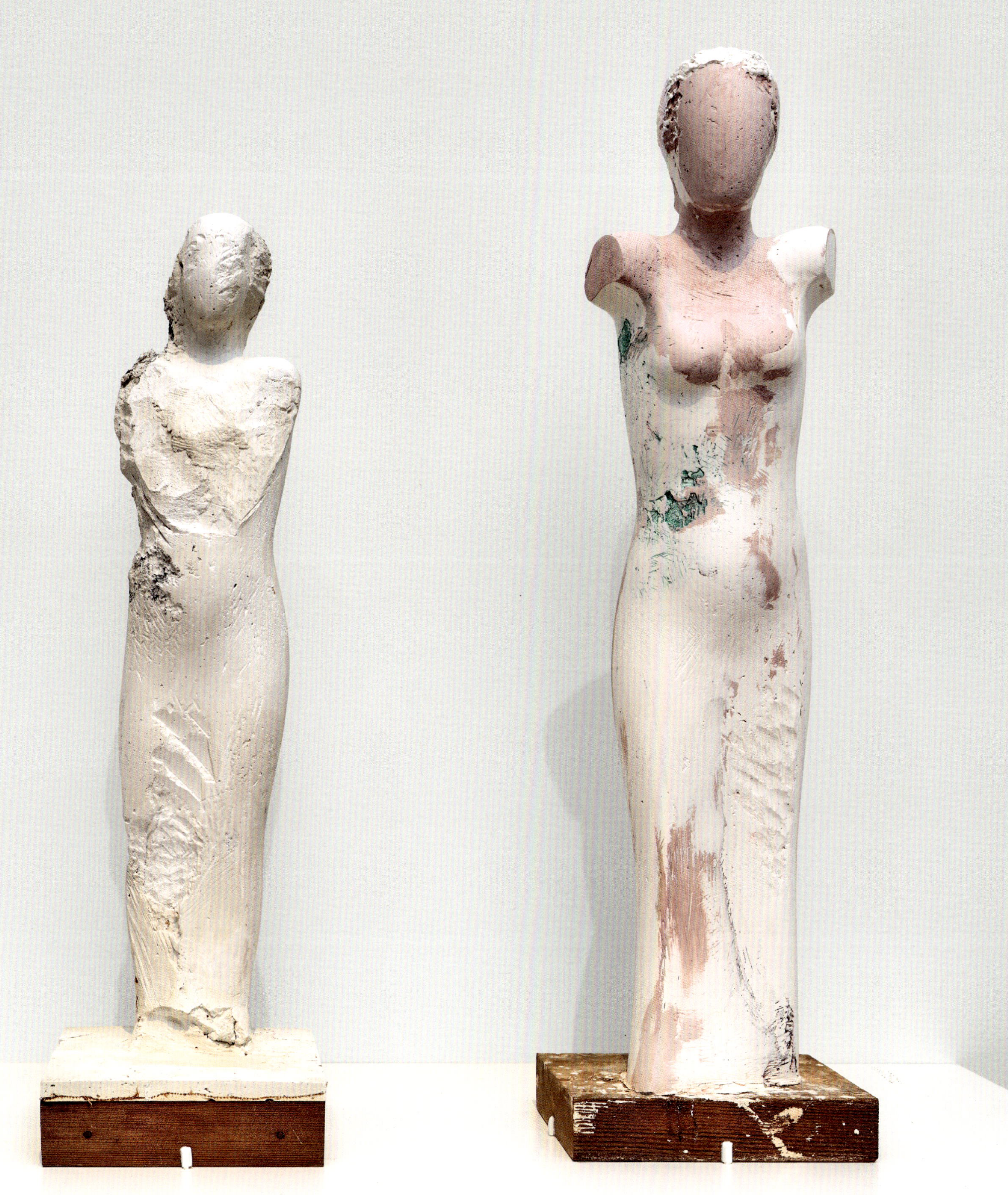

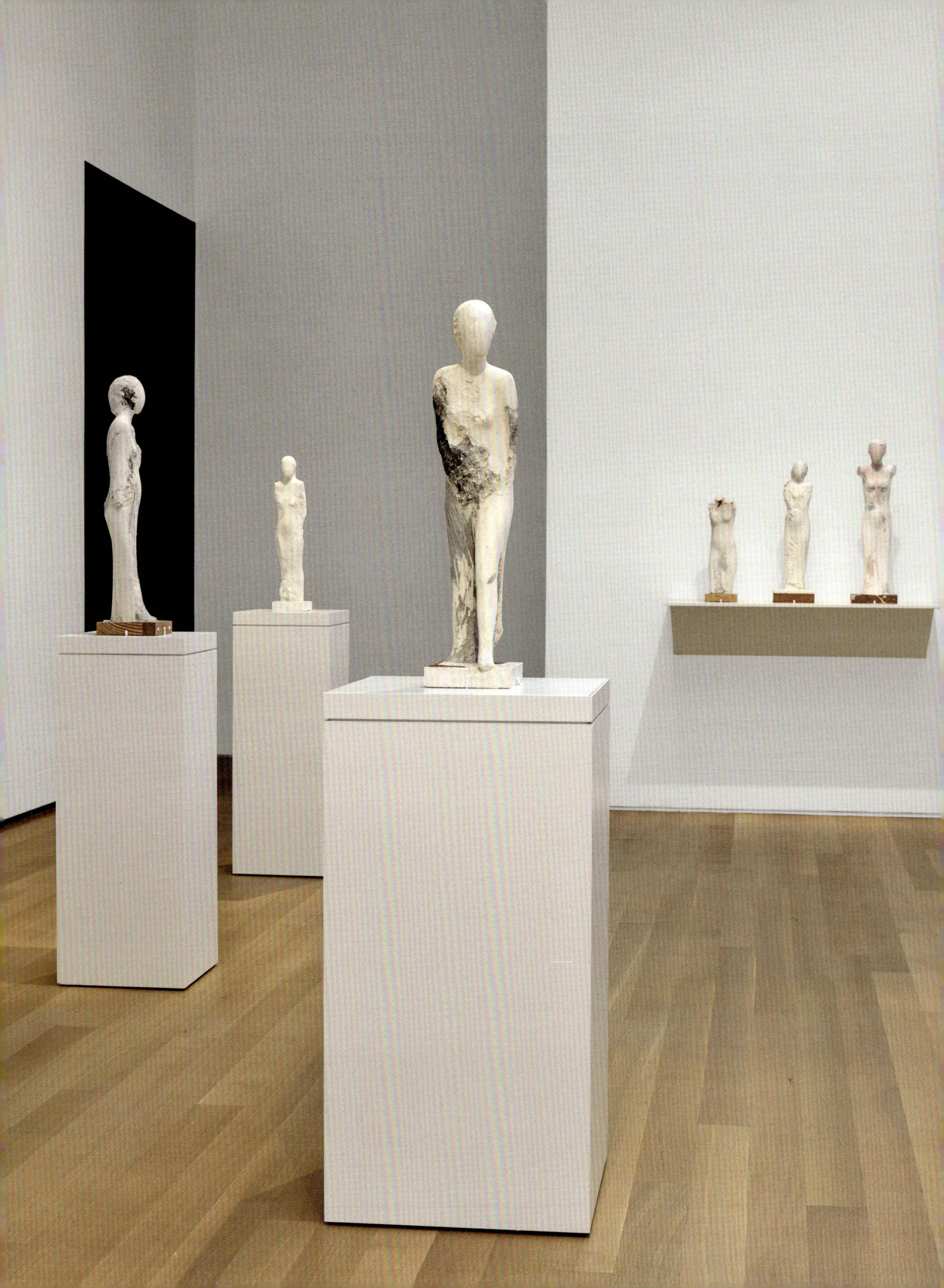

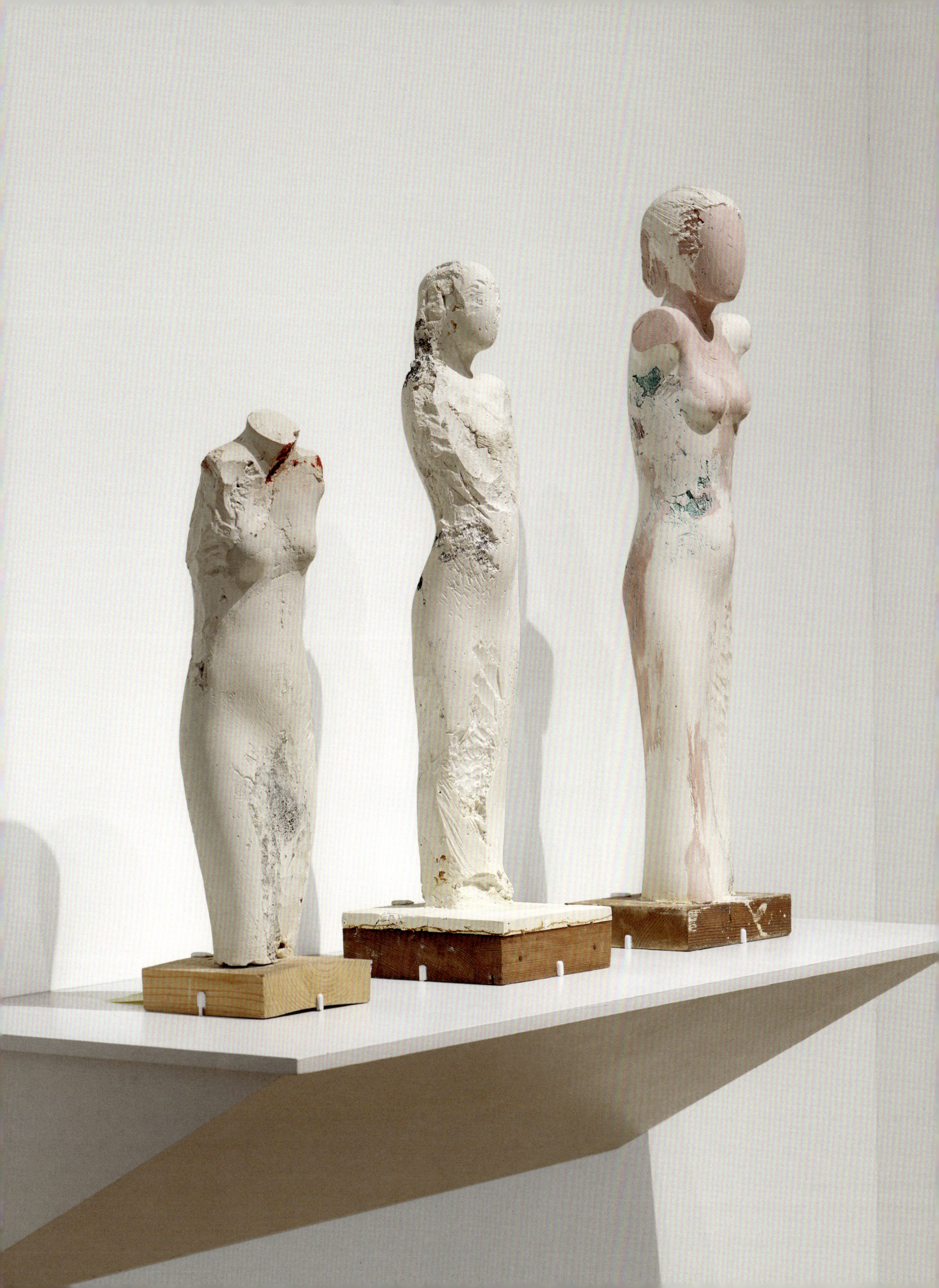

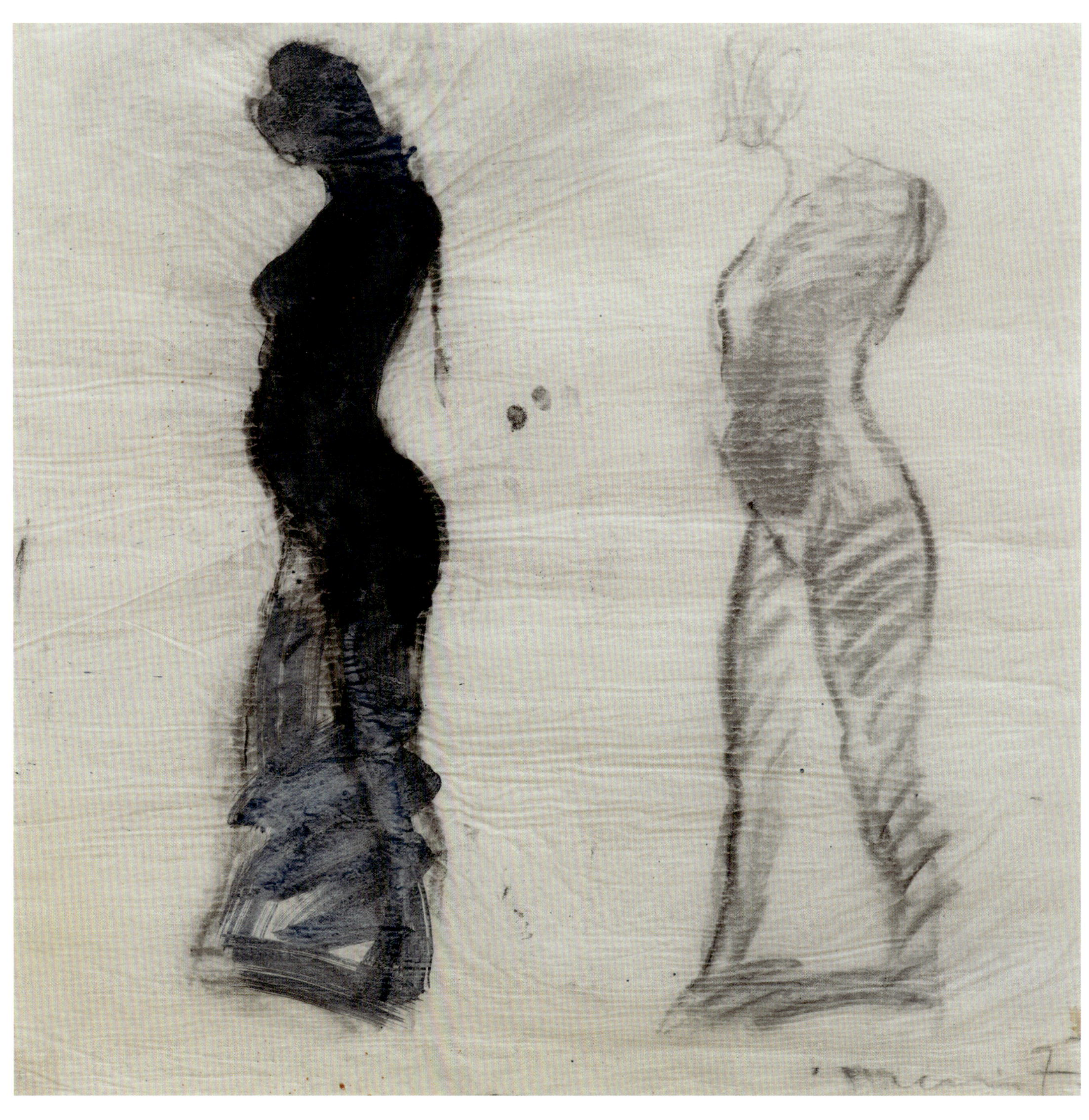

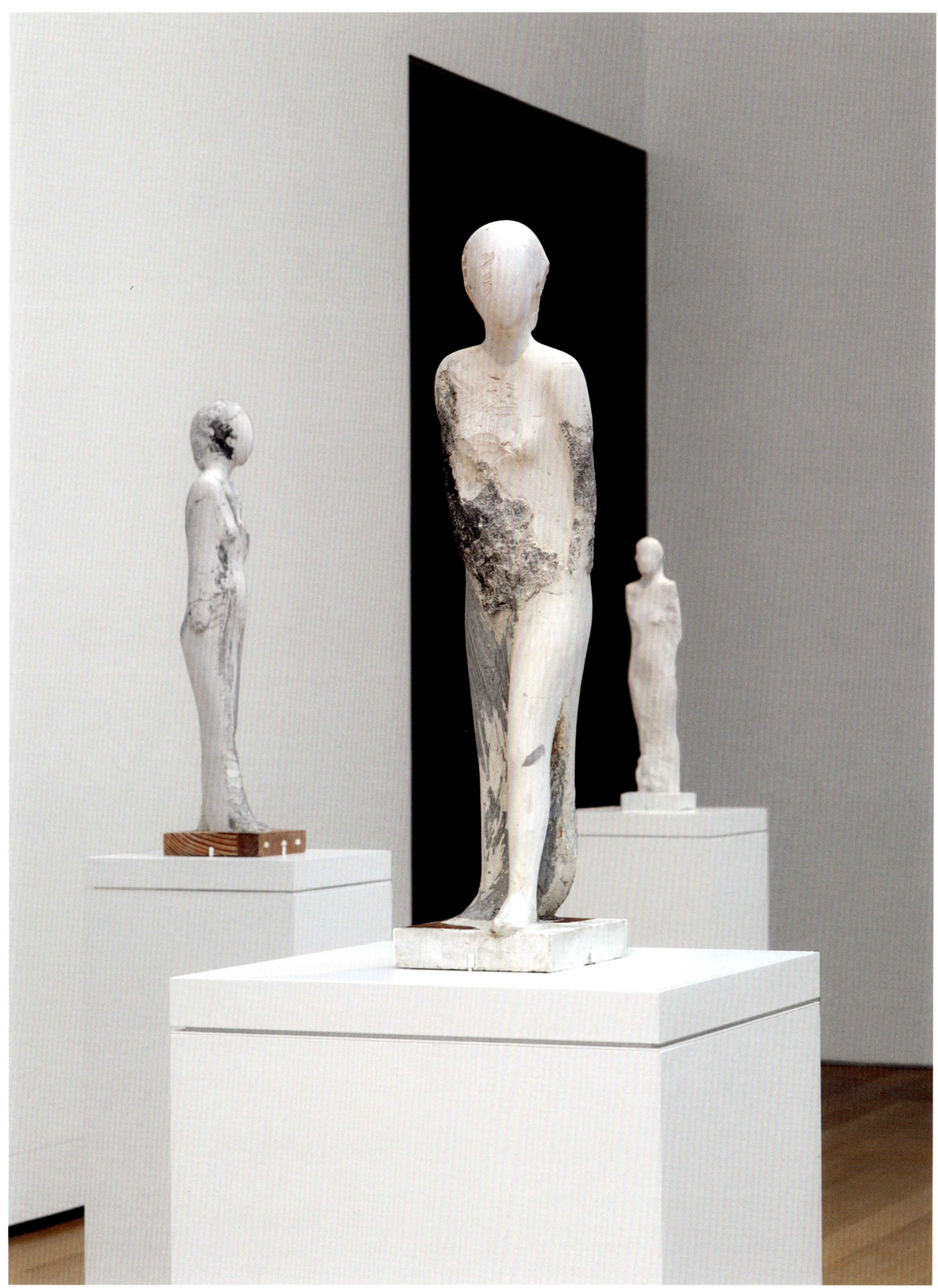

Exhibition Highlights

Exhibition Checklist

All works are by Manuel Neri (American, born 1930) and in the collection of the Yale University Art Gallery.

Casting Sketchbook, ca. 1959
Sketchbook with graphite, ballpoint pen, oil pastel, and ink
Gift of The Manuel Neri Trust
2017.88.131
Fig. 17

Head of Joan Brown, ca. 1959
Plaster with graphite
Janet and Simeon Braguin Fund
2018.4.1
Fig. 8

Plaster Mask IV, ca. 1960
Plaster with oil-based enamel and graphite
Promised gift of The Manuel Neri Trust

Shrouded Figure, ca. 1960
Plaster with water-based pigment
Gift of Philip Anglim, B.A. 1973
2017.86.1

Collage and Ink Figure Study No. 37, 1963
Opaque and transparent watercolor, charcoal, graphite, and paper collage on paper
Gift of The Manuel Neri Trust
2017.88.141

Head of Markos, 1963
Plaster with metallic paint and oil-based enamel
Gift of The Manuel Neri Trust
2017.88.3
Fig. 27

Joan Brown with Neri Sculpture II, 1963
Mixed media
Promised gift of The Manuel Neri Trust

Torso Studies, 1963
Mixed media with collage
Promised gift of The Manuel Neri Trust
Fig. 30

Female Head No. 1, ca. 1969, reworked 1972–74
Plaster, water-based pigment, and graphite
Gift of The Manuel Neri Trust
2017.88.2
Fig. 14

Male Head No. 1, 1969
Plaster with graphite
Gift of The Manuel Neri Trust
2017.88.4
Fig. 13

Mary Julia's Passion, 1973
Watercolor, charcoal, graphite, and ink on paper
Gift of The Manuel Neri Trust
2017.88.55
Fig. 29

Unos Actos de Fe Sketchbook, ca. 1974–76
Sketchbook with graphite, water-based pigment, ink, cut and pasted paper, and red pencil
Gift of The Manuel Neri Trust
2017.88.136
Fig. 18

Julia, 1976, reworked 2010
Plaster
Gift of The Manuel Neri Trust
2017.88.34
Fig. 21

Re-making of Mary Julia No. 6,
1976
Plaster with pigment
Gift of The Manuel Neri Trust
2017.88.35
Fig. 20

Untitled Head IV, 1976
Plaster with pigment
Gift of The Manuel Neri Trust
2017.88.5

Twins: Double Figure Study, 1977
Charcoal and watercolor on
paper
Gift of The Manuel Neri Trust
2017.88.56
Fig. 28

Coming in Last Thursday, 1981
Plaster
Gift of The Manuel Neri Trust
2017.88.33

*Mujer Pegada-Maquette for
Marble Relief I,* 1983
Plaster
Gift of The Manuel Neri Trust
2017.88.11

*Mujer Pegada-Maquette for
Marble Relief IV,* 1983
Plaster
Gift of The Manuel Neri Trust
2017.88.14

*Mujer Pegada-Maquette for
Marble Relief V,* 1983
Plaster
Gift of The Manuel Neri Trust
2017.88.7

*Mujer Pegada-Maquette for
Marble Relief VI,* 1983
Plaster
Gift of The Manuel Neri Trust
2017.88.8

*Mujer Pegada-Maquette for
Marble Relief VIII,* 1983
Plaster
Gift of The Manuel Neri Trust
2017.88.10

Annunciation No. 1, 1984
Plaster with water-based pigment
Gift of The Manuel Neri Trust
2017.88.31

*Arcos de Geso Plaster Maquette IV
(Mujer Pegada),* 1984
Plaster with pigment
Gift of The Manuel Neri Trust
2017.88.24

Arcos de Geso V, 1985
Plaster with pigment
Gift of The Manuel Neri Trust
2017.88.44

Arcos de Geso X, 1985
Plaster with pigment
Gift of The Manuel Neri Trust
2017.88.37

Strathmore Sketchbook, ca. 1987
Sketchbook with ink, oil stick,
graphite, and charcoal
Gift of The Manuel Neri Trust
2017.88.137
Fig. 16

Vestida No. 10, 1990
Plaster with pigment
Gift of The Manuel Neri Trust
2017.88.40

Bull Jumper III, 1989
Plaster with water-based pigment
Gift of The Manuel Neri Trust
2017.88.32
Fig. 15

M. J. Series III, 1989
Plaster with pigment
Janet and Simeon Braguin Fund
2014.63.1

*Sculpture for Love and Other
Differences: Ruth*, 1990
Plaster with water-based
pigment
Gift of The Manuel Neri Trust
2017.88.36

Ostrakon Plaster Maquette No. 3,
1998
Plaster with water-based
pigment
Gift of The Manuel Neri Trust
2017.88.26

Ostrakon Plaster Maquette No. 4,
1998
Plaster with water-based
pigment
Gift of The Manuel Neri Trust
2017.88.27

Ostrakon Plaster Maquette No. 5,
1998
Plaster with water-based
pigment
Gift of The Manuel Neri Trust
2017.88.43

Ostrakon Plaster Maquette No. 8,
1998
Plaster with water-based
pigment
Gift of The Manuel Neri Trust
2017.88.28

*Sor Juana: Crónica de mis años
peores* (Sister Juana: Chronicle
of My Worst Years), 1998
Opaque and transparent
watercolor and charcoal on
paper
Gift of Jane and John Fitz Gibbon,
B.A. 1956
2002.130.1

Vestida No. 6, 2002
Plaster with water-based
pigment
Gift of The Manuel Neri Trust
2017.88.39

Mary Julia's Passion, 2005
Acrylic on paper
Gift of The Manuel Neri Trust
2017.88.69

Caryatid II, 2007
Plaster with water-based
pigment
Gift of The Manuel Neri Trust
2017.88.25

Mary Julia VI, 2009
Watercolor on paper
Gift of The Manuel Neri Trust
2017.88.70

Acknowledgments

I embarked on this project to share the story of how my path as an artist came to intersect with Manuel Neri's, and to show that, despite the common perception of plaster and paper as pedestrian materials, in Neri's hands these two media have been repeatedly transformed into exceptional works of art. In addition, the project celebrates the recent gift by Neri of a large trove of his artworks to the Yale University Art Gallery.

Many people assisted in bringing this publication, and its attendant exhibition, to life. Lisa Scilipote, Senior Executive Assistant to the Director, deserves special thanks for keeping me on track and providing daily support throughout the development of the project.

In addition to the recent gift from the artist, works for the exhibition have been drawn from the Gallery's holdings. In the Gallery's Department of Modern and Contemporary Art, I thank Pamela Franks, Senior Deputy Director and the Seymour H. Knox, Jr., Curator of Modern and Contemporary Art, and especially Alexander Harding, Senior Museum Assistant, for his help in coordinating myriad details related to the gift, the exhibition, and the publication. In the Department of Prints and Drawings, I thank Suzanne Boorsch, the former Robert L. Solley Curator of Prints and Drawings; Suzanne Greenawalt, Senior Museum Assistant; and Rebecca Szantyr, the Florence B. Selden Senior Fellow.

Both paper and plaster are fragile materials, and for preparing the objects for exhibition, I acknowledge the work of my colleagues in the Conservation Department: Theresa Fairbanks Harris, Senior Conservator of Works on Paper; Emily Frank, Postgraduate Fellow; Anne Gunnison, Associate Conservator of Objects; Ian McClure, the Susan Morse Hilles Chief Conservator; Michaela Paulson, Postgraduate Fellow; and Carol Snow, Deputy Chief Conservator and the Alan J. Dworsky Senior Conservator of Objects. I also recognize independent conservator Mikhail Ovchinnikov, who worked with Neri for many years on minor repairs and patination of his sculptures.

For their expert assistance in mounting the exhibition, I am grateful to Jeffrey Yoshimine, Deputy Director for Exhibition and Collection Management, and Andrew Daubar, Exhibition Production Manager. The following museum technicians were also essential to the work on the installation: Patrick Brown, Andrzej Dutkanicz, Mark Geist, David Marshall, Tom Reilly, Alicia Van Campen, Christina Czap Vergara, and Kevin Wigginton. For coordinating the shipment of objects for both the exhibition and the incoming gift, I thank L. Lynne Addison, Registrar; Amy Dowe, Senior Associate Registrar; and Anne Goslin, Senior Associate Registrar. Thanks also go to the Advancement Department: Jill Westgard, former Deputy Director for Advancement; Brian P. McGovern, Associate Director of Advancement; and Valerie Richardson, Stewardship Manager.

For assistance in planning related programming to provide our visitors with a deeper engagement with the material, I am grateful to Molleen Theodore, Associate Curator of Programs, and Emily Arensman, Senior Programs Fellow. Joellen Adae, Director of Communications, working with Janet Sullivan, Communications Coordinator, oversaw publicity. In the Gallery's Business Office, Charlene Senical, Operations Manager, kept track of all aspects of the budget.

This publication has benefited from the guiding hand, keen eye, and attention to detail of the Department of Publications and Editorial Services. I am especially indebted to Madeline Kloss Johnson, former Assistant Editor, for her expert oversight of the project and her superb help in shaping the text and selecting images. I also thank Tiffany Sprague, Director of Publications and Editorial Services, who was assisted by Jennifer Lu, Editorial and Production Assistant. The beautiful design of the catalogue is the fine work of Christopher Sleboda, Director of Graphic Design, with the assistance of Chris Chew, Graphic Designer.

Photography for the project was undertaken by John ffrench, Director of Visual Resources; Anthony De Camillo, former Senior Photographer; and Richard House, Senior Photographer, with the assistance of David Whaples, Visual Resources Coordinator. Thanks go to Kathleen Mylen-Coulombe, Rights and Reproductions Coordinator, who cleared permissions for the photographs. For the many outstanding images of Neri in his studio, this publication is indebted to M. Lee Fatherree, who began photographing the artist and his work in 1979, and to The Manuel Neri Trust for kindly supplying digital files.

The Gallery extends special gratitude to Anne Kohs and Max Neri, co-trustees and stewards of The Manuel Neri Trust; thanks are also due to Diane Roby and Pam Evans of Anne Kohs and Associates, Inc. Above all, I thank Manuel Neri, who has been influential throughout my life both personally and professionally—not only because I admire his exceptional work and unique creative process, but also because he has been an important teacher, collaborator, and mentor to me and so many other artists.

Jock Reynolds
The Henry J. Heinz II Director
Yale University Art Gallery

Photo Credits

Every effort has been made to credit the artists and the sources; if there are errors or omissions, please contact the Yale University Art Gallery so that corrections can be made in any subsequent editions. Unless otherwise noted, all photographs courtesy Visual Resources Department at the Yale University Art Gallery.

Art © Estate of Robert Arneson/Licensed by VAGA, New York, N.Y.: fig. 1
© Estate of Joan Brown. Courtesy George Adams Gallery, New York: fig. 7
Photo: M. Lee Fatherree: cover, frontispiece
Photo: M. Lee Fatherree. Images from Price Amerson et al., *Manuel Neri: Early Work, 1953–1978*, exh. cat. (Washington, D.C.: Corcoran Gallery of Art, 1996), 338, 364: figs. 23–24, 32–34
Photo: Philip Galgiani: figs. 35, 37
Photo: Philip Galgiani. Image from Amerson et al., *Manuel Neri: Early Work, 1953–1978*, 98: fig. 36
Photo: Charles Ginnever. Image from Amerson et al., *Manuel Neri: Early Work, 1953–1978*, 315: fig. 10
Courtesy Hackett | Mill, representative of the Estate of David Park: fig. 5
Photo: Mary Julia Klimenko: essay frontispiece
Photo: Joanne Leonard: fig. 9
Photo: Fred Lyon. Image from Amerson et al., *Manuel Neri: Early Work, 1953–1978*, 316: fig. 4
© The Manuel Neri Trust: figs. 2, 12, 16–18, 27–30
© The Manuel Neri Trust. Photo: M. Lee Fatherree: figs. 8, 13–15, 20–21, 31
© The Manuel Neri Trust. Courtesy Jan Shrem and Maria Manetti Shrem Museum of Art, University of California, Davis. Photo: Cleber Bonato: fig. 19
Photo: James Mitchell: fig. 11
Photo: Steve Moore: figs. 22, 25
© Richard Diebenkorn Foundation: fig. 6
© Voulkos Family Trust: fig. 3
Photo: David Wakely: fig. 26